The Military Orders
From the Twelfth to the Early Fourteenth Centuries

The Military Orders

From the Twelfth to the Early Fourteenth Centuries

ALAN FOREY

University of Toronto Press
Toronto and Buffalo

First published 1992

Published in North America by
UNIVERSITY OF TORONTO PRESS
Toronto and Buffalo

ISBN 0–8020–2805–5 (cloth)
ISBN 0–8020–7680–7 (paper)

Published in the United Kingdom by
MACMILLAN EDUCATION LTD
Houndmills, Basingstoke, Hampshire RG21 2XS
and London
Companies and representatives
throughout the world

Printed in Hong Kong

Canadian Cataloguing in Publication Data
Forey, Alan *1933–*
The military orders: from the twelfth to the early
fourteenth centuries
Includes index.
ISBN 0–8020–2805–5 (cloth)   ISBN 0–8020–7680–7 (pbk.)
1. Military religious orders–History.   I. Title.
CR4701.F67 1992   271'.05   C91–094821–6

OCLC: 26543771

Contents

CONTENTS

Preface

Although I have long thought of writing a book on the military orders, it is doubtful whether, without Maurice Keen's invitation to write such a volume, the project would in fact have been carried out. I would therefore like to express my gratitude to him for providing the impetus, as well as for valuable suggestions during the course of writing.

In the first part of Chapter 2 and in the last part of Chapter 4 I have drawn on material which originally appeared in the *Journal of Ecclesiastical History* and *Viator*; and elsewhere I have made briefer use of articles which were published in *Speculum* and *Traditio*. I am grateful for the permission which has, where necessary, been granted for me to do this. I would also like to thank Vanessa Graham and Katherine Pym for the trouble they have taken in the production of the book. My wife has provided assistance at all stages, and my greatest debt is to her.

ALAN FOREY

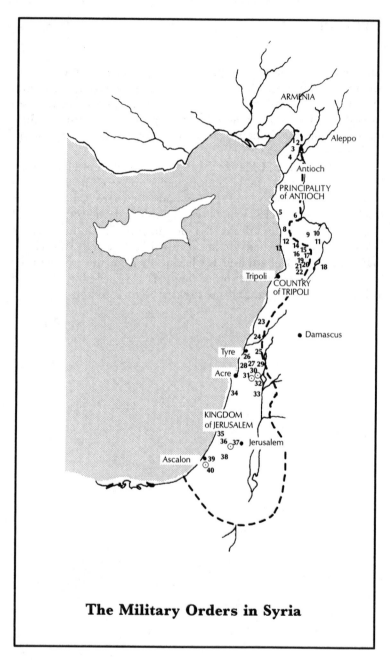

The Military Orders in Syria

The Military Orders in Syria

1. Roche Roussel (T)
2. Roche Guillaume (T)
3. Darbsaq (T)
4. Baghras (T)
5. Gibel (T/H)
6. Château de la Vieille (H)
7. Hamah
8. Margat (H)
9. ? Eixserc (H)
10. Bar'in (H)
11. Rafaniyah (H)
12. Tortosa (T)
13. Ruad Island (T)
14. Chastel Rouge (H)
15. Safitha (T)
16. Arima (T)
17. Tuban (H)
18. Homs
19. Crac des Chevaliers (H)
20. Castellum Bochee (H)
21. Lacum (H)
22. Felicium (H)
23. Sidon (T)
24. Beaufort (T)
25. Chastellet (T)
26. Montfort (T)
27. Castellum Regis (TO)
28. Judin (TO)
29. Safed (T)
30. Hattin
31. Cresson
32. Mount Tabor (H)
33. Belvoir (H)
34. Château Pèlerin (T)
35. Arsur (H)
36. Casal das Pleins (T)
37. Montgisard
38. Beit-Jibrin (H)
39. La Forbie
40. Gaza (T)

(T)   Temple
(H)   Hospital
(TO)   Teutonic Order
⊙   Site of battle
- -   Frontier in 1186

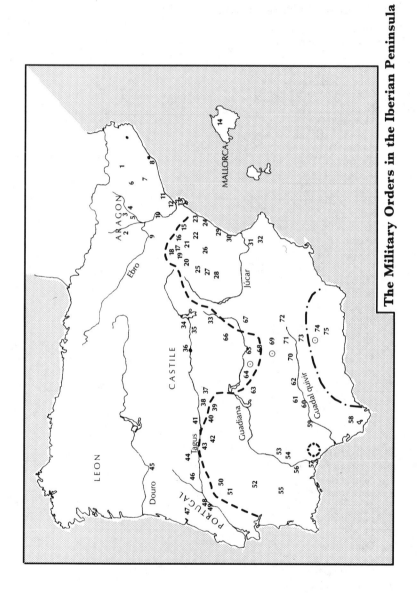

The Military Orders in the Iberian Peninsula

The Military Orders in the Iberian Peninsula

1. Puigreig (T)
2. Monzón (T)
3. Corbins (T)
4. LERIDA
5. Gardeny (T)
6. Grañena (T)
7. Barbará (T)
8. BARCELONA
9. Alcañiz (C)
10. Miravet (T)
11. Alfama (SJ)
12. TORTOSA (T)
13. Amposta (H)
14. Inca
15. Monroyo (C)
16. Castellote (M/T)
17. Aliaga (H)
18. Montalbán (S)
19. Orrios (M/T)
20. Alfambra (M/T)
21. Villarluengo (M/T)
22. Cantavieja (M/T)
23. Pulpís (T)
24. Chivert (T)
25. Teruel
26. Alcalá (G)
27. Villel (M/T)
28. Libros (M/T)
29. Burriana
30. VALENCIA
31. Anna (S)
32. Enguera (S)
33. Uclés (H/S)
34. Alharilla (S)
35. Oreja (S)
36. TOLEDO
37. Cabañas (Tr)
38. Albalat (Tr)
39. Sta. Cruz (Tr)
40. Trujillo (Tr)
41. Monfragüe (M/C)
42. Cáceres (S)
43. Alcántara (A)
44. Monsanto (S)
45. San Julián de Pereiro (A)
46. Castelo Branco (T)
47. Soure (T)
48. Tomar (T)
49. Belver (H)
50. Crato (H)
51. Avis (Av)
52. Évora (Av)
53. Moura (H)
54. Serpa (H)
55. Aljustrel (S)
56. Mértola (S)
57. Ayamonte (S)
58. Medina Sidonia (SM)
59. SEVILLE
60. Lora (H)
61. Setefilla (H)
62. CORDOBA
63. Capilla (T)
64. Alarcos
65. Calatrava (C)
66. Consuegra (H)
67. Alhambra (S)
68. Salvatierra (C)
69. Las Navas de Tolosa
70. Baeza
71. Úbeda
72. Segura (S)
73. Martos (C)
74. Moclín
75. GRANADA
76. Cartagena (SM)

(A)   Alcántara
(Av) Avis
(C)   Calatrava
(G)   Grande-Sauve
(H)   Hospitallers
(M)   Mountjoy/Monfragüe
(S)   Santiago
(SJ) San Jorge de Alfama
(SM) Santa María de España
(T)   Templars
(Tr) Trujillo
⊙   Site of battle
- -   Frontier in the mid-twelfth century
- · - Frontier in the mid-thirteenth century

The Military Orders
in Central and
Eastern Europe

1. Fellin (SB/TO)
2. Wenden (SB/TO)
3. Segewold (SB/TO)
4. Riga
5. Ascheraden (SB/TO)
6. Kokenhausen
7. Dünaburg (TO)
8. Doblen (TO)
9. Memel (TO)
10. Ragnit (TO)
11. Georgenburg (TO)
12. Königsberg (TO)
13. Balga (TO)
14. Kreuzburg (TO)
15. Frisches Haff
16. Elbing (TO)
17. Starogard (H)
18. Thymau (C)
19. Marienwerder (TO)
20. Kulm (TO)
21. Culmerland
22. Thorn (TO)
23. Dobrzyn (D)
24. Drohiczyn (D)
25. Luków (T)
26. Burzenland
27. Severin
28. Lamia (T)
29. Andravidha
30. Clermont

(C)   Calatrava
(D)   Dobrin
(SB)   Swordbrethren
(T)   Temple
(H)   Hospital
(TO)   Teutonic Order

The Military Orders in Central and Eastern Europe

The English Priory of the Hospitallers in the later thirteenth century

1. Torpichen
2. Mount St John
3. Beverley
4. Newland
5. Maltby
6. Ossington
7. Skirbeck
8. Dalby
9. Yeaveley
10. Halston
11. Yspytty-Ifan
12. Slebech
13. Dinmore
14. Grafton
15. Dingley
16. Melchbourne
17. Chippenham
18. Carbrooke
19. Battisford
20. Maplestead
21. Standon
22. Shingay
23. Hogshaw
24. Clanfield
25. Quenington
26. Brimpton
27. Clerkenwell
28. Sutton At Hone
29. Swingfield
30. Poling
31. Godsfield
32. Ansty
33. Fryer Mayne
34. Buckland
35. Bodmiscombe
36. Trebeigh

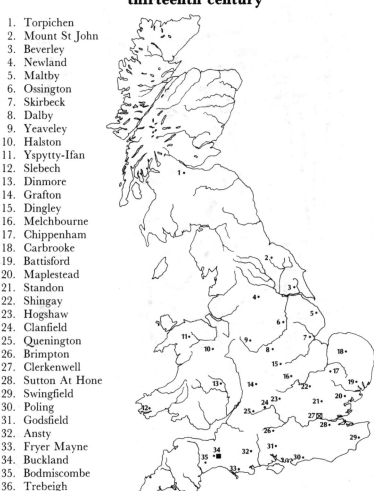

☒   Headquarters of the Priory
●   House of Hospitaller brethren
■   House of Hospitaller sisters

(from © Swanston *Atlas of Crusades*, Times Books)

xiv

CHATEAU PELERIN

1. N.W. Tower
2. N.W. Hall
3. North Hall
4. North Vault
5. North Alley
6. Inner or Upper Ward
7. West Undercroft
8. Bridge
9. West Hall
10. Ovens
11. S.W. Hall
12. South Hall
13. Round Church
14. South Undercroft
15. South Bailey
16. North Great Tower
17. South Great Tower
18. East Bailey
19. Middle Gate Tower
20. North Gate Tower
21. South Gate Tower
22. South Beach Gate
23. North Beach Gate
24. Ditch or Fosse
25. Harbour

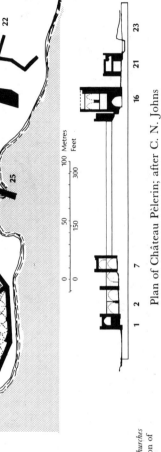

Plan of Château Pèlerin; after C. N. Johns

Reproduced from T. S. Boase, *Castles and Churches of the Crusading Kingdoms*, 1967, by permission of Oxford University Press.

1. Introduction

THOSE who in the seventeenth century perused the encyclopaedic works on military orders which were then appearing – such as Mennenius's *Deliciae equestrium sive militarium ordinum*, published in 1613 – were left in no doubt that they were reading about an institution which had been in existence for most of the Christian era. Many orders were reported to have been established well before the period of the crusades, although there were often conflicting opinions about the exact antiquity of particular foundations. The origins of the Spanish order of Santiago, which was in fact set up in 1170, were often traced back to the ninth century: yet while some associated its foundation with the supposed discovery of the body of St James during the reign of the Asturian king, Alfonso II, others linked its establishment with the legendary victory over the Moors at Clavijo, which was placed in the reign of Ramiro I. The accumulation of myth and tradition recorded in these encyclopaedias exercised a prolonged influence on historians of the military orders: disproof was not always sufficient to silence a persistent tradition. It is nevertheless clear that the Christian military order, in the sense of an institution whose members combined a military with a religious way of life, in fact originated in the Holy Land during the earlier part of the twelfth century. The first foundation of this kind was the order of the Temple, whose origins are probably to be placed in the year 1120. Whatever traditions and legends may later have developed, contemporaries were well aware that a new type of religious foundation was then being created. St Bernard of Clairvaux was clearly in no doubt, for he wrote of the Temple: 'a new kind of militia is recently reported to have arisen on earth...a new kind of militia, I say, and one unknown to the world'. The Templar rule itself referred to 'this new kind of religious order', and similar phrases are encountered in other twelfth-century writings.[1]

The Christian military order thus appeared in the wake of the first crusade. The Temple was founded in Jerusalem some twenty years after the city had been captured by the crusaders, and in the twelfth and thirteenth centuries the Templars and the brethren of other military orders which emerged in the Holy Land – such as the Hospital of St John and the Teutonic order – played an increasingly important role in the defence of the crusader states which had been established in Syria during and after the first crusade. But, just as crusades came to be preached against various enemies of Christianity and of the Church, so the role of the military order was extended. Templars and Hospitallers were fighting against Muslims in Spain by the middle of the twelfth century, when nearly half of the peninsula was still under Islamic rule, and local military orders were being established there in the third quarter of the century. In the thirteenth century, military orders were opposing pagans in central and eastern Europe: first the Swordbrethren and then the Teutonic order played a major part in the conquest of Livonia, while the acquisition of Prussia was largely the work of the latter. In the same century crusades were also being preached increasingly against Christians, and military orders were similarly employed against these. They helped to defend the Latin Empire of Constantinople, which was set up in 1204 at the end of the fourth crusade and which faced opposition from eastern Christians on both its European and its Asiatic frontiers; and several orders were founded within western Christendom to fight against heretics and other enemies of the Church.

Although the main characteristic of military orders was the combining of the military and the religious way of life, many of these institutions had other functions besides fighting. The Hospital of St John had been founded as a charitable institution in Jerusalem before the first crusade, and it continued to care for the sick and the poor after it had assumed military responsibilities. A number of other military orders similarly maintained hospitals, and several devoted time and resources to ransoming captives from the infidel. Nor, despite their primary purpose, were military orders necessarily all-male institutions. It was not uncommon for women to adopt a religious way of life by attaching themselves to a convent of a military order, and in the thirteenth century several of these orders had houses of sisters dependent upon them.

In this the military orders were not unlike many other religious foundations. They differed from the latter, however, not merely in function. The majority of the members of military orders were laymen, and these held most positions of authority. Whereas laymen could occupy only a subordinate role as *conversi* in

Cistercian monasteries, in military orders clerical brethren were either directly or indirectly under the authority of brothers who were not ordained. The military orders also marked a departure from contemporary monastic practice in the matter of organisation. Existing models, such as that of Cîteaux, did not meet their needs. New administrative structures were therefore evolved, which foreshadowed to some extent the forms of organisation adopted by the friars in the thirteenth century.

Although the military orders thus constituted a significant development in the religious life of the West and played an important role in the relations between western Christendom and its neighbours, and although the leading orders came to possess extensive properties and numerous convents in all parts of western Christendom, these foundations usually receive no more than limited attention in historical works of a more general nature. Histories of religious orders either ignore them completely or treat them in a perfunctory manner; studies of knighthood tend to focus on knights who remained part of the secular world; and works dealing with the relations of western Christendom and its neighbours – especially those concerned with the crusader states in Syria or the Spanish reconquest – devote attention only to the military exploits of these orders.

The historian who does seek to study the military orders admittedly encounters difficulties over sources. Although at the end of the thirteenth century and in the fourteenth several histories of conquests in the regions of Prussia and Livonia were written for the Teutonic order, most military orders produced little or no narrative material of their own, and reliance has to be placed on chronicle sources of a more general nature. And although rules, statutes and customs have survived for many orders, the bulk of the documentation which exists concerns property rights and privileges: little attempt was made to preserve documents of only temporary significance, but the orders were anxious to retain records of their rights, and often had their charters copied into cartularies. Not that material even of this kind has always been preserved: although the central archive of the Hospital of St John is now housed in Malta, where the Hospitallers established their headquarters in the sixteenth century, that of the Templars has long since disappeared: the Templar documentation which still exists mostly concerns lands and estates in the kingdoms of Western Europe. For some of the lesser military orders very little material of any sort has survived; and of course much that is of interest to the historian was never recorded in writing at all.

Nevertheless, the sources which do exist have in recent decades been the object of increased attention, and studies have appeared of individual orders or of aspects of their history. Numerous monographs have, for example, been published on the Spanish military orders. But little attempt has been made to consider the military order in general as an institution, and the form taken by more particular studies has often been dictated by the nature of the material which has survived: they are often primarily histories of the accumulation of estates. Questions to which the sources provide no ready and direct answer tend to be ignored or to receive only brief consideration. There is therefore scope for a more general study, which seeks to discern common trends and characteristics and which attempts to provide generalised comment. The nature of the documentation inevitably imposes limitations which cannot easily be overcome: it is necessary to write an institutional history rather than a study of individuals, for – with a few exceptions such as Pelayo Pérez Correa of the order of Santiago and the last Templar master James of Molay – it is usually difficult to discover the personalities behind the names. Even when some more institutional aspects are considered, the present state of research must make answers tentative and subject to modification as further detailed investigations are carried out. Yet sufficient research has been done to make a general study a feasible undertaking, even if in the present work there is not space to consider all topics fully.

Many military orders have a long history, and some still survive in a much modified form. This study will survey only the first stage in the development of the institution. This may be said to end in the early fourteenth century, when changes were taking place which affected the roles of many orders. The loss of the last western outposts in Syria in 1291 led the Hospital and the Teutonic order to alter the focus of their military activities, while lesser orders based in the Holy Land also had to reassess their function and purpose. In Spain, the halting of the reconquest in the second half of the thirteenth century led to a more gradual modification of roles. The most startling landmark in the early fourteenth century, however, was the abolition of the order of the Temple by Pope Clement V in 1312, after its members had been tried on charges of heresy, idolatry and immorality. Yet in Spain some Templar property was used to endow new military orders, and elsewhere it was assigned to the Hospitallers. Although in the later thirteenth century the orders had come under growing criticism, it was still thought that they had a role to perform.

2. Foundations and Locations

The Templars

> WE travelled from Joppa to the city of Jerusalem, two days' journey, by a mountainous route which is very difficult and dangerous, as the Saracens are always seeking to ambush the Christians: they lie concealed in the caverns of the mountains and the caves of the rocks, on the lookout night and day for anyone they can easily attack, either pilgrims travelling in small bands or exhausted stragglers separated from their companions.[1]

It is clear from this comment by the pilgrim Saewulf, who visited Jerusalem three or four years after the city had been captured by the crusaders, that the establishment of Western rule in parts of Syria had brought little security for those travelling in the Holy Land. The risks faced by pilgrims were also stressed by the Russian abbot Daniel of Kiev, who went to Syria a few years later and who described how the Muslims used Ascalon as a base from which to launch attacks on those journeying from the coast to Jerusalem. It was to provide necessary protection for such pilgrims that a group of Westerners formed themselves into a religious community in Jerusalem about the year 1120. Their leader was Hugh of Payns, who came from Champagne and who is thought to have been related to the ruling house of the county and to St Bernard of Clairvaux. He and his followers took the normal monastic vows of poverty, chastity and obedience but, with the approval of the patriarch of Jerusalem, devoted themselves to escorting and guarding pilgrims along the roads to Jerusalem. King Baldwin II assigned them a residence in part of his palace, the former al-Aqsa mosque, which the crusaders identified as the Temple of Solomon: hence the name adopted by the group. Within a few years, however, the community had extended its activities and its members were beginning to fight in the Christian armies of Syria against the infidel. By the time it obtained confirmation and received a rule at the Council of Troyes, which was apparently held in 1129, warfare against the Muslims had come to be regarded as its principal function.

In assuming a military role, as well as in providing protection for pilgrims, the Templars were answering an obvious need. Most of those who had participated in the first crusade had returned home shortly after the capture of Jerusalem. The contemporary chronicler Fulcher of Chartres reported that at the beginning of Baldwin I's reign the king had only three hundred knights and the same number of footsoldiers to defend the lands under Christian rule: garrisons had to be withdrawn from castles if a field army was to be mustered. In the following years the situation was exacerbated by a high mortality rate, which commonly left fiefs in the hands of widows and minors: it was not until the middle years of the twelfth century that a stable noble class emerged in the kingdom of Jerusalem. Bands of crusaders did, of course, continue to make the journey out to the Holy Land in the early twelfth century, but few settled in the East. Military service could also be sought from the native population, but this did not always provide a very reliable force; and although natives were at times hired as mercenaries, difficulty in paying troops was apparently already being experienced in Baldwin I's reign. Yet, although both in providing protection for pilgrims and in fighting against the infidel the Templars were supplying needed assistance, it has to be explained why those who formed the community sought to establish an institution which combined the use of force with a religious way of life.

Some writers have discerned the influence of Islamic models. In the early nineteenth century the Austrian orientalist Joseph von Hammer noted similarities between the Templars and the Shiite sect of the Assassins, and although much of his work has been discredited, Assassin influence has again been postulated more recently. But the parallels in dress and organisation to which attention has been drawn are based on questionable evidence and do not in any case explain the main characteristics of the Temple. Nor do twelfth-century sources suggest that Christian contemporaries considered the Templars and the Assassins to be very alike: although the chronicler William of Tyre employed the words 'master' and 'preceptor' – terms used in military orders – to describe the leader of the Assassins, he characterised the latter as a people (*populus*), not an order.

In 1820, two years after the appearance of Hammer's work, the Spanish historian José Antonio Conde advanced the view that the

origins of the Christian military order were to be found in the
Islamic institution of the *ribat*, which has been defined as a
fortified convent whose inmates combined a religious way of life
with fighting against the enemies of Islam; and his opinion has
continued to receive support, especially from Spanish historians.
The claim is not based on any direct evidence of borrowing, and
rests on the supposed similarities between the Islamic and Christian institutions, and on the assumption that the combining of a
religious and military way of life was alien to Christian tradition,
which forbade clerics to fight. The objection might, of course, be
raised that, if the gulf was so wide, Christians would not have
imitated Islam, but it has been maintained that the barrier which
had to be overcome was negotiated by a process of 'stimulus
diffusion': the divide was too great for the imitation to be
consciously acknowledged, but the Islamic concept acted as a
stimulus, which led to its reinvention on the Christian side as the
military order.

Advocates of this argument naturally cannot be expected to
produce evidence in support of their case; yet the theory would be
strengthened if it could be shown in the first place that Westerners
who had settled in the Holy Land after the first crusade knew
about the Islamic institution. Evidence concerning *ribats* is,
however, slight, and investigation is further hampered by the
fact that the term *ribat* was also used to describe buildings which
were not military strongholds. It has not been shown that there
were military *ribats* along the Muslim borders with the crusader
states in the early twelfth century; and as renewed Muslim interest
in holy war was only slowly aroused in this region of Islam in the
twelfth century, it may be doubted whether any *ribats* of this kind
were created during the early decades of the twelfth century in
districts bordering on the crusader states.

Even if it were accepted that the Franks in Syria knew of the
Islamic institution, it may still be questioned whether it could
have provided a model for the military order. Little is known of
the personnel of *ribats*, but it seems that at least in some cases these
fortresses were defended in part by garrisons of professional
troops, receiving assistance from volunteers who combined devo-
tional practices with fighting. These volunteers, who have been
seen as the model for the Templars, in some instances decided to
spend the rest of their lives giving service of this kind, but most

were men who served for only a limited period – often for a term of forty days or during Ramadan. Such volunteers, serving on a temporary basis, had little in common with members of Christian military orders. They were merely Muslims who led devout lives while fighting, and may be compared more readily with Western crusaders, who were expected to live soberly and devoutly and who in some instances had to serve for a fixed period in order to gain an indulgence. They may also be compared with the secular knights who lived with, and fought alongside, the Templars for a fixed term but did not become members of the order. Admittedly, it has recently been argued that the earliest Templars did not take the normal monastic vows and that before 1129 those giving only temporary service constituted at least a major element of the community; but the surviving evidence for the period up to the Council of Troyes hardly supports this contention.

The argument could, of course, be advanced that, even if those serving in *ribats* differed in their way of life from Templars, Westerners may not have fully comprehended the nature of the Islamic institution, and that – with the inevitable tendency to assimilate alien practices to Christian ones – they would have regarded the *ribat* as a kind of monastery. Yet there would still remain the further objection that the original function of the Temple differed from that of the *ribat*. The latter was a fortress near the frontiers of Islam, established for the purpose of warfare against the infidel; the Templars, on the other hand, adopted their characteristic way of life in the first instance to afford protection for pilgrims, and they had their residence in Jerusalem, not in a frontier stronghold. The later transition to fighting in Christian armies against Islam, which did not involve any fundamental change in the Templars' mode of life, is easily explained by the shortage of military personnel in the crusader states.

If the derivation of the order of the Temple from the *ribat* is to be rejected, it must be asked whether the emergence of an institution which combined a military and religious way of life can be satisfactorily explained in a purely Christian context. The question concerns its acceptability to the Church rather than to a laity apparently already long influenced by the militant tradition of the Old Testament.

That canon law forbade clerics to fight was not an obstacle, for the Templars and the members of later military orders who fought

were not clerics. In all of these orders a distinction was made
between chaplains and lay brethren, and only the chaplains
received the tonsure and were *clerici*. To the rest the prohibition
on bearing arms did not apply: they were merely laymen leading
a religious life.

Yet fighting might also appear at first sight to have been
incompatible in the eyes of the Church with the religious life,
by means of which men sought to express their love of God and to
devote themselves to His service away from the world and remote
from secular affairs and concerns. This form of life was characterised by a contempt for the world, and the individual who
practised it was expected, in the words of the Benedictine rule, 'to
cut himself off from worldly affairs'.[2] Certainly in the early
Middle Ages the gap between the military and the religious life
was seen to be wide. Smaragdus, abbot of Saint-Mihiel, writing in
the early ninth century, drew a stark contrast between monks
(*milites Christi*) and warriors (*milites seculi*):

> There are secular soldiers (*milites seculi*) and there are soldiers of
> Christ (*milites Christi*); but secular soldiers bear feeble and
> perilous arms, while those of the soldiers of Christ are most
> powerful and excellent; the former fight against their enemies in
> such a way that they lead both themselves and those they kill to
> everlasting punishment; the latter fight against evil so that after
> death they may gain the reward of eternal life; the former fight
> in such a way that they descend to Hell, the latter fight so that
> they may achieve glory; the former fight in such a way that
> after death they serve with devils in Hell, the latter so that they
> may possess the kingdom of heaven in eternity with the angels.[3]

In some ways the gulf would seem to have been widening in the
century before the emergence of the Temple, for – partly as a
reaction to current trends in the Church – there was a desire to
demarcate more precisely the various groups in society. John of
Fécamp complained that 'the clergy and the people, the priest
and the monk differ in no way either in their deeds or in their
conduct'.[4] One consequence of this attitude was a new emphasis
amongst religious on complete withdrawal from the world. Yet
while this further retreat represented one strand in the religious
life of the eleventh and early twelfth centuries, there was also at

that time a development of institutions, involving both clerics and laymen, which sought to adapt the religious life to more active pursuits such as charitable work and preaching, as is apparent from the establishment of hospices and hospitals as well as from the foundation of houses of regular canons. To some, an active life of this kind seemed superior to a purely contemplative existence. These forms of service might nevertheless appear to be far removed from the sordid business of fighting; but in seeking to explain the emergence of the military order in the early twelfth century it is necessary to take account of the role which the Church was then assigning to warriors and of the evaluation then being placed by the Church on some forms of fighting.

At the time of the Gregorian reform movement, ecclesiastics were beginning to attribute social and Christian obligations to all warriors, not just to kings and princes. Emphasis was placed on the warrior's responsibility to protect the weak and the poor, the Church and Christianity; he was also expected to refrain from fighting for his own glory or for material profit. *Militia* was thus contrasted with *malitia*. In the early 1090s, the Gregorian theorist Bonizo of Sutri defined the duties of warriors by stating that:

> It is their duty to obey their lords, not to covet booty, not to spare their own lives in protecting those of their lords, to fight to death for the welfare of the state, to make war on schismatics and heretics, to defend the poor, widows and orphans, not to violate their sworn fidelity and in no way to forswear their lords.[5]

Before the end of the eleventh century some of these ideas found a practical expression in the preaching of the first crusade, for Urban II made a general appeal for help, and did not turn just to kings and princes for aid. Those chroniclers who produced versions of his speech at Clermont assumed that he also called for an end to internal strife and feuding; while in a decree issued at Clermont those were singled out for approbation who went on the crusade 'out of devotion alone, not to obtain honour or money'.[6]

The emergence of the military order is obviously to be related to the Church's efforts to influence the attitudes of the warrior class. St Bernard of Clairvaux described both Templars and crusaders as belonging to the true *militia*, which he contrasted with the old *malitia*, and in his *De Laude novae militiae*, written in support of the Templars, he distinguished at length between the brethren of the Temple and secular warriors, who fought for worldly ends. In the prologue of the Templar rule it was further claimed that in the Temple 'the knightly order has again flourished and revived, for, abandoning its zeal for justice, it had not been defending the poor or churches, as was its function, but had been devoting itself to plundering, pillaging and killing'.[7]

Yet while the military order by the nature of its activities might be seen as exemplifying the true *militia*, its brethren obviously differed from crusaders and others by combining these functions with a religious form of life. This was possible because of the evaluation then being placed by the Church on some forms of warfare. Fighting in the true *militia* was becoming widely accepted as a new way of achieving salvation. The origins of this notion can be traced back at least as far as the ninth century, and it finds frequent expression in the sources for the first crusade, where those participating in the expedition were promised remission of sins and those dying on the crusade were regarded as martyrs. Warfare in the true *militia* was not devoted to the worldly ends of personal glory and material gain, and was ceasing to be regarded as a purely secular activity. It was coming to be seen as a work of charity and a way of expressing love for God and for one's neighbours and brothers. Urban II, in a letter to the inhabitants of Bologna in 1096, wrote that the crusaders 'have exposed their possessions and their persons for the love of God and their neighbour', while in Baldric of Dol's version of the Pope's speech at Clermont, Urban states that 'to lay down one's life for one's brothers is a sign of love'.[8] When Innocent II asserted in 1139 that by their deeds the Templars were fulfilling the words of the Gospel, 'greater love hath no man than this, that a man lay down his life for his friends', he was not expressing a new concept.[9] To fight in the true *militia* was therefore to abandon worldly concerns and material desires. Like monks, those who went on crusade were devoting themselves to the service of God, while the activities of the true knighthood were also comparable with the charitable work undertaken by religious institutions on behalf of the poor, the sick and pilgrims.

Despite the apparent contrast between the life of the monk and that of the warrior, the wide gulf which had earlier been seen to separate the religious from the military way of life no longer existed. Guibert of Nogent, in a frequently quoted comment, viewed the monastic life and participation in a crusade as alternative routes to salvation:

> In our time God has instituted holy wars, so that the equestrian order and the erring people, who like ancient pagans were commonly engaged in mutual slaughter, might find a new way of meriting salvation. They are no longer obliged, as used to be the case, to leave the world and to choose the monastic life and a religious rule; they can gain God's grace to no mean extent by pursuing their own profession, unconfined and in secular garb;[10]

and while Smaragdus and St Bernard both drew a contrast between the soldier of Christ (*miles Christi*) who sought salvation and the secular soldier (*miles seculi*) who would be damned, and used some of the same texts to support their arguments, in the *De Laude novae militiae* the *miles Christi* was a warrior and not the monk of the earlier work. It was, in fact, the bridging of the gap between the two that enabled the term *miles Christi*, which had formerly been used of the monk, to be applied now to the warrior. The way was therefore open for the two kinds of *miles Christi* to be combined in the same person, and for an institution to emerge 'in which a twin conflict is equally and indefatigably waged, both against flesh and blood and against the spiritual forces of evil in the heavens'.[11]

Although the Temple was the first military order to emerge, the institution had to some extent been foreshadowed by secular confraternities, devoted to the true purposes of fighting, which had been established in the eleventh century in areas away from the borders of Christendom and among men who had no knowledge of Islam. Wazo, bishop of Liège, is reported to have exacted an oath from a small band of warriors who undertook to support him and his church, and towards the end of the eleventh century a military confraternity of ten nobles was created for the protection of the monastery of Grande-Sauve near Bordeaux: their swords were consecrated in the monastery church and they promised to defend the monks and the monastery's property and also to protect pilgrims visiting the house. The importance of these confraternities should obviously not be exaggerated. They appear to have been loose associations with little formal organisation. Yet eleventh-century sources also contain not only references to monks who took up arms, but also defences of, and justifications for, their action. In the early eleventh century Bernard of Angers wrote approvingly of a prior of Conques who had been accustomed to wage war against malefactors. Bernard was little concerned that monastic regulations were being breached, and even commented: 'would that the lazy monk would put aside his idleness and act so bravely for the benefit of his monastery, rather than being inwardly a hiding-place for iniquity, while externally wearing the honoured habit of his order'.[12] The Cluniac chronicler Raoul Glaber was not so outspoken when he reported that monks in Spain had fought against al-Mansur, but he stated that 'they had wanted to fight out of brotherly love rather than for any glory of worldly praise', and said that a vision had revealed that those who had died had gained salvation.[13] Although on this occasion monks had taken up arms out of necessity, Raoul's comment provides a clear anticipation of twelfth-century attitudes towards the combining of a religious form of life with fighting.

Although the emergence of the Temple can be related to developments taking place within western Christendom, some Westerners nevertheless expressed doubts about the new foundation or voiced opposition to it. It would have been surprising if opinion had been uniformly favourable, for the changes which had been occurring in the West had not gained universal acceptance. Critics could quote many authorities which seemed to conflict with the new attitudes towards warfare, and the theoretical basis for the latter had still not been fully elaborated. Yet some evidence which might seem to imply doubts about, or hostility to, the Temple can be interpreted more satisfactorily in other ways. It is certainly true that in their early years the Templars gained little support, and this might be construed as an indication of uncertainty or opposition. William of Tyre's remark that after nine years there were still only nine brothers can be interpreted partly as a play on numbers, but the chronicler was implying that during that early period there was no marked increase in membership. There is similarly little record of patronage of the Templars in the West before the later 1120s. But this absence of support is to be attributed to a lack of awareness rather than to disapproval. When Hugh of Payns and several of his colleagues did travel to the West, probably in 1127, the order quickly began to receive gifts in various parts of Europe, and ecclesiastical approval was gained at the Council of Troyes, which was presided over by the papal legate, Matthew of Albano, and attended by the archbishops of Reims and Sens and their bishops and also by a number of abbots, including those of Cîteaux and apparently of Clairvaux.

It has, however, sometimes been argued that St Bernard gave only reluctant support to the Temple. He wrote the *De Laude novae militiae* only after three requests had been made by Hugh of Payns, and the letter which he wrote to Hugh of Champagne when the latter joined the Temple has also been seen as an indication of St Bernard's uncertainty. But in this letter St Bernard was not obviously doing anything more than mourning the absence of a friend, and although his claim that he was unfitted for the task of writing in support of the Templars may not provide the real reason for the tardy appearance of the *De Laude*, the delay is not necessarily a sign of misgivings about the order.

Yet both the *De Laude* and a letter written about the same time to the Templars by a certain Hugh – it has been attributed both to Hugh of Payns and to Hugh of St Victor – reveal that in the minds of some people there were misgivings and doubts. The *De Laude* is an answer to criticisms which were being voiced of the Templars, and Hugh's letter shows that some members of the order were themselves experiencing doubts as well as being censured by outsiders. But the grounds for doubt and hostility require definition.

In the first chapter of the *De Laude* St Bernard comments:

> When a bodily enemy is resisted by bodily force alone, I do not consider it strange, nor do I think it unusual; and when war is waged against evil or demons by spiritual strength, I would not say that this is extraordinary, although praiseworthy, since the world is seen to be full of monks. But when a man is powerfully girded with both swords and marked out nobly by the belt of each, who would not think this worthy of all admiration, even though it is certainly unusual?[14]

The wording of this extract, and particularly the last clause, implies that one ground for criticism was the common suspicion in this period of any innovation. That this was one element in the criticism of the Templars is also suggested by the fact that later in the treatise St Bernard adopted a tactic frequently employed by those seeking to rebut charges of novelty: he attempted to root the order of the Temple firmly in the past. He could not pretend that it was an ancient foundation, but he quoted several biblical prophecies concerning Jerusalem to demonstrate that there was scriptural warrant for the new order. In incurring criticism of this kind the Templars did not, of course, stand alone in the early twelfth century: all new orders were attacked on these grounds.

But some criticism was concerned more specifically with the Templars' manner of life. Although brethren were regarded as part of the true *militia*, in practice the habits of the old *malitia* were not easily overcome. In his letter to the Templars, Hugh wrote that the Devil sought to corrupt good works: 'the invisible enemy, who is always seeking to tempt... tries to instil hatred and frenzy when you kill, and greed when you despoil'.[15] Hugh did not consider that the Templars had succumbed, because in his view they hated not the man but iniquity and, because of their sins, infidels deserved to lose what was taken from them, while the Templars merited reward for their labours. But the inclusion of these remarks in the letter indicates one cause for concern.

According to Hugh, the Devil was also tempting the Templars to abandon their way of life in order to achieve spiritual progress, and he explained that he had heard that 'some of you have been disturbed by those of little understanding who suggest that your profession, in which you have dedicated your lives to bearing arms against the enemies of the faith and of peace for the defence of Christians, that your profession, I say, is either unlawful or pernicious, that is, either a sin or an impediment to greater advancement'.[16] Hugh was here referring to two criticisms, the second of which regarded the military order as inferior to other religious institutions, although not to be rejected completely: it was merely a hindrance to greater progress. This was restated later in the letter when Hugh wrote that the Devil 'grants that it is good, since he cannot deny it, but argues that the less good should be abandoned for that which is better'.[17] Certainly some outsiders, including St Bernard himself, regarded this form of life as inferior to that of the monk. But Hugh's statement also implies a more fundamental criticism, which regarded the Templar way of life as unlawful and sinful: to devote oneself in this way to fighting against the enemies of the faith was wrong. The whole concept of the military order was being called into question. This criticism was not, however, discussed in detail by Hugh, and clarification is to be sought rather in St Bernard's *De Laude*. He devoted a considerable amount of space to reassuring the Templars that to fight and kill the infidel for the sake of Christ and Christianity was not only permissible but also meritorious. The third chapter of the treatise thus begins:

> Indeed the soldiers of Christ fearlessly fight the battles of their Lord, in no way concerned about the sin of slaughtering the enemy or about the danger of being killed themselves, for a death either inflicted or suffered for Christ has nothing of sin in it but merits much glory.[18]

To St Bernard, the evaluation of warfare seems to have been the main issue of contention and the chief reason for criticism: once it had been established that fighting could be meritorious, he apparently saw no objection to combining a military and a religious way of life.

Other Military Orders in the Holy Land

DESPITE the widespread favour which came to be shown to the Templars, there is no evidence of attempts to found further orders of this type in the Holy Land during the twelfth and thirteenth centuries; but several existing religious institutions in Syria were transformed into military orders. These comprised the Hospital of St John of Jerusalem; the order of St Lazarus, which began as a leper hospital and which was first mentioned in the surviving sources in 1142; the Teutonic order, which grew out of the German hospital established outside Acre at the time of the third crusade (it is not necessary to consider here the vexed issue of the relationship between this hospital and an earlier German hospital in Jerusalem); and the order of St Thomas of Acre, which had originated as a house of regular canons, also founded during the third crusade.

The timing of the transformation is less certain in the case of the first two than in that of the others. The dating of the militarisation of the Hospital of St John has aroused much discussion, which has been encouraged by the lack of decisive evidence. The suggested dates have ranged between the 1120s and about 1160. The first date is probably too early, and the second is too late. The office of constable mentioned in a document written in 1126 may not have been a military post, and although the Hospitaller master Raymond of Le Puy was reported to be in the king of Jerusalem's company on an expedition against Ascalon in 1128, this does not necessarily indicate that the Hospitallers were then involved in fighting. On the other hand, although no unequivocal reference to military officials or military personnel is found in the surviving sources until the 1160s, earlier silence – given the nature of the documentation – is not necessarily of any consequence. It is, however, significant that in 1136 Fulk of Jerusalem granted the Hospitallers the newly-constructed castle of Beit-Jibrin, near the southern borders of the kingdom, and that Raymond II of Tripoli in 1144 assigned the Hospitallers a series of castles, including Crac, which lay in a district exposed to Muslim attack near the eastern frontiers of his county; he also surrendered to them rights of lordship over Montferrand (Bar'in) and Rafaniyah, which had been in Muslim hands since 1137. It has admittedly been argued that garrisons for the castles could have been provided not by brethren themselves but by paid retainers and by vassals settled in the surrounding districts. Yet it may be doubted whether reliable vassals would have been readily available: although there were some Christian settlers at Beit-Jibrin before the neighbouring city of Ascalon fell to the Christians in 1153, it was only later that the main work of establishing a Latin settlement there appears to have been undertaken successfully. To attract settlers to a frontier region was not easy, and it could hardly have been assumed that the defence of a stronghold could be guaranteed in this way. Native paid troops are certainly known to have been employed by the Hospital later in the century, but even if in 1136 the Hospitallers could have solved the problem of manpower in this way, it was necessary for such troops to be commanded and controlled, and this task would have fallen to the Hospitallers themselves, for Hugh of St Abraham, who had previously exercised lordship over

Beit-Jibrin, surrendered his rights of authority, just as William of Crac abandoned his claims to the castle of Crac in 1144. The Hospitallers were being assigned direct control over strongholds and were not just receiving rights of overlordship. To have entrusted frontier strongholds in these circumstances to an institution which contained no military element would have been foolhardy, and it is difficult to believe that Fulk would have asked Hugh of St Abraham to surrender his rights, or that the grant of Beit-Jibrin would have been made to the Hospitallers 'with the encouragement of the whole kingdom, both clergy and people',[19] if the Hospital had still been a purely charitable institution. And in 1144 the count of Tripoli would hardly have given an undertaking not to make truces with the Muslims without the counsel and assent of the Hospitallers if the latter had still been merely caring for pilgrims and the sick. It may be argued, therefore, that the Hospital was already being transformed into a military order in the 1130s.

Evidence about the militarisation of the hospital of St Lazarus is even sparser than that relating to the Hospital of St John. Although it has sometimes been assumed that it had taken on military obligations by the middle of the twelfth century, it is almost a hundred years later that the first firm reports of military activity occur: among the earliest engagements in which brethren of St Lazarus are known to have participated are the battle of La Forbie in 1244 (where, according to the patriarch of Jerusalem, they lost most of their forces), and Louis IX's Egyptian crusade six years later: their presence on this campaign was recorded by the English chronicler Matthew Paris.

The emergence of the Teutonic order and of St Thomas of Acre as military orders can be dated more precisely. It is generally accepted that the transformation of the former occurred in the last decade of the twelfth century, although there has been disagreement about the exact date. Some have maintained that military functions were already being assigned to the German hospital in 1193, when the ruler, Henry of Champagne, gave it a section of the defences of the city of Acre. But these were given to the brethren of the hospital on the condition that 'they repair and improve them, as may be necessary for the fortification of the city':[20] the obligation appears to have been a financial, rather than a military, one. There is, in fact, no evidence of military involvement until 1198. The *Narracio de primordiis ordinis Teutonici* relates that, when German crusaders were preparing to return home from the East in that year after hearing of the death of the emperor, Henry VI,

> it seemed advantageous and honourable to many of the German princes and magnates who were there that the rule of the Temple should be given to the aforesaid hospital. When this had been discussed, the German prelates, princes and magnates who were in the East met in the house of the Temple, and called the available prelates and barons of the Holy Land to give counsel on so salutary a matter. All were in full agreement that the aforesaid house should have the regulations of the Hospital of St John concerning the sick and the poor, as in the past, but for the rest should have the rule of the Militia of the Temple with regard to clerics, knights and other brothers.[21]

Admittedly, this account was probably not written until the middle of the thirteenth century, but some details contained in it are corroborated by a letter of confirmation which Innocent III issued in 1199.

If one of the hospitals established during the third crusade had become a military order by the end of the century, the transformation of the other did not take place until thirty years later. Peter of Roches, the bishop of Winchester, on whose initiative the militarisation of St Thomas of Acre was undertaken, is known to have arrived in the Holy Land by the autumn of 1227, and the institution was called a *militia* for the first time in an English document, which cannot be dated later than the autumn of the following year.

The surviving sources provide little direct information about the reasons for the transformation of these institutions. A precedent had obviously been set by the Temple, but it is usually not clear why it was followed. In the Hospital, the first step towards militarisation may have been taken by extending its obligations to pilgrims and adopting the Templar practice of protecting them, for a letter of Innocent II states that:

> servants, whom the brothers of the house maintain at their own expense especially for this purpose, devotedly and diligently

ensure when necessary that pilgrims can journey more safely to the holy places consecrated by the bodily presence of our Lord.[22]

The further argument has been advanced that the Hospitallers were compelled to adopt a military role because of the competitive power of the Templars, who had a wide appeal and who threatened to overshadow a purely charitable order. Yet it has recently been doubted whether the Templars were in any condition to arouse jealousy in the 1130s, since – as has been seen – in their early years they gained little support and some brethren had qualms about their vocation. But once the Temple had become known in the West this support was soon forthcoming, and in the 1130s the order was in fact becoming a strong contender for patronage, although it would be difficult to prove that the favour shown to the Templars was a serious threat to the fortunes of the Hospital: increased patronage of the Temple may have been largely at the expense of older monastic foundations.

The transformation of the German hospital has been interpreted as an attempt to maintain and strengthen German influence in the Holy Land and even to further imperialist plans; but the reality of the latter may be questioned, and arguments concerning political considerations can be no more than hypotheses. The same is true of the suggestion that the change was viewed as a way of ensuring the future of the foundation. This last consideration is more clearly apparent in the transformation of St Thomas of Acre. When confirming its change of function, Gregory IX stated that 'the canons of that house did not have sufficient resources to sustain themselves adequately, and the future of the foundation, which was weighed down by poverty and near to collapse, was for a long time in doubt'; he also said that the bishop of Winchester had acted 'on account of the dissoluteness and negligence of the canons'.[23] But, if the hospital was in a poor state, it is necessary to explain why the decision was made to convert it into a military order, and here the outlook and attitudes of the bishop of Winchester should be taken into consideration, for Peter of Roches had in the past played the part of the warrior bishop, and during his stay in the Holy Land he also contributed towards the costs of restoration work on the defences of Jaffa and Sidon.

Yet, when altering the character of St Thomas of Acre, he was also acting on the advice of the patriarch of Jerusalem and of the magnates of the kingdom, just as the local prelates and barons had advised on the future of the German hospital at the end of the twelfth century; and they would no doubt have stressed the military needs of the Holy Land. The lack of manpower there was obviously a constant factor in the transformation of charitable institutions into military orders. Throughout the twelfth and thirteenth centuries Western settlement in Syria remained limited, and there was a need for institutions which could help to remedy the deficiency of troops. The foundations which became military orders must therefore either already have had men who could fight – this might in itself help to explain the assumption of military functions – or have been able to obtain them. It has been pointed out, for example, that the law-book known as the *Livre au roi* stipulated that knights and sergeants who contracted leprosy should join the order of St Lazarus, and that Templar regulations similarly expected a leprous brother to transfer to St Lazarus. As it is not known when the leper hospital became a military order, the significance of these rulings must remain uncertain, but presumably from the outset St Lazarus was likely to include some men who were capable of fighting, especially as the term *lepra* was loosely applied in the Middle Ages to a variety of diseases which were not always incapacitating. The historian James of Vitry, writing in the second decade of the thirteenth century, was of the opinion that the transformation of the German hospital was largely to be explained by the existence of members who were capable of fighting:

> since men not only of lesser rank, but also of knightly status and some German nobles...bound themselves by vows to the hospital...they thought that it would be pleasing and agreeable to God, and more meritorious, not only to serve the poor and sick, but also to lay down their lives for Christ, and by defending the Holy Land from the enemies of the faith of Christ to engage in both spiritual and bodily warfare for Christ.[24]

Some German crusaders may have decided to stay out in the East in 1198, although the *Narracio* reports the recruitment only of the German noble Hermann of Kirchheim at that time. The existing personnel of St Thomas of Acre could not, on the other hand, have provided a nucleus of fighting men when it became a military order, for the canons were subject to the canonical prohibition on fighting; they were removed, and presumably the bishop of Winchester, who according to one chronicler was 'well-supplied with a force of warriors', provided a military element from amongst his followers.[25]

The Iberian Peninsula

IN the early twelfth century, the Hospitallers were already attracting patronage in Spain as in other parts of the West: the first known gift in the peninsula was made in Catalonia in 1108. Two decades later donations there were also beginning to be made to the Temple: some were received in 1128 by Raymond Bernard, who was one of the Templars dispatched to various parts of the West at that time to solicit gifts. In the early decades of the century the Hospital was, of course, still a purely charitable institution, but once the Templars appeared in Spain Christian rulers there quickly sought to involve them in the reconquest. In 1128 the Countess Teresa promised them the frontier stronghold of Soure in Portugal, and three years later, on the other side of the peninsula, the border castle of Grañena was granted by the count of Barcelona 'for the defence of Christianity according to the purpose for which the order was founded'.[26] This wording was repeated when Armengol VI, Count of Urgel, in 1132 assigned the Templars another castle near the Muslim frontier at Barbará. The naming of the Templars as one of his three heirs by Alfonso I of Aragon in 1131 probably also had the purpose of bringing the order into the reconquest. Yet the hopes of the Spanish rulers were not immediately fulfilled: it is clear from surviving sources, for example, that the castle of Grañena was not immediately garrisoned by the Templars. In the early 1130s the order still regarded Spain merely as a source of manpower and revenue, and at this stage of its development was no doubt wary of committing itself to fighting on a second front against Islam. The Christian rulers nevertheless persisted in their efforts to gain military assistance from the Templars – a step which might also ensure that recruitment by the order within the peninsula did not drain manpower away from Spain to the Holy Land. An undertaking given in 1134 by Raymond Berenguer IV of Barcelona and a group of Catalan nobles, to serve with the Templars for a year, seems to have been part of a plan to prevail upon the order to establish a convent at Grañena. Yet it was not until nine years later that the count of Barcelona – after lengthy negotiations which also concerned the order's claim to a third of Aragon – finally persuaded the Templars to participate in the reconquest. This was the import of the count's declaration in 1143 that

> for the defence of the western church which is in Spain, for the defeat, overcoming and expulsion of the race of Moors and the exaltation of the holy Christian faith and religion, I have decreed that a militia shall be formed, on the model of the militia of the Temple of Solomon in Jerusalem which defends the eastern church, to be subject to the Temple and to follow that militia's rule and customs of holy obedience.[27]

Raymond Berenguer was, of course, interested in involving the Templars in the reconquest only on the eastern side of the peninsula, but the 1143 agreement clearly affected the order's role throughout Spain, and within a few years the Templars were fighting against the infidel in other parts of the peninsula. In 1144, Templars were reported to have been campaigning in the neighbourhood of Soure in Portugal, and probably by the middle of the century they were defending the castle of Calatrava in Castile.

Although by 1143 the Hospitallers appear to have adopted a military role in the Holy Land, it is clear from the negotiations concerning Alfonso I's will – in which the Hospital had also been named as an heir – that they were not then being brought into the Spanish reconquest. In those negotiations, the Hospitallers acted not with the Templars but with the third heir, the canons of the Holy Sepulchre; and while in 1143 the Templars received from the count of Barcelona a number of strongholds and a share in future conquests, the Hospitallers – like the canons of the Holy Sepulchre – received only minor concessions in return for the renunciation of their claims to the Aragonese kingdom. Yet, if in Spain the Hospital was still regarded as a charitable institution in 1143, five years later some brethren of the order were present at the siege of Tortosa, near the mouth of the Ebro, and it was apparently in 1149 that Raymond Berenguer IV assigned the Hospital the frontier castle of Amposta. In the charter of donation the count stated, in phrases reminiscent of the 1143 agreement with the Templars, that he was making the grant

> for the exaltation of the church of Christ, for the propagation of the faith and religion of holy Christianity, and for the defeat and confounding of the Moorish race;[28]

and it is clear from the wording of the document that the Hospitallers were expected to take up residence in the castle. The Hospital of St John therefore appears to have become involved in the Spanish reconquest by the middle of the twelfth century.

At that time the Temple and Hospital were the only military orders in the peninsula, although several military confraternities had earlier been set up there, and Alfonso I had apparently tried unsuccessfully to establish a military order, modelled on the Temple, at Monreal del Campo in the south of his kingdom. In the third quarter of the century, however, local military orders were being established in all of the peninsular kingdoms except Navarre. In Castile the order of Calatrava was founded in 1158, and Santiago was established in the neighbouring kingdom of Leon in 1170. It was also in Leon that San Julián de Pereiro, later known as the order of Alcántara, was created, although the precise date of its foundation is unknown. A chronicle of uncertain date assigns its establishment to the year 1156, but serious doubts have been expressed about the reliability of this account, and the earliest documentary reference to the order relates to the year 1176. This is also the year of the first documentary evidence of the foundation established in Portugal at Evora, which later became known as the order of Avis. Attempts have been made to trace the origins of this foundation back before the middle of the century, but no evidence has been produced to justify such claims, and constitutions which bear the date of 1162 have been shown to be forgeries. Evora had been conquered from the Muslims in 1165, but in the later 1160s and early 1170s the Portuguese ruler was favouring the Temple and then Santiago, and the Portuguese order was probably founded only shortly before 1176. In Aragon, on the other side of the peninsula, the order of Mountjoy was established, apparently in 1173, and in the next year the monastery of Grande-Sauve set up a dependency with military functions at the castle of Alcalá, which lay near the Aragonese border with Valencia. Most of the Spanish military orders were founded within a few years of each other in the third quarter of the twelfth century. Between the later 1170s and 1300 only two further orders are known to have been created: San Jorge de Alfama, which was established at the turn of the twelfth and thirteenth centuries in Aragon, and Santa María de España, which was set up in Castile in the 1270s.

All of these Spanish foundations had military functions from the outset: their foundation dates are therefore also the dates of their entry into the reconquest. In this they differ from the military orders which emerged in the Holy Land. The reasons for this can only be conjectured. Possibly in the Holy Land, where there was a constant shortage of manpower, the creation of entirely new institutions which could make a worthwhile contribution to Christian forces was not felt by most people to be a feasible undertaking. The bishop of Winchester, admittedly, appears to have been able to supply the personnel needed for the transformation of St Thomas of Acre, but this remained a very small establishment, playing only a limited role in the defence of the Holy Land. In Spain, on the other hand, the opportunities for recruitment were more favourable.

The Spanish military orders were clearly founded to further the reconquest, and were established in imitation of the Temple and Hospital. But an explanation of their creation should also take account of the particular aspirations of the founders and original members, and also of the various expectations of those – especially kings – who provided the patronage necessary for the creation of new military orders. Even the identity of the founders and original members is, however, not always known with certainty. Although in 1176 Gómez, the master of San Julián de Pereiro, was referred to as the 'first founder' of that order,[29] according to a chronicle account it was set up by a certain Suero of Salamanca. When the founder or first master is known, there is often little information concerning the identity of his colleagues. Since Alexander III in 1175 made reference to a council of thirteen in the order of Santiago, it has sometimes been argued that there were thirteen original companions of the founder, who was the Leonese noble Peter Fernández, and some historians have attempted to identify their names; but the whole argument lacks any factual basis. Since the founder of Mountjoy, Roderick, former count of Sarria, had previously been a member of the order of Santiago, it is possible that some of his early companions had similarly been brothers of that order: this supposition is corroborated by Alexander III's subsequent ruling that 'from now on' Roderick should accept no brothers of Santiago into his order.[30] But none of the early Mountjoy documents provides any further comment about Roderick's companions. Some of the early members of Calatrava may likewise have been drawn from the lay brethren of the Cistercian monastery of Fitero, whose abbot in 1158 acccepted responsibility for the defence of the stronghold of Calatrava and who established the order which took its name from that castle. But the account of the foundation given by the thirteenth-century chronicler Roderick Jiménez de Rada suggests that the original intention was to defend Calatrava with crusaders and mercenaries, rather than to create a new military order: he states that the archbishop of Toledo offered indulgences to those undertaking the defence of the castle and that this appeal met with a widespread response, while the abbot brought goods from his monastery, together with 'a multitude of warriors to whom he supplied wages and provisions'. And Roderick implies that it was from crusaders that the first members of the new order were drawn: 'then many who had been inspired by devotion received their order, having modified the habit as military activity demanded'.[31]

When the motivation of founders or original members is mentioned in the sources, it is usually explained merely in terms of pious endeavour. The prologue of the rule of Santiago thus records of the founders that:

> Inspired by the grace of the Holy Spirit, and realising the indescribable danger which threatened Christians, unless it could be overcome, they placed on their breasts the cross in the form of a sword and invoked the name of the blessed James, so that they might curb the attacks of the enemies of Christ and defend the church of God, and so that they might stand like a wall of fidelity against the frenzy of the infidel.[32]

But there were no doubt also more particular and personal reasons, which are only rarely noted in the sources. Roderick, the founder of Mountjoy, was reported to have left Santiago so that he could follow a stricter way of life: one cause of his discontent was said to be Santiago's practice of allowing members to have wives. His action was, however, seen less charitably by others as a sign of inconstancy.

Spanish kings obviously hoped that new orders would provide military assistance against the Muslims. The order of Santiago was first established at the castle of Cáceres, which lay near the Muslim frontier and which had recently been gained by Fernando II and was therefore in need of defenders. The order of Mountjoy was patronised by the Aragonese king, Alfonso II, to gain assistance in holding recently conquered territories in the district of Teruel, while the problem of securing frontier regions is also apparent in the foundation of San Jorge de Alfama, for Alfama, which lay near the frontier with Valencia, was described at the time as being a 'deserted place'.[33] The order of Santa María de España was founded when only Granada remained in Muslim hands and when much of the conflict with the Muslims centred on the control of the straits of Gibraltar, and it was apparently favoured by Alfonso X of Castile as a means of gaining naval assistance, for the order seems at first to have been mainly concerned with fighting at sea: in the cortes of Zamora in 1274 it was assigned certain revenues 'for the affairs of the sea',[34] while its headquarters were establised at Cartagena, and its other early establishments were also on the coast.

Yet, given the need for military or naval assistance, it is necessary to explain why Spanish rulers should have lent their support to new orders instead of just relying upon Templars and Hospitallers. In some cases the explanation lies in the inadequacy of the international orders. In 1158, the Templars informed Sancho III of Castile that they could no longer undertake the defence of Calatrava. New guardians had to be found for the stronghold, but no nobles were willing to assume the task; Sancho therefore agreed to the proposals which led to the foundation of the order of Calatrava, even though at the time some considered the abbot of Fitero's offer to be misguided. Yet this was not the only consideration. Local orders could devote all of their resources to warfare in the Iberian peninsula and did not have to send men and money to the Holy Land, as the international orders did. It may also have been thought desirable to encourage several institutions rather than to place too much power in the hands of one or two foundations. At the time of the Templar trial in the early fourteenth century the Aragonese king, James II, certainly claimed that his predecessors had patronised various orders with the intention that power and authority should be shared among many. That this was a justified claim is suggested by the actions of Alfonso II in the later twelfth century. Although the agreement made with the count of Barcelona in 1143 gave the Templars a claim to a fifth of Aragonese conquests, they were excluded from the territories gained by Alfonso in the second half of the twelfth century. The Aragonese king extended his patronage instead to Mountjoy and Grande-Sauve. He may have been wary of allowing too much power to the Templars, who were already firmly entrenched along the lower reaches of the Ebro. A similar concern may also explain why Alfonso's son, Pedro II, gave Alfama as the base for a new order.

There are also indications that Iberian rulers envisaged using the Spanish orders against their Christian enemies as well as against the infidel. Although Fernando II's early charters to Santiago refer to its fighting for the defence of Christianity, Cáceres had been gained from Portugal and not from the Muslims, with whom Fernando was at peace in 1170. The more immediate threat was therefore likely to come from a Christian neighbour. This factor is further illustrated by the gift of the castle of Monsanto made to Santiago by the Portuguese ruler Afonso Henriques in 1172, for the condition was attached that it should not be subjected to a commander of another kingdom and that the brother in charge of the stronghold should always receive Afonso's son or daughter there, if they held the kingdom, even if they were at war with Christians. In fact, however, in the later twelfth century the Spanish orders quickly adopted a neutral stance in the conflicts between Christian kingdoms in Spain.

Although the Spanish orders received considerable support from the Christian rulers of the peninsula, not all flourished. In 1186 an attempt was made to amalgamate Mountjoy with the Templars: it was done in the absence of the master, Roderick, who may by then have been dying or have lost interest in his foundation, and lack of a leader may have been one of the reasons for the proposed union. The plan was not, however, implemented, possibly because of opposition from the Aragonese king, Alfonso II, who was still trying to prevent the Templars from gaining influence in southern Aragon. Instead, Mountjoy was amalgamated in 1188 with the ransom hospital of the Holy Redeemer which had recently been founded by Alfonso at Teruel. But difficulties continued, and in 1196 Alfonso was obliged to agree to the union of the order with the Templars: it was reported that he feared that the frontier castles held by the order would not be defended and had therefore commanded the master of Mountjoy to surrender them to the Crown or give them to an order which could protect them. In the circumstances, amalgamation with the Temple was seen to provide the best solution. This union was not, however, accepted by all members of Mountjoy, and a group led by Roderick González refused to abide by the master's decision and established itself at the Castilian castle of Monfragüe, situated on the river Tagus near the Muslim frontier. The dissident group became known as the order of Monfragüe, but it in turn was soon beset by problems. At the Lateran Council in 1215, the master of Calatrava reported that the brethren of Monfragüe wanted to enter his own order, and this proposal was implemented in 1221, when Monfragüe was in serious financial difficulties, although again there were some brothers who resisted amalgamation. While Mountjoy's and Monfragüe's existence came to an end because of internal problems, Santa María de España lost its identity at least in part because of difficulties encountered by the order of Santiago. In 1280 the latter suffered a serious defeat at Moclín, not far from the city of Granada: the master and other leading brothers were killed. It was apparently to make good these losses that an amalgamation took place, with the master of the smaller order becoming the new head of Santiago.

Although the Spanish military orders had been founded to fight against Muslims in the Iberian peninsula, and although their activities were in practice concentrated there, an enlargement of their role was on various occasions envisaged and sometimes attempted. A natural extension of their activity would have been to North Africa. Thus when a group of men from Avila joined the order of Santiago in 1172 they stated that 'if, when the Saracens have been driven from Spanish lands on this side of the sea, the master and chapter should decide to fight in the land of Morocco, they would not cease to assist them as brothers'.[35] An opportunity to extend Santiago's interests to North Africa appeared to have occurred in 1245, when it was reported that Zeid Aazon, the Muslim ruler of Salé on the Atlantic coast of North Africa, wished to become a Christian and was ready to cede his realm to the order of Santiago. Innocent IV gave his approval, but nothing came of the project. It has been suggested that military commitments within the peninsula prevented the order from acting on this offer, but it seems more likely that the report concerning Zeid Aazon, like so many rumoured conversions of infidel rulers, proved to be unfounded.

There were also at times proposals to establish some of the Spanish military orders in the Holy Land. On some occasions the initiative came from the West. In the later 1170s the master of Mountjoy went to Syria and was given various properties, including rights which were granted by Reginald of Châtillon and confirmed by Baldwin IV on the condition that the order fought continuously against the infidel in the Holy Land. It was, in fact, at this time that the order adopted the name of Mountjoy, taken from the hill from which pilgrims gained their first sight of the city of Jerusalem. The master's action is perhaps to be seen as an example of the widespread concern amongst Spaniards for the defence of the Holy Land, despite the presence of the infidel in the peninsula. There was a more particular reason behind a plan to dispatch brothers of Calatrava to the East in 1206: the king of Castile was at that time at peace with the Muslims, and Calatrava could no longer fulfil its functions in Spain. A further proposal to establish the order in Syria was put forward in 1234. The circumstances in which this suggestion was made are not known, but it is clear that the initiative came from the order itself. On the other hand, a plan to establish Santiago in northern Syria in 1180 seems to have been initiated by Bohemund III of Antioch. He was no doubt anxious to secure manpower from any possible source, and promised the master of Santiago several strongholds in the principality of Antioch on condition that the order sent a force of men out to the East within a year. In fact, none of these plans concerning the Holy Land bore fruit. They are known only from the documents in which the proposals were first set out, and no further evidence survives to indicate why the

Spanish orders failed to become established in Syria. But it is to be presumed that changing circumstances within the peninsula, or an inability to supply the expected aid, provide the explanation. In addition to these proposals concerning the Holy Land there were, however, also attempts to involve Spanish orders in conflicts against pagans and schismatics in Central and Eastern Europe.

Central and Eastern Europe

THE Hospital and the Temple were the first military orders to establish themselves in Central Europe: they were already acquiring properties in parts of the region in the twelfth century. Yet although in 1198 the Hospitallers were assigned Starogard, which lay near the Prussian border in Pomerelia, most early acquisitions were not situated near the pagan frontiers, and there is no evidence to indicate that in their early years in this region the Templars or Hospitallers took up arms against pagan opposition. Gifts appear to have been made to them in order to provide resources for the Holy Land and for charitable work rather than for fighting against neighbouring pagans. When in 1225, for example, a Polish duke, Ladislas, confirmed donations which had been made to the Hospitallers of Poznan by his father, Mieszko III, it was stated that the object of the gifts was the maintenance of local pilgrims and the poor, and that any surplus income was to be sent to the Holy Land. Despite their early appearance in the region, the Temple and Hospital were not, in fact, the first military orders to be employed against pagans in Central and Eastern Europe. Reliance was at first placed on new foundations and on other orders which were called in from Spain and the Holy Land.

In the early decades of the thirteenth century two new military orders were founded to fight in the Baltic region. The Militia of Christ of Livonia – also known as the order of the Swordbrethren – was established at Riga in 1202, and the order of Dobrin, which took its name from the stronghold of Dobrzyn on the Vistula, was founded in 1228 or shortly before. The circumstances of the two foundations were similar: when Gregory IX issued a confirmation for the latter order in 1228 he in fact stated that it had been set up 'on the model of the Militia of Christ of Livonia'.[36] Both were established in connection with missions. By 1202, missionary activity had been in progress in Livonia for some twenty years but had achieved little lasting success. Albert of Buxhövden, who was appointed bishop of Livonia in 1199, was not the first to realise the necessity of force, which was needed not only to protect Christians in the region but also as a means of subjugation and conversion. It could also, of course, help to further plans for the creation of personal empires. Albert relied mainly on crusaders, but their recruitment was not always easy and they had the disadvantage of providing only short-term service. A more permanent force was required and to answer this need the order of the Swordbrethren was founded. According to the chronicler Henry of Livonia, the initiative came from Albert's helper, Theoderich, a monk from the Cistercian monastery of Loccum near Hanover, who,

> anticipating the perfidy of the Livonians and fearing that he would not be able to withstand the multitude of pagans, therefore established certain brothers of the knighthood of Christ in order to increase the numbers of the faithful and to preserve the church among the people.[37]

In the same way, the creation of the order of Dobrin was linked with the missionary efforts of Bishop Christian of Prussia. He had started missionary work in the first decade of the thirteenth century, but had encountered difficulties similar to those experienced in Livonia. Like his counterparts there, he realised the necessity of force and, like them, he at first sought the help of crusaders. He then turned to the idea of establishing a military order, although in this instance the secular power also had a say in its foundation. The Polish duke, Conrad of Masovia, wanted assistance both in defence and for offensive campaigns, and gave the stronghold of Dobrzyn with its surrounding territories as a base for the new order. In both cases the first recruits appear to have been drawn mainly from regions with which the founders had close links. Some early members of the order of Swordbrethren came from places lying in the district to the south of Loccum, and some brothers of Dobrin had their origins in Mecklenburg, Nordelbeland and Pomerania.

At about the time when Dobrin was being founded, further down the Vistula a convent of the Spanish order of Calatrava was being established near the Prussian border at Thymau in Pomerelia. In 1229, the master of the brothers of Calatrava in Thymau was a witness to a charter in favour of the monastery of Oliva, and in the following year several brothers of Thymau witnessed a further agreement. It has been suggested that the immediate occasion for Calatrava's arrival in this region was the destruction of the abbey of Oliva by the Prussians in 1226. Oliva was a Cistercian house, and Calatrava's links with the Cistercians may well explain its appearance on the Prussian frontier at this time. But the circumstances are not revealed in the surviving sources.

Of greater import, however, was the establishment of the Teutonic order in Central and Eastern Europe. This first occurred in Hungary. In 1211, the Hungarian king, Andrew II, granted to it the district of Burzenland, which lay on the borders of the kingdom to the north of the Transylvanian Alps, and which was described at the time as being deserted and uninhabited. The purpose of the grant was not only defence against attack from the Cumans, but also expansion. Andrew's summoning of the Teutonic order is probably to be explained in part by the influence of the German element at the Hungarian court following the king's marriage, and it is perhaps also significant that, shortly before the Teutonic order was called in, Andrew had been conducting negotiations for the marriage of his daughter to the son of Hermann, the landgrave of Thuringia, whose vassals included the family of Hermann of Salza, the recently appointed master of the Teutonic order. In deciding to accept Andrew's offer the master was probably influenced by the order's relative insignificance at that time in the Holy Land, where it had as rivals two well-established military orders and where opportunities for expansion were limited because of the meagre extent of Christian territories: Hungary was possibly seen as providing more scope. A contingent was quickly sent there under the leadership of a brother called Theoderich, and in 1212 the king could write that 'they have been placed like a new foundation on that frontier, and in withstanding the constant onslaughts of the Cumans and in providing a strong defence for the kingdom they do not fear to expose themselves to death every day'.[38] Yet the Teutonic order stayed in Hungary for less than fifteen years.

Already, before 1222, Andrew had made one attempt to rid himself of it, and although in that year he issued a confirmation of the order's rights, which had by then considerably increased, he expelled the brethren in 1225. The background to these events is not clearly explained in the surviving sources, but when Gregory IX was later seeking restoration of the order's rights, it was objected that this would displease the king's sons and the baronage. Opposition to the Teutonic order is therefore probably to be related to more general trends in Andrew's reign, which was marked by anti-German feeling and by calls for the recovery of rights alienated by the Crown. But there were also claims that the order had exceeded and abused its rights and it was said of the brethren that 'they are to the king like a fire in the breast, a mouse in the wallet and a viper in the bosom, which repay their hosts badly'.[39] Certainly, in 1224, Honorius III (at the order's petition) placed Burzenland in the *ius* and *proprietas* of St Peter, and he asserted that the brethren wanted their territories in Hungary 'to be subject to the special lordship of the apostolic see'.[40] The order appears to have been seeking to withdraw itself from the authority of the Hungarian king.

The order's intentions are more clearly apparent in Prussia. The possibility of transferring its interests there occurred at about the time when it was losing its rights in Hungary. The Prussians were then exerting increased pressure on Poland, which was itself divided by internal rivalries and ambitions. Conrad of Masovia needed help against the Prussians and offered the district of Culmerland to the Teutonic order. The negotiations which followed have given rise to considerable controversy, with the authenticity of some documents being questioned and the ambiguous wording of others occasioning varying interpretations. The order's attitude is apparent, however, from the Golden Bull of Rimini, which Hermann of Salza persuaded the emperor, Frederick II, to grant in 1226 and which promised the order considerable powers and independence. Relying on political theories rather than political realities, Frederick not only confirmed the donation of Culmerland made by Conrad, but also granted to the order whatever it could gain in Prussia, with the rights which other princes of the empire enjoyed; he also decreed that his grant should not be violated by any secular or ecclesiastical power. The way was being prepared for the creation of an independent state,

thus averting a repetition of what had happened in Hungary. Yet
Frederick's concession could not, in fact, automatically destroy all
other claims, and it did not lead to the immediate involvement of
the Teutonic order in warfare against the Prussians. In 1228,
when Conrad issued a brief confirmation of the grant of Culmerland in return for a promise of military aid, the duke was
apparently also seeking alternative assistance through the creation of the order of Dobrin, and at this time the Teutonic order
was itself pursuing other possibilities in the eastern Mediterranean. In 1230, however, Conrad appears to have ceded to the
Teutonic order full rights not only over Culmerland but also over
whatever it could gain from the Prussians. Yet claims to both
Culmerland and Prussia were also asserted by Bishop Christian on
the basis of earlier grants from the Polish duke and from the Pope.
In 1230, Christian relinquished his possessions in Culmerland to
the Teutonic order, but he sought at the same time to assert his
lordship over the order and, in 1231, basing his claims on papal
concessions, he agreed to allow the master and brethren only a
third of conquests in Prussia. Yet in 1234 – the year following the
bishop's capture by the Prussians – the Teutonic order obtained
from Gregory IX a privilege in which the Pope took into the *ius*
and *proprietas* of the papacy the lands which the order already held
and whatever it acquired in future in Prussia, and granted these
territories back to the master and brethren. Bishop Christian was
ignored. He voiced the expected protests when he finally secured
his release from captivity, and it was later agreed that a third of
acquisitions in Prussia should go to the episcopate, but the
foundations had been laid for a state under the control of the
Teutonic order, and by 1230 its brethren had already begun to
establish themselves in the territories assigned to them.

   Within a few years, as rivals disappeared, the Teutonic order
was apparently the only military order fighting against pagans in
Central and Eastern Europe. After 1230 nothing more is heard of
Calatrava's house at Thymau, and the orders of Dobrin and of
the Swordbrethren were soon swallowed up by the Teutonic
order. New religious orders almost invariably encountered difficulties, and the greater strength and resources of the Teutonic
order could have exercised both an oppressive and an attractive
influence. The background to the amalgamation of Dobrin with
the Teutonic order in 1235 is not known in detail, but the former

was clearly not in a strong position. According to the fourteenth-century chronicler Peter of Dusburg, it consisted originally of only a master and fourteen brethren; and Bishop Christian's capture in 1233 deprived it of a protector. Yet it is clear from later evidence that the master and some of the brethren were unhappy with the amalgamation, and the initiative may not have come from them. Conrad of Masovia was also dissatisfied, as he wanted Dobrin's lands to revert to him. It is therefore possible that the initiative lay with the Teutonic order, which may have seized a favourable opportunity to take over the properties of the smaller order. Already, before this, the Teutonic order had also been conduct-ing negotiations with the Swordbrethren. These had been begun by the latter, who were experiencing difficulties; but at first little progress was made, partly because the Swordbrethren were anxious to maintain some degree of autonomy within the Teuto-nic order. But the defeat of the Swordbrethren in 1236 at the battle of the Saule, in which fifty brothers were reported to have been lost, was apparently decisive in bringing about an amalga-mation in the following year, and with it the extension of the Teutonic order's interests to Livonia.

Although rivals to the Teutonic order were disappearing, there was still a place for other military orders in Poland and Hungary. After the expulsion of the Teutonic order from Hungary and its establishment as an independent force in Prussia, the rulers of Hungary and Poland were likely to turn elsewhere for assistance. Attempts to establish other military orders in the frontier regions of these two kingdoms in the thirteenth century were, however, of little lasting consequence. In 1237 the stronghold of Drohiczyn on the river Bug, together with territory which bordered on the lands of the pagan Jadzwings, was assigned by Conrad of Masovia to the brothers of Dobrin who had opposed the union with the Teutonic order. When, however, the master of the revived order was captured in the following year, the experiment came to an end. In 1245, the Polish dukes Przemysl and Boleslav appealed to the Cistercian chapter for some knights from Calatrava: the chapter referred the matter to the abbot of Morimond, to which Calatrava was affiliated, but apparently nothing further hap-pened. Already, before this, contingents of Templars had assisted in the battles of Liegnitz and Mohi against the invading Mongols, and in the mid-1250s the Templars were assigned Luków, which lay on the eastern borders of Poland. But plans to establish the Temple on that frontier quickly foundered and nothing further is heard of the Templars at Luków. Further south, in Hungary, Bela IV sought in 1247 to make use of the Hospitallers. He granted them the district of Severin, which stretched from the Transylvanian Alps to the Danube, together with rights over Cuman-held territory to the east of the river Olt. In return, the Hospitallers undertook, amongst other obligations, 'to take up arms against all pagans, of whatever race'.[41] This agreement was confirmed in 1251 by Innocent IV, who three years earlier had exhorted the Hospitallers in Hungary to defend the kingdom against the Mongols, but there is no evidence to suggest that it was ever implemented: when Severin was invaded in 1260 it was not being defended by the Hospitallers.

Although the rulers of Poland and Hungary had been seeking assistance from military orders mainly against pagan neighbours, Bela IV's agreement with the Hospitallers also placed them under an obligation to give service against Bulgars and other schismatics; and in Livonia the Swordbrethren and later the Teutonic order were at times in conflict with Russian princes, whose spheres of interest clashed with those of the orders. Yet while in these districts warfare against schismatics was of secondary importance, further south the Latin Empire of Constantinople faced Greek opposition on both its European and its Asiatic frontiers, and it was also opposed in the north by the Bulgars. In the first decade of the thirteenth century, when the Latin Empire was being established, crusades were beginning to be preached against Christians, and participation in such expeditions – as in those against infidels – was becoming accepted as a means of salvation. Fighting against heretics and schismatics could therefore be regarded as a legitimate function for a military order. Thus James of Vitry, writing in the second decade of the century, could state, without feeling the need to provide any special justification, that

> the brothers of a military order have been assigned the task of defending the church of Christ with the material sword, especially against those who are not Christians, namely the Saracens in Syria, the Moors in Spain and the pagans in Prussia, Livonia and Cumania, but also at the command of their superior against schismatics in Greece and against heretics wherever they exist in the universal church. . . .[42]

When, later in the century, St Thomas Aquinas discussed whether a
religious institution could be founded for military purposes, he
concluded that it could, provided it did not devote itself to worldly
ends: he did not limit its competence to warfare against infidels.

In the Latin Empire, military orders were expected to, and did,
contribute to its defence. Although some early gifts made there to the
Templars and Hospitallers were said to be for the aid of the Holy
Land, and may have had the purpose merely of providing resources
for Syria, it was reported in 1210 that after the Templars had
received the lordship of Lamia in Thessaly they had built a castle
there for the defence of the Empire. That brethren of the orders in
the Empire were expected to assume military responsibilities is also
apparent from the wording of a document drawn up in 1237
concerning a proposed amalgamation between the hospital of St
James at Andravidha and the Teutonic order: Geoffrey of Villehar-
douin, the hospital's patron, stated that the brethren of the Teutonic
order 'are to have a house in our castle of Clermont (Chloumoutsi)
and, if it is necessary for the defence of the castle, the whole convent
is to take up residence there'.[43] The most precise evidence about
military commitments in the Empire, however, concerns the Spanish
order of Santiago. In 1246, when he was touring the West in search
of aid, the Latin emperor, Baldwin II, entered into an agreement
with Santiago's master, Pelayo Pérez Correa, who undertook to take
three hundred knights, two hundred archers and a thousand foot to
the Latin Empire and stay for a period of two years; it was also
agreed that a convent of Santiago should be established permanently
at Constantinople to provide military assistance to the emperor.
Because of changing circumstances in the Iberian peninsula and
Baldwin's inability to find the sum of 40,000 marks which he had
promised to Santiago, this agreement was never implemented; but
there is no doubt that some military orders were involved in the
defence of the Empire and later of the remaining Frankish territories
in Greece.

Within Western Christendom

ALTHOUGH in the thirteenth century there were crusades within
western Christendom against heretics and other opponents of the
church, and also in support of secular rulers whose cause was

favoured by the papacy, popes made little attempt to involve the established military orders directly in campaigns of this kind in Western Europe. On some occasions the papacy sought financial contributions from the leading orders, but brethren were not usually called upon to give military service. The only pope who is known to have invoked the miltary aid of Templars or Hospitallers within Christian lands in Western Europe was Clement IV. In 1267, when Charles of Anjou was seeking to establish his authority in south Italy and Sicily and to oust the last Hohenstaufen claimant, the Pope, in a letter to the Hospitallers, broached the question of fighting in support of the Angevin cause. But the approach was made in a half-hearted manner: Clement did not order the Hospitallers into the field, but merely gave them permission to take up arms against the Hohenstaufen; and this licence was to be valid for only a year. The Hospitallers did, however, put a force into the field on this occasion under the leadership of the provincial prior, Philip of Egly.

The papacy was more ready to seek the intervention of military orders in conflicts among Western Christians in the eastern Mediterranean. In 1218, shortly after the accession of the infant king Henry I, Honorius III commanded the Templars and Hospitallers to assist in quelling disorders in the kingdom of Cyprus, and they were again asked to give aid and counsel to Henry in 1226. Their assistance was also sought in Syria. In 1235, for example, when Frederick II's officials were encountering baronial opposition, Gregory IX instructed the orders to give military aid, if it was necessary, for the defence of Tyre and other places under imperial authority. Towards the end of the next decade, however, the papacy was seeking to ensure that Hohenstaufen claims in the Holy Land received no support. In 1248, Innocent IV wrote to the military orders stating that some elements in the kingdom wanted it to be under the rule of Frederick and his son Conrad; the Pope ordered that 'as far as it is in your power, you are not to allow anyone to make any major change in the government of that kingdom'.[44] Later in the century Nicholas III was ready to deploy the orders in defence of local church interests: when Paul, bishop of Tripoli, complained that Bohemund VII had despoiled him of his possessions and ejected him from his see, the Pope threatened to coerce the prince by calling in the Templars, Hospitallers and brethren of the Teutonic order.

The papacy's reluctance to invoke the aid of the orders in western Europe is probably to be partly explained by the fact that they could not be relied upon to provide contingents which were both trustworthy and substantial. There was sometimes the likelihood, or at least the fear, that the orders would refuse to support the papacy. During the Albigensian crusade the Hospitallers in southern France appear to have remained on good terms with Raymond VI of Toulouse, and when the papacy was in conflict with Frederick II, the loyalty of the Teutonic order was inevitably suspect. And in Aragon in 1285, the military orders openly sided with the deposed Pedro III against the French even though the latter were seeking to implement Martin IV's award of the Aragonese crown to Charles of Valois. On this occasion, of course, the pope could have called upon brethren in France to give service, but in areas away from the borders of western Christendom the leading military orders could not supply a very substantial contingent of well-equipped brethren. Although the Templars and Hospitallers had convents scattered throughout western Christendom, these usually contained very few brothers, and most of those resident in western Europe were not fighting brethren; and inventories compiled in the early fourteenth century after the arrest of the Templars reveal that few arms and little military equipment were kept in most of the houses in the West. It was only in the regions where they were engaged in the struggle against the infidel that these orders could furnish a substantial and well-equipped force.

The papacy was, of course, at times under pressure from secular rulers who might benefit militarily or financially from demands made on the orders. It is clear, for example, that in the 1260s Clement IV's actions were influenced by the wishes of Charles of Anjou. But royal pressure was not always effective, and some popes may have been more influenced by the fear of providing further ammunition to those critics who were claiming that the papacy was neglecting the interests of the Holy Land: this consideration was likely to be particularly significant when the fortunes of the Franks in Syria were at a low ebb.

Although the established orders were little used within western Europe, the thirteenth century saw the foundation of several new military orders whose purpose was to curb the activities of certain fellow Christians in Western countries. In sources surviving from the year 1221, when the Albigensian conflict was still continuing, several references occur to a Militia of the Faith of Jesus Christ, which was being set up in the south of France. Permission was sought from Honorius III for its members to adopt Templar observances and to fight in the south of France just as the Templars did in the East. The purpose of the institution was defined as the defence of the person and lands of Amaury of Montfort and also 'the seeking out and destruction of evil heretics and their lands and also of those who rebel against the faith of the holy church'.[45] Nothing more is heard of this foundation, however, and it may have failed at this stage to become firmly established. It is certainly to be differentiated from the order – first mentioned in a letter sent by Gregory IX in 1231 – which was later known as the order of the Sword or of the Faith and Peace, and whose properties lay mostly to the west of Toulouse, in the dioceses of Auch, Lescar, Comminges and Bayonne. According to Gregory IX, the order was founded on the initiative of Amanieu, the archbishop of Auch appointed in 1226, and the Pope explained its establishment by stating that:

> Since in the province of Auch the wickedness of the proud and the pride of the wicked had so increased that, with truth publicly spurned and justice corrupted, peace had altogether perished and those who abstained from evil were subject to the assaults of the perverse, while repute was proportional to the degree of savagery displayed, you, inspired by zeal for the faith and peace and equipped with the arms of God for the defence of both, worthily determined to fight against the enemies of peace and of the faith.[46]

Yet little is known of its history and activities, and it was soon in decline. In 1262 the master sought to amalgamate the foundation with the Cistercian monastery of Feuillant. This proposal did not, however, mark the end of the order of the Sword, for five years later Clement IV was deposing its master, claiming that it had declined because of the malice and neglect shown by this official and by others, and an attempt to revive the foundation was made by the archbishop of Auch, who in 1268 bought the hospital of Pont d'Artigues from Santiago for it and who appointed his nephew as master. But the attempted restoration was clearly unsuccessful and references to the order cease after the next decade.

If attempts to establish military orders in the south of France met with limited success, one founded in Italy in the thirteenth century did last rather longer. It was known as the order of the Blessed Virgin Mary and it received its rule from Urban IV in 1261. In this the Pope defined the military responsibilities of the brethren:

> they are to be allowed to bear arms for the defence of the catholic faith and ecclesiastical freedom, when specially required to do so by the Roman church; for subduing civil discords they may carry only defensive weapons, provided they have the permission of the diocesan.[47]

Among the order's founders was Loderingo degli Andalò, who came from Bologna and belonged to a Ghibelline family; and he and another brother called Catalano di Guido, who was a member of the Guelph house of the Catalani, were given governmental authority in Bologna in 1265 in an attempt to bring peace between rival factions there. In the following year they were similarly placed in charge of the city of Florence by Clement IV, following the defeat and death of the Hohenstaufen Manfred at Benevento. But the activities of Loderingo and Catalano in Florence soon aroused criticism, which finds expression in various sources, including Dante Alighieri's *Inferno*. The reputation of the order quickly fell, and the way of life of its members earned them the epithet of 'jovial brothers' (*fratres gaudentes*). But the order did not quickly collapse. These foundations within western Europe were nevertheless of very minor significance. Throughout the twelfth and thirteenth centuries the military order was an institution which was used mainly against Muslims and pagans on the borders of western Christendom.

3. Military Activities

AN examination of the orders' military activities must focus on warfare against infidels in Syria, Spain and the Baltic. Although in the thirteenth century military orders were being used against Christians, little record has survived of their military undertakings in this sphere: their contribution was presumably too limited to merit much comment in narrative sources. Chronicles, charters and letters provide fuller information about fighting in the frontier regions of Christendom. Even in these districts, however, the military activities of some lesser orders, such as St Thomas of Acre or San Jorge de Alfama, have left little trace: they are rarely mentioned in chronicles or letters, and direct references to participation by minor orders in campaigns and sieges are encountered in very few charters. It is only the actions of the more powerful orders which can be discussed at all fully. A consecutive account of these orders' military operations would necessitate extended narrative surveys of crusades to the Holy Land and of the crusader states, the Spanish reconquest and Baltic expansion. These have been provided by others. Here a more analytical approach will be adopted, and the objective will be to define the orders' military roles and to assess the importance of their contribution in conflicts between western Christendom and its non-Christian neighbours.

Roles and Functions

ALTHOUGH on all fronts the orders engaged in both defensive and offensive operations, garrisoning strongholds as well as fighting in the field, the balance between defence and offence varied from region to region. By the time that military orders were emerging in the Holy Land, the political fragmentation which had characterised neighbouring Muslim territories in the early twelfth century was being replaced by a greater degree of unity, first under Zangi and then under Nur ad-Din and Saladin. The crusader states came under increasing threat and suffered severe setbacks: after the defeat at the hands of Saladin at Hattin in 1187, large stretches of territory were quickly lost by the Franks.

Even after the gains made during the third crusade, the kingdom of Jerusalem comprised no more than a narrow coastal strip running from Tyre to Jaffa. Pressure was relieved by the death of Saladin in 1193 and by renewed Muslim disunity, which allowed limited Christian expansion in the first half of the thirteenth century, especially through the agreements negotiated by Frederick II in 1229 and by Theobald of Champagne and Richard of Cornwall in 1240 and 1241. But for the rest of the century the crusader states were again on the defensive. The Mamluks extended their power from Egypt into Syria, defeating the Mongols in 1260 and exerting increasing pressure on the Franks, who lost stronghold after stronghold. The end came in 1291 when Acre and the few other remaining western bases fell, although the Christian kingdom of Armenia did survive for most of the fourteenth century.

While the crusader states collapsed and the Franks were driven out of Syria, in the Iberian peninsula and in the Baltic region Christian frontiers were in the long term being advanced. Although in the middle of the twelfth century little more than half of the Iberian peninsula was in Christian hands, by 1250 the Muslims held hardly any lands outside Granada. The Christian advance had been particularly rapid in the second quarter of the thirteenth century, following the break-up of the Almohad empire in Spain and North Africa: during this period Mallorca, Valencia, Murcia and much of the rest of southern Spain, including Córdoba and Seville, were gained. Progress was not, of course, continuous and there were setbacks at the hands of the Almohads, especially in the last decade of the twelfth century: in 1191 Alcácer do Sal and several other Portuguese strongholds fell to the Muslims, while in the centre of the peninsula territories were lost after the severe Christian defeat at Alarcos in 1195. But overall the Christians had the upper hand, even if the reconquest did come to a halt after 1250 and Granada remained under Muslim rule until towards the end of the fifteenth century.

By the end of the thirteenth century a considerable amount of territory had similarly been brought under Western control in the Baltic region, although – as in Spain – there were also some setbacks. In the early decades of the century much of Livonia and Estonia was conquered, while in Prussia the Teutonic order advanced down the Vistula and along the Frisches Haff in the

1230s before proceeding to secure the hinterland. But there were major revolts by conquered peoples in 1242 and 1260, which were only slowly overcome, and the Teutonic order failed to establish a permanent link between its Prussian and its Livonian lands, while in the fourteenth century few further advances were made against the Lithuanians.

Variations between regions may also be noted in the nature and objectives of offensive warfare. On all fronts aggressive action could, of course, serve the purposes of defence, but such operations also had more positive avowed ends, which were not the same in all areas. In the Mediterranean region, offensive action against Muslims was seen to have the primary purpose of asserting control over land. In Syria and the Iberian peninsula, the orders' task was to assist in the recovery of territories which were thought rightfully to belong to Christendom and which Islam was unjustly detaining. Admittedly, at the time of the first crusade there had been considerable slaughter of Muslims and some forced conversions, but among those who remained in the East attitudes quickly changed. Successful campaigns in Mediterranean lands were certainly followed by the establishment, or re-establishment, of the Latin Church in conquered territories, and conquests might serve more generally to promote the interests of Christianity, but conversion of the infidel was not a significant issue. It is true that in 1175 Alexander III maintained that the brethren of Santiago should fight against the Muslims, partly 'in order that they may win them over to the cult of the Christian faith',[1] and this statement was incorporated into the rule of Santiago; and during the thirteenth century friars both in Spain and in the Holy Land were seeking to convert Muslims living under Christian lordship. Yet, although conquest might facilitate conversion, and although those captured in war sometimes adopted Christianity immediately, expansion was not usually undertaken specifically for the purpose of converting the infidel.

In the Baltic the situation was rather different, even if historians have not always agreed on the exact extent of the difference. The territories conquered in the thirteenth century, such as Prussia and Livonia, had never before been under Christian rule, and conquests could not be justified on the grounds that territories which had formerly been part of Christendom were being recovered. Although it was the accepted ecclesiastical view that

infidels should not be forced to become Christian, the campaigns
fought against the pagans of this region were regarded in part as
wars of conversion, which was to be secured through ruthless
expeditions characterised by slaughter and devastation. Men were
killed and women and children seized; property was burnt or
pillaged. The nature and purpose of such expeditions are illustrated by comments made by the contemporary chronicler Henry of
Livonia, about a campaign into Ungannia in 1215; he wrote of the
Christians that

> laying waste that land with nine armies, they left it desolate
> and deserted so that afterwards neither men nor victuals were
> found there; for their intention was to go on fighting until either
> those who remained came to seek peace and baptism or the
> pagans were completely wiped out.[2]

Henry provides further evidence about the link between warfare
and conversion by the words he puts into the mouths of Christian
leaders at times when pagans were suing for peace. Brother
Rudolph of the Swordbrethren is reported to have said to
inhabitants of Wierland in 1219:

> No peace will be given to you – except the peace of that true
> Peacemaker ... who instructed his disciples, saying, 'Go, teach
> all peoples, baptizing them'. If, therefore, you wish to be
> baptized and to worship the one God of the Christians with
> us, we will give you that peace which he gave us, which he left
> to his followers when he ascended, and we will receive you into
> the fellowship of our brotherhood for ever....

In the same year Volquin, the master of the Swordbrethren, was
supposed to have said to the Warbolians: 'If you wish to worship
with us the one God, to be washed by the fount of holy baptism,
and to give your sons as hostages, we will make everlasting peace
with you'.[3] The early-fourteenth-century chronicler Peter of
Dusburg in turn provides numerous examples from Prussia of
pagans' agreeing to adopt, or to return to, Christianity when they
could no longer resist the Germans. He reports, for example, that
in 1242

since the Prussians of Warmia, Nattangia and Bartia had through God's decree been weakened by the brethren and the said duke [Otto of Brunswick] and could no longer resist, they made a virtue out of necessity, gave hostages and subjected themselves to the faith and to the lordship of the brethren....

He further relates that when the king of Bohemia was in Prussia in 1255 some pagans

in order to escape the carnage which he had inflicted on others, all offered their sons as hostages and bound themselves on pain of their lives to obey the mandates of the faith and of the brothers.[4]

Killing and devastation were seen in part as a means to an end, which was the acceptance of Christianity, although Henry of Livonia's comment on the expedition in 1215 would also imply that slaughter itself was an objective if conversion could not be achieved, and there are other sources as well which seem to regard killing as an end in itself. The author of the *Livonian Rhymed Chronicle* writes of the Swordbrethren's rejoicing in killing, and of a later attack by the Teutonic order on the Samites he reports that the brethren said that 'they wished to make a raid and, with God's assistance, create widows and orphans'.[5]

The brethren of the Teutonic order in Prussia and Livonia were thus fighting a different kind of war from their colleagues in the Holy Land, although, of course, raiding took place in Mediterranean regions just as in the north, for on all fronts this form of warfare could help to weaken the enemy and provide resources. Explanations of the orders' activities in the Baltic region must take into account the fact that pagans in that area were treated differently from Muslims in Mediterranean lands. Arguments which could be applied to warfare against all infidels cannot provide a satisfactory answer. It could, of course, be maintained that for some Christians in the Baltic region the conversion of pagans was merely a justification for actions which had more material objectives – in this context it may be noted that Peter of Dusburg mentions the pagans' acceptance not only of Christianity but also of the Teutonic order's overlordship – but even then it would be necessary to explain why conversion took the form it did. The explanation of the differing attitudes to pagans and Muslims seems to lie in the perceptions which Christians had of the enemy. Pagans in central and eastern Europe appear to have been seen as primitive and warlike peoples with only a rudimentary religion. The only possible approach was to convert them, which formed an important part of the civilising process, or to destroy them. Some who had gone on the first crusade had regarded Muslims as being little different from pagans, and this would explain some of the more brutal episodes of that expedition. But those who lived permanently near the Muslim frontiers of western Christendom understood that both in material and spiritual matters Islam was much more advanced than paganism, and that the policy of repression adopted towards pagans was scarcely appropriate.

Because of the nature of the climate and terrain, the conditions of warfare in the Baltic region also differed from those in Mediterranean lands. In Prussia and Livonia movement was often hampered by extensive forest and marsh; but in the winter the ground froze and seas and rivers were iced over. The launching of winter campaigns therefore became an accepted practice in these regions. Henry of Livonia describes how the master of the Swordbrethren in 1214 led a force across the frozen sea to Rotalia, and two years later the island of Oesel was reached in the same way. There were, of course, drawbacks to campaigning in winter. In some years snow was so deep that armies had to march in single file, as happened in the winter of 1219–20, when the Germans were moving northwards into Estonia. Fighting was also sometimes hampered by the intensity of the cold: in 1322–3 the severity of the winter prevented the launching of any expedition. On the other hand, a mild winter could equally limit military operations. Peter of Dusburg tells of a crusader in the mid-1250s who

> came to the land of Prussia in the winter, but because the winter was mild, he could not go against the neighbouring enemies of the faith; for there were marshes in between... which froze only in the most intense cold, and since they had not frozen, movement was impossible.[6]

Winter campaigns nevertheless constituted an important part of military operations in the Baltic region. The situation was obviously very different from that in Mediterranean lands, where difficulties were caused by heat and aridity.

All fronts were similar, however, in that the military orders usually comprised only one of several elements in the Christian forces; but they played a more independent role in Syria and the Baltic than in the Iberian peninsula. The leadership of the Spanish reconquest was in the hands of the Christian rulers of the peninsula, and these sought to maintain a firm control over military activity. When Alfonso IX of Leon gave the stronghold of Alcántara to the order of Calatrava in 1217 he decreed that 'you are always to make war from there and also peace whenever and with whomsoever I command',[7] and this statement was echoed in many other charters issued to military orders in Spain. They were expected not only to make war at the king's command but also to observe royal truces and peaces with the Muslims. These restrictions were not, however, always readily accepted by the papacy. In 1193 Celestine III commanded the military orders in Spain to continue the struggle against the infidel despite the truces which then existed between Christian rulers and the Muslims, and in 1225 Honorius III similarly told the orders to assist the Castilian noble Alfonso Téllez in defending the castle of Albocácer from Muslim attack even at times when the Spanish kings had truces with the infidel. In 1221, the orders of Santiago and Calatrava themselves agreed in principle to a minor breach of royal truces when they undertook to aid each other if they were attacked by the Muslims after the king had made a truce. Yet although in 1193 Celestine threatened to excommunicate any who tried to prevent the orders from fighting, royal wishes seem usually to have prevailed, and royal truces were observed by the orders. In 1205 the Aragonese king, Pedro II, sought permission from the Pope to use the order of Calatrava on the Aragonese frontier because its brethren did not dare to break the truce which the Castilian king then had with the Muslims; and, as has already been mentioned, it was because of enforced inactivity in Spain that the proposal was made in the following year to transfer Calatrava's forces to the eastern Mediterranean. The overriding weight of royal influence was further demonstrated in 1220, when Calatrava complained to Honorius III that it was being forbidden to retaliate against Muslim attacks.

Spanish rulers were not, however, seeking to stifle all independent initiatives: only those which clashed with royal policy were
proscribed. Brethren in Spain were, in fact, often encouraged to
act on their own initiative by the terms included in royal charters,
for these not infrequently promised to military orders the territories which they succeeded in gaining from the Muslims. In 1173
Calatrava received from Alfonso VIII of Castile the concession of
'every castle which from now on you can gain in any way from the
Saracens';[8] and other charters encouraged action in particular
localities by allowing orders to expand existing lordships at the
expense of the Muslims. When Alfonso II of Aragon granted the
castle of Villel to the order of Mountjoy in 1187 he also ceded
'everything which you can gain from the Saracens from there',[9]
and a similar concession was made by his successor Pedro II in
1202 when he gave the frontier stronghold of Fortanete to the
Hospitallers.

In Spain the orders did, in fact, on numerous occasions fight
independently of royal forces. A Muslim letter records a raid
undertaken by *ifrir* – the word used to designate brethren of the
military orders – and the inhabitants of Avila into the Córdoba
region in 1173, and among the undertakings of this kind mentioned in chronicle and annal sources is the conquest of a number
of castles by Santiago and Calatrava in the late 1220s and early
1230s, while charter evidence shows that the Templars captured
the stronghold of Pulpís in northern Valencia about the year
1190. In some instances it is not clear whether the orders were
acting on their own initiative or at the king's command, but
several entries in the *Chronicle of James I* reveal that the initiative
did not always rest with the king. The attack on the Valencian
castle of Villena which took place in 1240 was decided upon by
Calatrava and a group of Aragonese nobles, and the wording of
that chronicle also implies that the Templars and Hospitallers
took the initiative in negotiating the surrender of Chivert and
Cervera in the same region a few years earlier.

Military orders nevertheless enjoyed greater freedom of action
in the eastern Mediterranean. In the county of Tripoli independent activity received early encouragement from Raymond II
when he assigned to the Hospital in 1144 rights of lordship over
Rafaniyah and Bar'in, which were in Muslim hands: the order was

expected to undertake the recovery of these strongholds. In 1168 Bohemund III of Antioch similarly granted the Hospitallers rights over territories under Muslim control; he also allowed them to make war and negotiate truces as they wished, and promised to observe any cease-fire agreed by them. He further accepted that if he himself made truces without their counsel, they were not obliged to observe these. In 1210, Leo II of Armenia followed Bohemund's example by allowing the Hospitallers to open hostilities or to make truces, which he undertook to observe; he also promised to break any truces which he himself had with the infidel if this was necessary for the defence of Hospitaller lands. There is no record of concessions of this kind by kings of Jerusalem in the twelfth century, and on several occasions during that period the Crown appears to have punished orders when they took independent action which conflicted with royal interests. William of Tyre reports that, in the mid-1160s, Amaury hanged twelve Templars who had surrendered a frontier castle beyond the Jordan when the king was on his way to relieve it; and, according to the same chronicler, Amaury in 1173 imprisoned the Templar Walter of Mesnil, who was held responsible for the killing of an envoy of the Assassins, with whom the king was then negotiating.

Towards the end of the twelfth century, however, monarchical authority in Jerusalem was declining, and in the thirteenth century the orders were able to pursue their own policies throughout Syria. In the early decades of that century they were undertaking aggressive action in the more northerly regions, which enabled them to exact tribute from neighbouring Muslim rulers. In 1213, for example, an attack on Homs and Hamah which had been planned by the Hospitallers was bought off, and in 1230 the Templars and Hospitallers marched against Hamah to enforce the payment of tribute which had been promised. On this occasion they were defeated, but a more successful campaign was launched in 1233. Two years earlier, Gregory IX had ordered the Templars not to contravene the peace which Frederick II had made with Egypt, and the orders' independent stance in the south was also made apparent at the time of the crusades of Theobald of Champagne and Richard of Cornwall, when agreements were negotiated, first with Damascus and then with Egypt: the Hospitallers are reported to have refused to adhere to the truce with Damascus, while the Templars ignored the settlement with

Egypt. In the second half of the century, as Mamluk power in Syria grew, the orders were making private truces to secure their own interests. In 1266, the Templars were offering half of Gibel to Sultan Baibars in order to obtain peace, and in the same year the Hospitallers had to renounce various tribute payments before they could secure terms from him. In 1280, the Hospitallers were similarly negotiating a ten-year truce with the Mamluk sultan, Kalawun, and two years later he also agreed to a ten-year peace with the Templars. The latter had admittedly been castigated by the crusader king Louis IX in the early 1250s, for conducting negotiations on their own initiative with Damascus: he insisted on the banishment of the Templar marshal Hugh of Jouy, who had been the order's envoy and who had subsequently to be found a post in Spain. Yet for most of the thirteenth century there was no one in a position of overall authority who could effectively limit the orders' independence. The consequences of this lack of authority were most apparent in periods of Muslim disunity, when Templars and Hospitallers were sometimes pursuing conflicting foreign policies and siding with different Muslim powers. Admittedly, when the neighbouring Muslim world was fragmented the crusader states were usually in no serious danger, but it could be argued that greater co-operation among Christians would have allowed them to derive more benefit from divisions among the infidel, although adherence to a consistent policy would at times have been made difficult by the fluidity of political relationships among Muslim powers. It could also be maintained that more unified action by Christian forces would also have been beneficial when the Muslim threat was greater; but it should be remembered that much medieval fighting was of a localised character, focusing on particular strongholds or districts, and that local truces and local agreements were a common feature of medieval warfare.

It was in the Baltic, however, that military orders consistently enjoyed the greatest freedom of action. Although the Teutonic order could not always dictate policy to those who came out on crusade, in Prussia it was subject to no superior power. In Livonia, the Swordbrethren and later the Teutonic order did not in theory enjoy such complete independence, but in the field no one held authority over them. After reporting the election of Volquin as master of the Swordbrethren in 1209, Henry of

Livonia wrote that 'he afterwards fought the battles of the Lord, leading and commanding the army of the Lord on every expedition, whether the bishop was present or absent'.[10] In these regions, however, the consequences of independence were militarily not as significant as in the Holy Land.

Military Personnel

IN the leading orders, the brethren who could give military service included both knights and sergeants-at-arms. Although there was a clear-cut distinction of rank between the two groups, in military matters they differed in degree rather than in kind. Templar regulations on military equipment state that the sergeants-at-arms 'can have everything which the brother knights have',[11] with certain exceptions: instead of a hauberk they were to have a *haubergeon*, which was probably shorter and lacked *manicles* protecting the hands; the *chausses* of the sergeants were to be without *avant-piés*, covering the foot; and whereas the knights wore either a helm or *chapeau de fer*, the sergeants were equipped only with the latter, which was lighter and did not protect the whole head. Both knights and sergeants-at-arms could give mounted service in the field, though their allowances of mounts differed, and usually only the knights had squires to assist them. In the Temple a knight was normally permitted three mounts and one squire, while a sergeant was restricted to a single mount, although when there was a plentiful supply of horses the allocation was raised to four and two mounts respectively. That the allowances of animals in the Teutonic order were usually the same is suggested by a clause in its Customs which states that 'when the master allows knightly brothers to have four mounts, other brethren-at-arms should by his favour have two mounts':[12] the norm was presumably three for knights and one for sergeants. By contrast, early thirteenth-century Hospitaller decrees fixed the normal allocation at four mounts for knights and two for sergeants; but some later sources refer to a usual complement of three animals for knightly brothers.

The differences in equipment probably made it easier for sergeants than for knights to fight on foot, and their limited allocation of mounts no doubt meant that it was often necessary for them to do so. Yet the weapons and equipment of both groups were essentially similar, and the sergeants-at-arms did not constitute a light cavalry of the kind found in some Muslim armies.

In addition to sergeants-at-arms, the leading orders also had non-military sergeants who could, if necessary, be pressed into service. The Templar Customs refer to the purchase of 'Turkish arms' for these brothers, but clearly not very much was expected of them, for the Customs also include the comment that

> if they fight well, they will please God and the brethren. But if they see that they cannot withstand the enemy or if they are wounded, they can withdraw if they wish, without seeking permission, and they will not be censured by the order for doing so.[13]

Apart from brethren who committed themselves for life to a military order, there were also individuals who lived and fought alongside them for a term, without taking the normal monastic vows. In the Templar rule three clauses were devoted to this group, and in several other clauses lifelong members were classified as 'permanent brothers' (fratres remanentes) in order to distinguish them from those serving for only a term. Presumably men coming out to the East on crusade sometimes stayed with the Templars and formed part of their contingents in the field: an early example is apparently provided by Fulk of Anjou, who travelled out to Jerusalem about the year 1120 and who, according to Ordericus Vitalis, 'stayed there for a time as an associate of the knights of the Temple'.[14] Yet it was not only crusaders in the East who gave temporary service with the Templars. In 1134, at least twenty-six Catalan nobles, as well as the count of Barcelona, promised to serve with the Templars in Spain for a year, and although in this instance the undertaking was not fulfilled, there were certainly others who did serve with the Templars for a term in the peninsula. In the dating clause of one Catalan document, for example, 1148 was referred to as the year in which 'García Ortiz served God in Corbins with those brothers'.[15] By the middle years of the twelfth century, however, temporary service may have been of declining significance: although the clauses about those serving for a term were retained in the French version of the order's rule, which appears to have been made about 1140, in this redaction the term *frater remanens* was rendered merely as *frere*, as though the earlier distinction was no longer thought necessary; and the later Customs of the Temple make no more than an occasional reference to temporary members. Yet service of this kind did not altogether disappear. When Pope Adrian IV learned in 1158 that the Templars and their lands in Spain were in serious danger, he ordered the archbishops of Narbonne, Auch and Tarragona to try to persuade any who had vowed to go to Jerusalem to assist the Templars in the Iberian peninsula instead and to serve with them for a year or two in remission of their sins. The murderers of Archbishop Becket were apparently to give more lengthy assistance, for it was reported that a penance was imposed on them of serving with the Templars in Jerusalem for fourteen years. In the early thirteenth century, Innocent III issued a decree directed against those who undertook to serve the Temple for a period and left before the term had expired, and a century later a secular knight who gave evidence during the Templar trial in Cyprus testified that he had lived with the Templars for a month. That service of this kind in fact remained fairly common is suggested by a thirteenth-century French tale called *La fille du comte de Ponthieu*, which has the count spending a year with the Templars when he went on pilgrimage to the Holy Land. Nor was service of this kind limited to the Temple. In 1220, Honorius III promised indulgences to any who assisted the order of Calatrava in fortifying and defending its frontier castles, and that the Swordbrethren had help of this kind in Livonia in the thirteenth century is implied by a privilege granted by the same pope which stated that 'if any pilgrims coming to Livonia to defend or extend the Christian faith in those parts want to stay of their own accord in order to guard your castles or serve you in other ways, you may freely retain them for as long as they are willing'.[16]

In theory, the Teutonic order could at times claim authority over all crusaders fighting in Baltic campaigns, not just over those who entered into particular agreements, for contingents going to Prussia or Livonia were sometimes instructed by the Pope to place themselves under the command of the Teutonic order: thus in 1260, Alexander IV named the order's provincial master in Prussia as the captain and 'principal leader' of the crusaders who were then preparing to fight against the Mongols in that region. In practice, however, leading crusaders appear to have been reluctant to accept a subordinate position. Peter of Dusburg gives the impression that Ottokar of Bohemia was in command during his expedition to Prussia in 1255, and was even giving advice to' brethren of the Teutonic order. The authority and independence of leading crusaders were assured both by their rank and by the size of their following.

Orders could also obtain military assistance from their own vassals, who in some regions could provide mounted as well as foot service. Even in Spain, where they enjoyed the least independence, military orders commonly received privileges which exempted men under their lordship from military obligations to the Crown: these vassals were to give service instead only to their immediate lords.

Mercenaries provided the remaining source of manpower for the military orders. In the Holy Land the paid troops employed by the leading orders included *turcoples*, who were recruited from the native population and who were sometimes mounted and equipped with a bow. The term was, however, probably applied to troops of various kinds, and *turcoples* should not always be equated with the light cavalry of the kind used by the Turks. Although *turcoples* are mentioned in the statutes of the three leading orders in the Holy Land, these provide little precise information about them. In the Temple and the Hospital these troops were usually under the command of a brother called a *turcoplier*, but in the Teutonic order this post does not seem to have been continuously in existence, for according to that order's Customs, a *turcoplier* was to be appointed only when he was needed. Yet, although in the Holy Land the Teutonic order may not have made as much use as the Templars and Hospitallers did of paid troops, chronicle sources for the Baltic region make frequent references to *armigeri*. Those designated by this term were too numerous to have been the knights' squires, and the word must signify men-at-arms, at least some of whom would have been in the orders' pay. Mercenaries may also have been employed by the military orders in Spain, but no clear evidence of their use in the twelfth and thirteenth centuries has survived: the *mercenarii* mentioned in early statutes of Calatrava were not necessarily paid troops.

In examining the contribution made by these forces in warfare against the infidel on the frontiers of western Christendom, it will be convenient to consider the garrisoning and fortifying of strongholds separately from military activities in the field, although of course to contemporaries this distinction would have appeared somewhat artificial.

Castles and Strongholds

ON all fronts, military orders became responsible for a very considerable number of strongholds, which served various purposes. Although castles by themselves could only exceptionally deny an enemy access to a region, an invader who could not capture opposing strongholds was restricted to raiding and plundering: as long as these held out, permanent occupation of territories was prevented. For defensive purposes castles also provided a place of refuge as well as a base from which reconnaissances could be made and sorties launched against invading forces. They could similarly be used as a base for more offensive operations. Lastly, castles not only furnished a means of dominating the inhabitants of a district, but also served as administrative centres. Some of these functions are mentioned in comments reputedly made at the time of the reconstruction of the Templar castle of Safed in the Holy Land in 1240: it was apparently claimed that the new fortification

> would provide defence and security against the Saracens and be like a shield for the Christians as far as Acre; it would also be a strong and formidable point of attack, and from there it would easily be possible to launch incursions and raids into Saracen territories as far as Damascus; and through the construction of the said castle the sultan would lose a lot of money and much support and service from the men who would be subject to the stronghold and from their lands. He would also in his own territories lose villages, agricultural land, pasture and other rights, because men would not dare to work the land for fear of the castle. His territories would be turned to waste and solitude, and he would have to undertake large expenses and engage a considerable force of mercenaries to defend Damascus and the surrounding districts.[17]

In the crusader states in Syria in the twelfth century, the Templars and Hospitallers were entrusted with a growing number of strongholds. These were either given or sold to them by rulers and nobles who lacked the manpower or resources to defend them adequately. Because of the loss of Templar archives, however, more is known in detail of Hospitaller acquisitions. It has been calculated that by 1160 the Hospitallers had possession of seven or eight castles in Syria, and that they acquired a further eleven or twelve in the 1160s. In 1180 the number of Hospitaller castles had risen to about twenty-five, and altogether during the twelfth and thirteenth centuries they held at one time or another some fifty-six strongholds.

It has been seen that in the southern part of the kingdom of Jerusalem the orders were beginning to be assigned castles well before the middle of the twelfth century. William of Tyre explained that in 1136 Beit-Jibrin was constructed partly as a defence against attacks launched from Ascalon; and Gaza, which was given to the Templars at the end of the following decade, served a similar purpose. Among the most important castles held by the orders in the kingdom of Jerusalem during the twelfth century were those at Safed, in northern Galilee, and at Belvoir, which dominated the Jordan valley to the south of the Sea of Galilee. The former was given to the Temple by Amaury about the year 1163 and Belvoir was sold to the Hospitallers in 1168. Lesser fortifications included several which lay on pilgrim routes and provided refuges for those journeying to Jerusalem or other holy places. It is reported that during the third crusade it was thought essential to restore the Templar castle of Casal des Pleins, which lay a few miles inland from Jaffa, 'for the sake of pilgrims journeying by that route',[18] and in his *Libellus de locis sanctis*, the twelfth-century German pilgrim Theoderich mentioned a number of forts and towers which the Temple held along the road from Jerusalem to the river Jordan. A visitor could apparently even gain the impression that most strongholds in the kingdom of Jerusalem were subject to the orders, for Thoros of Armenia, journeying through the kingdom in the 1160s, reputedly said to Amaury:

When I came to your land and inquired to whom the castles belonged, I sometimes received the reply: 'This belongs to the

Temple'; elsewhere I was told: 'It is the Hospital's'. I found no castle or city or town which was said to be yours, except three.[19]

He may have been referring, however, to the crusader states in general, rather than to the kingdom of Jerusalem alone, for in the twelfth century the Hospitallers and Templars held more lands and strongholds in Tripoli and Antioch than in the kingdom itself.

During the twelfth century, much of the northern part of the county of Tripoli passed under the control of the orders. To the north of the Nahr el Kebir, only the lordship of Maraclea was not under their authority: the count retained responsibility for defence only from Gibelacar southwards. Besides Crac, in 1144 the Hospitallers received from Raymond II Castellum Bochee, Felicium and Lacum. Although the Hospital had only recently become a military order, the advantage of having these places under its control was already thought to be such that the count was prepared to buy out the secular nobles who had previously held authority in them. The Hospitallers later received Chastel Rouge, on the road from Tortosa to Rafaniyah, from Raymond III, and also the exposed stronghold of Tuban, while the difficulties encountered by the nobility are illustrated by the sale of Eixserc to the Hospitallers by William of Maraclea in 1163. In the county of Tripoli, the Templars gained less than the Hospitallers, but in 1152, when Tortosa 'remained deserted and destroyed after it had been wretchedly seized and burnt by the Turks', the order was given rights in the city by the local diocesan 'so that the aforesaid bishop and his successors and the men living in the city may be more secure, and that the church of the holy virgin Mary, mother of God, may be maintained and services held there more safely'.[20] By this time the Templars had already been assigned Safitha (Chastel Blanc), inland from Tortosa, and they also acquired Arima, a little to the south.

Further to the north, in 1168, Bohemund III of Antioch gave the Hospitallers a large tract of territory lying on both sides of the river Orontes, part of it situated near lands which they held in the county of Tripoli; but much of this district was in fact then in Muslim hands. In the long term a more important acquisition was the stronghold of Margat, near the coast in the south of the principality, which the Hospitallers received in 1186 from its lord Bertrand le Mazoir, 'since he realised that he could not hold the castle of Margat, as was necessary in the interests of Christianity, because of excessive expenses and the very close proximity of the infidel'.[21] Templar holdings in the principality were, by contrast, centred further north, in the region of the Amanus mountains. They included Baghras, near the road from Cilicia into Syria which went through the Belen Pass, and also the strongholds of Darbsaq and Roche Roussel (Chilvan Kale), which dominated the Hajar Shuglan Pass, further to the north. It is not known exactly when the Templars acquired these castles, but the Amanus march appears to have been assigned to them in the 1130s and is perhaps the earliest example of the entrusting of a border district to a military order. For Saladin's secretary and biographer, Imad ad-Din, Baghras and Darbsaq were 'two redoubtable weapons for the protagonists of infidelity'.[22]

Most of the strongholds held by the military orders in Syria during the twelfth century were, however, lost in the aftermath of the battle of Hattin: the only important castles which remained in Hospitaller hands were Crac des Chevaliers and Margat, while the Templars retained only Tortosa and Roche Guillaume, which lay in the Amanus march. Yet some were later recovered, and other castles were acquired by the Templars and Hospitallers in the thirteenth century, while the Teutonic order was also then participating in the defence of the Christian states in Syria. The Templars recovered Baghras in 1216, although it had in the meantime passed into the hands of the Armenians, and following the peace with the Muslims in 1240 the same order also regained Safed. Beaufort, which, like Safed, had come under Christian control in 1240, was purchased by the Templars twenty years later, together with Sidon, which had recently been subjected to Mongol attack and which Julian Garnier sold 'because he did not have the resources to restore the walls which had been destroyed'.[23] Among the new responsibilities of the Hospital was Château la Vieille in the principality of Antioch, which passed into their possession in 1218, while further south they took control of Ascalon in 1244, after it had been entrusted to them by Frederick II; and in 1261 they were renting Arsur from Balian of Ibelin. The Teutonic order assumed defensive responsibilities, particularly in the hinterland of Acre, where its acquisitions included the strongholds of Castellum Regis and Judin, but in 1236 it also received the nucleus of a march on the eastern frontiers of Armenia from King Hetoum. In the same way, Leo of Armenia had earlier created a march under Hospitaller authority in western Cilicia. In the early decades of the thirteenth century, the main responsibilities of the Templars and Hospitallers, in fact, lay in the north: it was mostly in the middle decades of the century that they were acquiring strongholds in the kingdom of Jerusalem. Yet, besides manning the strongholds which were assigned to them, the orders also, of course, assisted at times in the defence of cities, such as Acre and Tripoli, which were not under their lordship.

Nor were the orders' responsibilities limited just to supplying manpower for the defence of fortresses: they also undertook the building of new castles as well as the repair and extension of existing strongholds. In some instances donors placed military orders under a specific obligation of this kind. In 1152, the bishop of Tortosa required the Templars to build a new castle there, and when a few years earlier Baldwin, lord of Mares, had given Platta and surrounding lands to the Hospital, he had made it clear that the gift would be reclaimed 'if those brothers were not prepared to fortify the said place within a year from next Pentecost'.[24] On other occasions building was undertaken on the initiative of an order, as appears to have been the case at Chastellet, which was constructed by the Temple in 1178 near the Jordan crossing called Jacob's Ford, and of which a description survives in a letter written by Saladin's administrator, al-Fadil:

> The width of the wall exceeded ten cubits; it was built of enormous slabs of stone, each of which measured seven cubits across, more or less. The number of the slabs was more than 20,000, and each slab which was put in place and fixed in the structure cost not less than four dinars, and perhaps more.[25]

Imad ad-Din likened the walls to the rampart of Gog and Magog, and Saladin was reported to have offered the Templars 100,000 dinars to have the castle dismantled.

Chastellet was, in fact, very rapidly destroyed by Saladin, but the Templar castle of Château Pèlerin, which was begun in 1218, was among the last strongholds in the crusader states to fall to the Muslims. It was situated on a promontory on the Syrian coast, surrounded on three sides by water. In the twelfth century there had been a small observation tower near there, but after the losses sustained at the hands of Saladin it was decided to construct a much larger fortification. The promontory was 280 metres long and 168 metres wide, and the whole area was built upon in the thirteenth century. The most formidable constructions were on the eastern side, where the land was flat. These comprised first a revetted counterscarp, and then a ditch running across the neck of the promontory: this was almost 200 metres long and 18 metres wide; behind this was an outer wall with three towers. The eastern defences were completed by a bailey and then a higher inner wall with two large towers, which were sited between those in front, so that all could be used for firing on an attacker. In his *Historia Damiatina*, Oliver of Paderborn provides an early description of the new fortifications:

> At the front of the castle two towers were erected out of stones hewn into squares of such size that one stone could scarcely be pulled in a cart by two oxen. Each tower is a hundred feet in height and seventy-four in width. Inside them are two vaults. They rise up to a height which exceeds that of the headland. Between the two towers a high wall with ramparts has been newly completed, and has been so constructed that armed knights can ascend and descend inside. Item, at a short distance from the towers another wall extends from the sea on one side to that on the other, enclosing a well of running water.[26]

The Templar castle which was built at Safed in the early 1240s remained in Christian hands for little more than two decades, but in the early 1260s it was said that 'its outstanding and excellent construction seemed to have been achieved not by man alone but rather by God's omnipotence', and twenty years later the pilgrim Burchard of Mount Sion wrote that 'in my judgement it is more beautiful and stronger than any other castle I have seen'.[27]

The castle of Montfort, to the north-east of Acre, which the Teutonic order began to build in the later 1220s, was hardly as impressive. It was not in a strategically important position, and served mainly as an administrative centre and a place of refuge and defence, for which it relied to a considerable extent on the natural advantages of its site. It was situated on a long, narrow ridge, 110 metres long and between 20 and 30 metres wide, which was separated from higher land on the eastern side by a ditch. The main buildings consisted of a keep measuring 13 metres by 10 metres, a chapel and a hall which was 17 metres square. These ran from east to west along the ridge; but there were apparently also attempts at strengthening the slopes on the northern and southern sides with walls.

More imposing was the Hospitaller castle at Belvoir, which – like Montfort – has been excavated. This stronghold, which was built in the second half of the twelfth century, has been described as a '*castrum* within a *castrum*',[28] since the quadrilateral of the outer enceinte enclosed a square inner castle, which had towers at each of the four angles. Better preserved is the stronghold of Crac des Chevaliers, where the Hospitallers undertook extensive repair and construction work. The extent of the castle when it passed into the hands of the Hospital is not known precisely, and it is not clear on what scale the Hospitallers were engaged in building operations at an early stage. But damage caused by earthquakes in 1170 and 1202 had to be repaired, and it was at about the turn of the century that a new outer enceinte was constructed at a distance varying between 16 and 23 metres from the earlier outer wall. This new structure, which was provided with semi-circular towers, allowed further work to be undertaken on the inner enceinte, including a great talus along the west wall, round the south-west corner and along the south front. Among the last additions made by the Hospitallers at Crac was a barbican protecting the postern on the north front: this bears an inscription ascribing its construction to Nicholas Lorgne, at one time master of the Hospital, and it may have been erected in the period between 1254 and 1269.

Less is known about the orders' role in the construction of castles and strongholds in the Iberian peninsula. An obligation to undertake building operations was certainly sometimes imposed on them: when Afonso II of Portugal granted Avis to the master and brethren of Evora in 1211, he included the condition that 'you are to build a castle in the aforesaid place of Avis',[29] and a similar obligation was specified by Sancho II of Portugal when he gave Crato to the Hospitallers in 1232. Construction work was clearly undertaken by the orders – in the second half of the twelfth century, for example, the Templars were fortifying Tomar in

Portugal – but more detailed investigation of sites and structures is needed before the importance of their contribution can be accurately assessed.

Yet if relatively little is known of building operations undertaken by the military orders in the peninsula, it is clear that a large number of frontier castles passed under their control, although the importance of individual orders varied from region to region. In the lower valley of the Ebro, conquered by the count of Barcelona in the middle years of the twelfth century, the Temple and Hospital were the orders to whom strongholds were mainly assigned. In 1153, for example, Raymond Berenguer IV, 'wishing to entrust to safe guardians the castle of Miravet which by divine mercy and with great labour I have captured',[30] granted both that stronghold and neighbouring lesser castles to the Templars, just as a few years earlier he had given Amposta to the Hospitallers. On the other hand, in the territories in the district of Teruel conquered during the second half of the twelfth century by Raymond Berenguer's successor, Alfonso II, the order of Mountjoy was chiefly favoured by the Aragonese king, who also entrusted the castle of Alcañiz to the order of Calatrava. The Templars gained a footing there only at the end of the century, and although the Hospitallers acquired the castle of Aliaga in this region by private grant in 1163, they were not given any strongholds there by the Aragonese crown until the opening years of the thirteenth century. The Templars and Hospitallers also received a series of castles in the northern and central parts of the kingdom of Valencia when it came under Christian control in James I's reign; but some of these acquisitions had already been promised to the orders by James's predecessors, and in the period immediately following the conquest they were not assigned castles in the more southerly regions of Valencia beyond the river Júcar. In this part of the kingdom Santiago was the order chiefly favoured by James, from whom in 1244 it received the castles of Enguera and Anna.

On the other side of the peninsula, in Portugal, the international orders of the Temple and the Hospital similarly became firmly established in the more northerly regions. In the twelfth century the Templars undertook the defence of a considerable number of castles and territories to the north of the Tagus, including Castelo Branco as well as Soure and Tomar; and the

Hospital was given land to fortify at Belver, on the Tagus, as well as at Crato, a little further south. Yet although the Hospitallers also received Mora and Serpa, to the east of the Guadiana, after these strongholds had been reconquered in 1232, most of the castles which were entrusted to military orders in more southerly districts – brought permanently under Christian lordship mainly in the first half of the thirteenth century – were assigned to Avis or Santiago. Sancho II thus gave the latter order a group of castles in the Baixo Alentejo and Algarve districts, including Aljustrel, Mértola and Ayamonte.

The Templars and Hospitallers were of least significance in the central regions of Spain. Even in the twelfth century, when they were being assigned numerous castles in other parts of the peninsula, the Leonese and Castilian kings made them responsible for few frontier strongholds. Although the Templars had early been assigned Calatrava, they appear to have been given little else in the Castilian frontier area during the second half of the twelfth century. In 1163, the castle of Uclés was granted to the Hospitallers, but in 1174 it passed into the hands of Santiago, and the Hospital was apparently given compensation in the form of lands further north, away from the border region. The only important stronghold which the Hospitallers held near the Muslim frontier in Castile in the later years of the twelfth century was Consuegra, granted by Alfonso VIII in 1183. He favoured mainly the Spanish orders. Of these, Santiago was assigned strongholds chiefly in the eastern sector of the frontier region: among its acquisitions in this area were Alharilla and Oreja as well as Uclés. Calatrava predominated in the central portion of Castile's border area, and in the second half of the twelfth century seems to have possessed more frontier castles than any other order in Castile; but in the last decade of the century a district in the western part of the frontier region was granted to Trujillo, the name given to the Castilian branch of San Julián de Pereiro: in 1195, Alfonso VIII gave it the castles of Albalat, Santa Cruz, Cabañas and Zueruela, which all lay near Trujillo itself. The pattern was similar in the thirteenth century. Although the Templars received the stronghold of Capilla from Fernando III in 1236, and the Hospitallers in 1241 were given Lora, Setefilla and Almenara, between Córdoba and Seville, the Spanish orders were again favoured in the districts conquered by the Leonese and Castilian kings during the first half of the thirteenth century. Calatrava and Santiago were both entrusted with a number of castles in the Alto Guadalquivir region, where Calatrava's holdings were centred on Martos, and Santiago's on Segura de la Sierra. Santiago, in addition, in the first half of the century, received strongholds in Extremadura, where Alcántara also became firmly established. The Spanish orders were, however, assigned less in the middle and lower parts of the Guadalquivir valley, which were dominated by the cities of Córdoba and Seville.

In the Baltic region, the military orders built strongholds as the conquest progressed: they did not merely take over existing fortifications. Pagan defences were usually primitive structures of wood, which were often fired during the course of assaults and which were not designed to withstand the onslaughts of Western catapults and other siege machinery. In describing the Swordbrethren's use of catapults against the Estonian fort of Fellin in 1211, Henry of Livonia commented that 'the Estonians had never seen such things, and had not fortified their houses against such attack'. He then described how the Germans 'used fire and burned the fort'.[31] Yet most of the fortifications which the orders erected in the early stages of conquest were themselves constructed of wood and earth, and built quickly with the available materials and manpower; and there are numerous references to the burning of such defences by the orders' enemies in the middle decades of the thirteenth century. It was not until later that more sophisticated structures became the norm, with extensive use being made of brick.

In Prussia during the early 1230s, forts were built by the Teutonic order along the Vistula at Thorn, Kulm and Marienwerder, and later in the decade along the Frisches Haff at Elbing and Balga. Further castles were constructed in the interior as this region was brought under control and also further north, as the Teutonic order advanced into the Samland peninsula. There the fortress of Königsberg was established in 1255. In the second half of the thirteenth century several strongholds were also built along the Niemen, as the Teutonic order extended its power into Lithuanian territory: these included Georgenburg and Ragnit. Because the Teutonic order's authority in Prussia was so extensive, its construction of strongholds there was not dependent on individual grants of land, as the orders' castle-building activities were in the Holy Land and Spain; but in Livonia the Teutonic order, like the Swordbrethren earlier, had more limited rights, although both orders made a significant contribution in that region to the defence of conquered territories. The Sword-brethren early established themselves to the north-east of Riga at Segewold and Wenden, on the river Aa, and they also soon had a stronghold further north at Fellin. Yet the most heavily fortified frontier was in the south. On the Dvina itself the Swordbrethren held Ascheraden, and much later in the century the Teutonic order built a castle at Dünaburg, much further up the river. But most of the Teutonic order's castles in this area lay further to the west, in Semgallia and the more northerly districts of Kurland, while down the coast the fortress of Memel was established when the Livonian branch of the Teutonic order advanced that far in 1252. Apart from garrisoning their own castles, however, the brethren of the Teutonic order also at times assisted in the defence of those subject to other lords: thus according to the *Livonian Rhymed Chronicle*, in the 1280s a brother of the Teutonic order was in charge of the castle of Kokenhausen on the Dvina, which was under the lordship of the archbishop of Riga.

On all frontiers of western Christendom military orders clearly played a major role in holding and defending frontier castles, but the size of the garrisons which they could provide is difficult to assess because of lack of adequate evidence. The author of the *Gestes des Chiprois* claimed that in 1280 the Hospital had 600 mounted troops at Margat, and according to one version of the *Annales de Terre Sainte*, l000 men, including eighty Hospitallers, were killed or captured when Arsur fell in 1265. But another redaction of the same source gives a figure of 410 brothers, and a later chronicle puts the loss at ninety brothers, while another annalist had heard that 180 brethren, including some Templars, were led away into captivity from Arsur. Figures provided by narrative sources are obviously to be viewed with caution. More credence should be given to the numbers mentioned in papal letters written in 1255 in response to Hospitaller appeals for financial help: these show that Alexander IV had been informed by the Hospitallers that they intended to maintain sixty mounted troops (*equites*) permanently at Crac des Chevaliers and forty at a fortress to be built on Mount Tabor. These figures may be compared with those given in an account of the reconstruction of the castle of Safed, in which it was said that fifty knightly brothers and thirty brother sergeants, together with fifty *turcoples* and 300 archers, were necessary for the garrisoning of the stronghold. This account was written shortly before the castle was lost in 1266, and the figures were said to have been obtained from the Templars themselves; they are also to some extent borne out by a statement made during the Templar trial by a group of brethren in Paris, who claimed that when Safed fell to the Mamluks, eighty brothers were executed on the orders of the sultan. The garrisons needed to defend castles would obviously vary in size, but it would seem that even in the most important strongholds in the Holy Land the numbers of brothers are to be reckoned in tens rather than in hundreds, and this view is supported by a letter from the Hospitaller master, Hugh Revel, in 1268, which implies that in the whole of Syria the Hospital had only 300 brothers. It was admittedly claimed by some Templars during their trial that the order had lost three hundred brethren in the defence of Acre in 1291, but probably most Templar manpower was then concentrated there, even though the order still retained a few strongholds elsewhere in the Holy Land at that time. The evidence from Safed would also suggest that for permanent garrisons the orders relied heavily on mercenary troops, and this is also the conclusion to be drawn from the pilgrim Wilbrand of Oldenburg's assertion that when he visited the Holy Land in 1211 he was told by the Hospitallers that Crac des Chevaliers was defended by 2000 men: if this is an accurate figure, brethren would have comprised only a small proportion of the garrison.

Information about the size of garrisons in the Baltic region has to be derived mainly from the writings of chroniclers, and the figures these provide concerning brethren of the orders are remarkably small. Peter of Dusburg claims that when Thorn was built in 1231, only seven brothers were stationed there, and he also reports that in the following decade twelve brothers were left to garrison the newly-built castle of Potterberg. The largest force of brethren mentioned by him in any of the Teutonic order's Prussian castles was at Ragnit, where a commander and forty brothers were said to have been stationed in 1289. Peter of Dusburg is sometimes at pains to contrast the size of a garrison

with that of opposing forces, and it might be argued that he
deliberately underestimates the numbers of brethren in the
Teutonic order's strongholds. But at times he also draws a
contrast between the numbers of brethren and of those assisting
them. Thus at Potterberg there were said to be numerous men-at-
arms (*multi armigeri*), and at Ragnit the forty brothers were said to
have been accompanied by a hundred *armigeri*. He is not always
trying to present the total Christian force as minimal, and it
would seem that his assessment of the numbers of brethren was
not necessarily biased. His figures are also paralleled by those
given in the *Livonian Rhymed Chronicle*, which mentions, for example, that there were only fifteen brothers at Terweten in 1279
when it was attacked by the Semgallians. It appears, therefore,
that in defending strongholds in the Baltic region the military
orders, as in Syria, relied heavily on what were presumably paid
troops, and that the manpower of an order itself comprised in
numerical terms only a small proportion of defenders.

Figures for the Iberian peninsula are even rarer than those for
other fronts, but Templar evidence drawn from Aragon again
suggests that strongholds usually housed only a few brothers. The
largest number of Templars recorded at any one time in the castle
of Castellote is ten, and when Templars stationed in the order's
strongholds in southern Aragon were taken into royal custody in
1308, the number of brethren arrested varied from three at Villel
to eight at Castellote and fifteen at Cantavieja; and it should be
remembered that not all would have been warrior brethren. By
that time, however, these castles were no longer near the Muslim
frontier. Yet if the surviving numerical information is sparse, it is
clear from Templar sources in Aragon that brethren did not
themselves garrison all the fortified places which they were
assigned in frontier regions. Of the group of strongholds along
the lower Ebro granted by Raymond Berenguer IV in 1153, only
Miravet became the site of a Templar convent: although references to commanders of the nearby castles of Algás and Gandesa
occur in the thirteenth century, these were merely subordinate
administrative officials. In the same way, the order did not
garrison all the castles in southern Aragon which it inherited
from Mountjoy at the end of the twelfth century. At first, groups
of castles were placed under the control of brothers who were
often already heads of convents further north. Templar convents

were in due course established in some of Mountjoy's strongholds, such as Alfambra, Castellote and Villel, but the commander of the castle of Libros mentioned in several documents in the first half of the thirteenth century was merely an administrative official, and there is no evidence that Templars were stationed at Villarluengo or Orrios when these still lay near the Muslim frontier. Some fortifications were, of course, little more than watchtowers, but clearly not all of the fortified places under the control of the Aragonese Templars in the frontier region were constantly guarded by members of the order.

The defence of strongholds obviously did not depend entirely on garrisons which were permanently maintained. Vassals from surrounding districts could be called upon in times of danger. These would often include inhabitants who had been subjugated as the Christian frontiers advanced. Thus, in Mediterranean lands, Muslim communities were sometimes expected to give assistance in the defence of strongholds: in 1234 a surrender agreement between the Templars and the Muslim population of Chivert in northern Valencia included the provision that the latter should give service if Chivert was itself attacked by either Christians or Muslims. But conquered elements were not always reliable or very large. Western colonisation was often necessary before adequate aid from vassals could be obtained, and resettlement sometimes constituted a significant stage in the process of securing and maintaining Christian control in border districts, and defending frontier castles.

The area for which there is least evidence of colonisation is the Holy Land, and it was there, in fact, that least settlement occurred. It is quite clear that there was a perennial shortage of manpower and that settlers could not easily be attracted from the West. It is therefore not surprising that only isolated examples are known of colonising activity by the orders. William of Tyre reports the emergence of a settlement – though not necesarily of Westerners – at Gaza, which was under Templar lordship, and a Hospitaller charter from the year 1168 alludes to a Frankish settlement at Beit-Jibrin which had apparently been created after the nearby city of Ascalon had fallen to the Christians in 1153. But further evidence is lacking.

During the twelfth and thirteenth centuries there was much more extensive Christian settlement in lands gained from Islam in the Iberian peninsula; and as the military orders were assigned numerous frontier strongholds, together with the surrounding territories, they inevitably became heavily involved in the work of colonisation. Numerous settlement charters (*cartas de población*) have survived which were issued by the orders in various parts of the peninsula from the late twelfth century onwards. Yet military orders were confronted by the same problems as other Christian lords, and resettlement on the orders' lands, as on those of others, was a slow and laborious process. It might be thought that the orders would be able to recruit settlers from their own estates in the more northerly parts of the peninsula, and there are occasional examples of the transfer of men from an existing estate under an order's lordship to a new settlement under its control: in 1231, for example, land in a new settlement at Castellnou, near Lérida, was assigned by the Templars to inhabitants of Riudovelles and other nearby places under Templar authority. The evidence provided by tenants' names also suggests that in other Templar settlements some colonisers came from estates belonging to that order. But settlers' names do not suggest that the majority were recruited in that way. Those who took up residence in conquered lands under Templar lordship in the *Corona de Aragón* appear to have come from all parts of Aragon and Catalonia and possibly also from southern France. The orders would certainly not have wanted to recruit settlers primarily from their own estates, for it is clear that the surplus of manpower in the more northerly regions was not large: in the thirteenth century many lords in these districts were, in fact, suffering from a lack of tenants because of migration to rural estates further south or to growing urban communities in various parts of the peninsula. In the middle of the thirteenth century, for example, Christian settlers in the cities of Seville and Murcia included men who had been attracted away from estates further north which belonged to the order of Santiago. The consequences of such desertions can be seen in the Templar lordship of Puigreig in northern Catalonia, where a new settlement charter, favourable to tenants, was issued in 1281 in an attempt to check emigration and to attract newcomers; eleven years later, however, permission to alienate Puigreig was being given by the Templar master because it was no longer profitable to the order. In fact the military orders, like other lords in Spain and elsewhere, sometimes found it convenient to delegate the task of finding settlers. In the early thirteenth century the order of Santiago assigned the castle of Alhambra to the Castilian noble Alvaro Núñez de Lara, who was to resettle it. The Hospitaller grant of La Cenia in 1232 to William Moragues, an inhabitant of the nearby city of Tortosa, was made for the same purpose, and in the same district the Hospitallers in 1239 similarly allotted Alcanar to five named settlers on the condition that 'you, the aforesaid, settle it and send there twenty-one settlers'.[32]

Yet, whatever the method employed, the progress of resettlement on the estates of military orders was no more rapid than in other lordships in Spain: along the lower Ebro, which had been conquered in the middle years of the twelfth century, the settlement of lands assigned to the Templars and Hospitallers did not make much progress until the turn of the century, at which time the work of colonisation was also being undertaken by other lords in the district. Nor were all ventures immediately successful: at Pinell, on the lower Ebro, *cartas de población* were issued by the Templars in 1198 and 1207 to different groups of tenants, which suggests that the first attempt at settlement had foundered; and that this was not uncommon is indicated by a Templar charter recording a lease of land in the district of Lérida in 1174, for it included the provision that 'if it happens that all the other settlers of that field leave it, we have the power to recover these three *fanegadas*'.[33] Colonisation, particularly in rural districts, tended to be slow: new settlements were still being created along the lower Ebro in the later thirteenth century. But progress was gradually made on the estates of the military orders as on those of other lords, although some districts had ceased to be frontier areas by the time that any considerable settlement took place.

In the thirteenth century, resettlement in Spain was certainly proceeding more rapidly than colonisation in Prussia and Livonia. In the early stages of conquest in the Baltic region the only settlement was of burgesses and nobles. In Prussia, large estates situated near the eastern borders of the districts under German control were at that time being assigned to immigrant nobles. Among the more important grants was that of a castle and 300 *Hufen* made to Dietrich of Tiefenau in 1236; but most were of lesser extent. Peasant settlement in Prussia did not progress until the closing years of the thirteenth century, after the Prussians had

finally been subdued. Villages were then quickly founded on the
Teutonic order's lands, particularly in the more westerly parts of
Prussia: in a period of forty years, 1200 *Hufen* were settled with
peasants in the district of Elbing. The work of organising such
settlements was usually delegated to agents (*locatores*), which
suggests that the order did not usually transfer men from its
own estates further west, as has sometimes been suggested. To
have done so would probably have created the same problems as
in Spain. In Livonia, however, there was never any large-scale
settlement by Western peasants.

Nevertheless, even where colonisation was limited, the orders
played an important role in defending frontier strongholds, and
sources can easily be found which praise their work in this sphere.
In the later twelfth century, William of Tyre – although ready to
criticise the Templars and Hospitallers – conceded that they had
guarded Gaza and Beit-Jibrin with diligence; even a Muslim
source relates that the Westerners fought fiercely in the defence
of the Templar castle of Safed in 1266, and the contribution made
by some, though not all, brethren to the defence of Acre in 1291
elicited praise from the propagandist Thaddeus of Naples. In
Spain, the Castilian king, Alfonso VIII, referred to the orders
more generally as providing a constant wall and shield in defence
of the faith, and in 1210 the Aragonese king, Pedro II, rewarded
the Hospitallers, 'taking into consideration how great a concern
they continually display for the defence of the faith'.[34]

Numerous instances can also be quoted where brothers offered
stout and prolonged resistance. After the disaster at Hattin in
1187, the Hospitaller castle of Belvoir held out for more than a
year, and Saladin was unable at this time to take either Margat or
Crac des Chevaliers from the Hospitallers. In 1211, the Castilian
castle of Salvatierra, which then housed the headquarters of the
order of Calatrava, similarly maintained a lengthy and determined resistance when it was attacked by the Almohad caliph: the
chronicler Roderick Jiménez de Rada claims that it fell only after
a siege of nearly three months, when large numbers of the
defenders had been killed and the towers and wall almost
destroyed, while according to the *Crónica latina de los reyes de
Castilla* it was only on the king's order that it finally surrendered.

On the other hand, there were occasions when little effective
resistance was offered. After the battle of Hattin, the Hospitaller

castle of Beit-Jibrin surrendered without a fight, as did the Templar stronghold of Gaza, and in Spain a few years later, several of Calatrava's castles were quickly lost after the defeat at Alarcos: according to some Muslim sources, those living in Calatrava itself fled even before Muslim forces arrived. In northern Syria, the Muslims similarly found the Templar stronghold of Baghras deserted in 1268, and in the second half of the thirteenth century a number of the orders' castles in the Holy Land fell to the Mamluks after sieges lasting weeks rather than months: the Hospitaller master Hugh Revel commented disdainfully in 1268 that 'Safed, concerning which the Templars had spoken so fulsomely, could not defend itself for more than sixteen days',[35] and he claimed that the Templar castle of Beaufort, which should have been able to resist for a year, had fallen within four days, although, according to Muslim sources, the siege was a little more prolonged. He prided himself on the fact that at Arsur the Hospitallers had managed to hold out for as long as forty days. A few years later, however, he was himself the recipient of a Muslim letter which stated: 'we bring the news that God has granted us an easy conquest of Hisn al-Akrad (Crac des Chevaliers). You fortified it, built it up and adorned it, but you would have been more fortunate had you abandoned it'.[36] In the Baltic region, castles belonging to the Teutonic order were in the same way quickly lost in the wake of native rebellions. In 1260, for example, the recently-built castles of Karshowen and Doblen in Semgallia were abandoned, while many other strongholds, both in Livonian and in Prussian lands, could offer little effective resistance.

In some instances it is possible to discern particular factors which helped to determine the outcome of sieges. Gaza was surrendered by the Templars after the battle of Hattin in order to secure the release of their captured master. At Belvoir, on the other hand, the besiegers' lack of vigilance enabled the Hospitallers early in 1188 to launch a successful sortie, by which they gained supplies as well as inflicting casualties on the enemy; and later in the year the Muslim besiegers were hampered by incessant rain. According to Islamic sources, it was the exceptional position and strength of the stronghold of Margat that allowed it to remain under Christian lordship at that time. Yet although the Hospitaller strongholds of Margat and Crac des Chevaliers held out at a time of Muslim dominance, it tended to be the general military and political situation rather than more particular factors which decided the fate of strongholds and cities. After severe Christian defeats in battle, such as those at Hattin in the East, and Alarcos in Spain, it was difficult to retain castles, especially as it had often been necessary to reduce or remove garrisons beforehand in order to put a viable force into the field. And as Mamluk power grew in Syria during the second half of the thirteenth century, the orders found themselves incapable of resisting the advance of the Muslims, who attacked stronghold after stronghold. Faced by large infidel forces and deprived of help from relieving Christian armies, garrisons could not hold out, despite increased fortifications and the stern efforts of defenders, who sought to answer bombardment with counter-bombardment, and mining with counter-mining. And when the situation became desperate, it was often thought better to surrender in return for a safe-conduct for the garrison than to fight to the bitter end. It was in this way that a number of the orders' castles in Syria, including Crac and Montfort, finally passed into Muslim hands in the later thirteenth century. In Prussia numerous castles of the Teutonic order similarly fell in the early 1260s following widespread rebellions, because they did not have the resources to maintain very prolonged resistance and could not be relieved: of Kreuzburg, for example, Peter of Dusburg writes that in 1263 'the brothers and their *familia*, after many glorious battles there, left the castle secretly by night, when supplies were completely exhausted'.[37]

Yet, if in adverse circumstances military orders could not be relied upon to retain their strongholds, they were of value in providing garrisons at all, for they were undertaking a task which could not easily be fulfilled by others. As has been seen, the order of Calatrava owed its existence to the fact that no secular noble was prepared to assume responsibility for the defence of the castle of Calatrava; and when the Aragonese king, Pedro II, gave the stronghold of Monroyo to the same order he asserted that 'there is no one in our land who wants to receive that castle for colonising'.[38] Sometimes conquests in Spain just had to be abandoned for lack of necessary resources, as happened at Ubeda in 1212. It has also been seen that in Syria castles passed in increasing numbers into the hands of the military orders because secular lords found themselves unable to defend them adequately; and although in the Baltic region some strongholds were assigned to immigrant nobles, the main task of defence in Livonia and Prussia inevitably fell on the Swordbrethren and the brothers of the Teutonic order.

In the Field

IT is difficult to obtain reliable information for any region about the size of contingents which the military orders could put into the field. Much of the surviving evidence emanates from chronicles and is therefore to be treated with caution; and statements about numbers made by the orders themselves are few. The sources also often fail to distinguish between brethren and secular troops under their command, and they rarely indicate whether all available manpower was being used: obviously, the size of the contingents put into the field would vary according to the nature of the operation being undertaken. Despite the limitations of the evidence, however, it is clear that the numbers of brethren who could give field service on the frontiers of western Christendom were relatively small, even by medieval standards, and that in the field – as in the garrisoning of castles – there was a heavy reliance on auxiliary troops.

In Syria, military orders were not obliged to provide a fixed number of men in return for their lands, and the only precise figures about military establishments in the eastern Mediterranean are those contained in capitular decrees issued by the Hospital in 1301 and 1302. The number of knights and sergeants-at-arms at the order's headquarters was then fixed at eighty, but by that time the Holy Land had been lost and the order was based in Cyprus. Other statements made in the East by Templars and Hospitallers themselves about the contingents they could, or did, put into the field are difficult to evaluate. In the middle of the twelfth century the seneschal of the Temple reported that he had taken a force, including 120 knights and totalling up to 1000 troops, to Antioch following the death of the prince in 1149; but it is not clear how many of these were Templars. Twenty years later the Hospitaller master, Gilbert of Assailly, promised the service of 500 knights and 500 *turcoples* for the invasion of Egypt then being planned, but again it is not known whether the knights would all have been members of the order. Similarly, it is unclear how many brethren were among the nearly 2000 men whom the Temple and Hospital were each reported by the papal legate Pelagius to be maintaining at the siege of Damietta during the fifth crusade. Statements made by chroniclers are no easier to assess, even if the figures they provide are accepted at their face value. The twelfth-century Muslim writer Ibn al-Qalanisi states that a force of Templars and Hospitallers travelling to Banyas in 1157 totalled 700 horsemen, but it is evident that this figure included some who were not brethren of the orders. The same comment can be made about a Christian source which relates that the Hospital's contingent on an expedition against Hamah in 1233 comprised a hundred knights, 400 mounted sergeants and 500 foot. William of Tyre, on the other hand, reports that eighty Templars took part in the victory over Saladin at Montgisard in 1177, but whereas in 1233 the Hospital was said to be using all its available manpower, some Templars were engaged elsewhere at the time of the battle of Montgisard.

Reports concerning losses often provide more precise information about brethren themselves. A papal letter of the year 1157, for example, states that in the defeat suffered to the north of the Sea of Galilee in June of that year the master of the Temple was captured and eighty-seven of his brethren killed or taken, together with 300 other knights. Adrian IV did not indicate the proportion of brothers lost, but some later letters are more informative on this point. A Templar letter to the French king, Louis VII, reports the loss at Artah in 1164 of sixty Templars, besides *turcoples* and *fratres clientes*, who were perhaps men serving for a term with the order: only seven brothers survived. In 1187, the grand commander of the Temple informed his colleagues in the West that the order had lost sixty brothers at Cresson in May and that 230 brethren had been killed at Hattin: the central convent had been 'almost completely annihilated'.[39] After the defeat at La Forbie in 1244 the patriarch of Jerusalem sent letters to the West in which he stated that 312 Templar knights and 324 of their *turcoples* had been killed, and that the Hospital had lost 325 brother knights and 200 *turcoples*, while 400 men of the Teutonic order had been lost. He also reported that only thirty-three Templars and twenty-six Hospitallers had escaped. These figures do not, of course, provide absolutely reliable information: the master of the Hospital put the number of survivors at eighteen Templars and sixteen Hospitallers. In the confusion following a severe defeat it would inevitably have been difficult to obtain accurate information, and it would be surprising if all reports had tallied exactly. It may also be noted that the patriarch wrote only of knightly brethren, and it is to be surmised that he was, in fact, referring to sergeants as well as knights, while the figure for the Teutonic order's losses may have included some secular troops. Despite reservations about the reliability of the evidence, it would seem not unreasonable to suggest that in the kingdom of Jerusalem the Templars and Hospitallers were each capable of putting into the field a force of some 300 brothers, and this figure would tally with that given by the Hospitaller master in 1268, provided, of course, that he was referring only to warrior brethren and that garrisons were severely depleted when a large field army was needed. If this figure is valid, it would mean that the contingent of brothers which the Temple and Hospital together could provide would in the second half of the twelfth century have been not very different in size from the knightly force supplied by the feudal levy of the kingdom of Jerusalem. But it should be remembered that the military orders' forces would presumably have included sergeants-at-arms, whereas the king of Jerusalem could in theory call upon the service of some 5000 sergeants in addition to the levy of knights. But it is clear that the orders also furnished considerable numbers of *turcoples* and other auxiliary troops, and already, before the end of the twelfth century, the secular forces which the king could summon had been much reduced as lands and service were lost. In the twelfth century the orders were making a major contribution to the forces which the crusader states put into the field; but their importance was even greater in the thirteenth.

They were less significant in the Iberian peninsula. Only in isolated instances were orders in Spain under an obligation to provide a fixed number of troops in return for lands assigned to them, but towards the end of the thirteenth century the Aragonese kings did begin to demand contingents of fixed size for frontier service. In 1287, Alfonso III ordered the Templars and Hospitallers to station thirty knights each on the Valencian border, while Calatrava was required to provide twenty. In the autumn of 1303, when preparations were being made to repel a threatened attack from Granada, James II of Aragon demanded a hundred knights from the Temple, sixty from the Hospital, thirty from Calatrava and twenty from Santiago. Some of these figures are not very large when compared with the military obligations of leading Aragonese nobles; nor should it be assumed that contingents of the size demanded were always, in fact, furnished. Further summonses to the Aragonese Templars in 1303 and 1304 merely asked them to send as large a force as possible, and in October 1304 the king was ready to be satisfied with a Templar contingent of twenty to thirty knights.

The size of contingents provided at the turn of the thirteenth and fourteenth centuries is not, of course, necessarily indicative of the number of troops supplied by military orders at earlier stages of the reconquest. It has been seen that in 1246 the master of Santiago felt capable of taking 300 knights to Constantinople to assist Baldwin II; but it was stipulated that the knights did not all have to be members of the order, and the Infante Alfonso sought to ensure that not more than fifty knightly brothers were sent. Since the project foundered, it is also not clear whether Santiago could, in fact, have supplied a force of 300 knights. As James I noted in his *Chronicle*, however, that order later failed to provide the aid it had promised for his crusade to the Holy Land: although Santiago had undertaken to furnish a hundred knights, in fact its contingent consisted of twenty.

This last figure is not very different from some found in accounts of thirteenth-century expeditions within the peninsula. It is recorded in the *Chronicle of James I* that when the Aragonese king set out towards the Muslim city of Valencia in 1238, those accompanying him included a Templar commander with about twenty knights: among other contingents were those of the nobles William of Aguiló and Roderick of Lizana, which numbered fifteen and thirty respectively, while the king's own retainers totalled between 130 and 140 knights. But these figures refer to an early stage of the campaign, before all available forces had been mobilised. More revealing are comments about the siege of Seville in 1248 contained in the *Primera crónica general*. This reports that in the early stages of the siege the master of Santiago had 280 knights under his command, although these were not all brethren of the order; it also states, however, that towards the end of the siege the master was accompanied by only twenty-five brothers of

Santiago. It has further been calculated that the Templars had about 100 knights or their equivalent in the attack on Mallorca in 1229, but these may not all have been members of the order; and when the provincial prior of the Hospitallers arrived on the island he was said to have been accompanied by only fifteen brothers.

The losses incurred by military orders in serious defeats in the peninsula also suggest that their numerical contribution was of only moderate importance. According to the *Kalendario* of Uclés, nineteen brothers of Santiago died in the disaster at Alarcos in 1195, and in the further defeat at Moclín in 1280 the master and fifty-five brethren of the same order were killed. The author of the *Crónica del rey Alfonso X* nevertheless claimed that in this battle 'the great majority of the brothers of the order of Santiago died';[40] and, as has been seen, the loss was sufficiently serious to occasion the amalgamation with the order of Santa María de España.

Evidence of a different kind is provided by the *repartimiento* recording the allocation of conquered lands in Mallorca, for this gives an indication of the relative significance of the various contingents participating in the expedition in 1229. All who had taken part in the campaign were allotted shares of the conquered lands in proportion to the size of contingent provided. The Templar allocation amounted to a little under a twenty-fifth of the whole. It was only a small share, even though the Temple was the leading military order in James's lands. But clearly Christian rulers in Spain could call upon larger contingents of secular Christian troops than their counterparts in Syria could mobilise, for Western Christians comprised a much larger proportion of the population of the peninsular kingdoms than of the crusader states. Apart from the service provided by the nobility, Spanish kings commonly made use of a more general obligation of military service, and the militias provided by townships provided both infantry and the mounted troops known as *caballeros villanos*.

The most precise information concerning contingents of the military orders in Central and Eastern Europe refers to obligations which were never in fact fulfilled. It has been seen that the master of Santiago undertook to provide a fixed number of troops for the defence of the Latin Empire in 1246. When in the following year the district of Severin was granted to the Hospitallers, they similarly agreed to furnish the king of Hungary with the service of a hundred brothers if the kingdom was invaded by pagans, Bulgars or other schismatics, and sixty if the Mongols attacked. Further north, however, in the Baltic region, where the military orders were of greater significance, the evidence is less precise, and is contained mainly in chronicle sources. These suggest that both in Livonia and Prussia the contingents of brethren were never very large and that they made up only a small proportion even of the forces which were recruited locally. The most informative comment is that found in the *Livonian Rhymed Chronicle* concerning an expedition against the Russians in 1268: the provincial master of the Teutonic order was reported to have assembled all the brothers he could mobilise, and these totalled about 180 in an army which was said altogether to comprise some 18,000 mounted troops and 9000 seamen. The numbers given for the total force seem to be somewhat exaggerated, but the figure of 180 appears not unreasonable as a maximum contingent of brothers. Certainly, other figures provided by this source and by Peter of Dusburg are always smaller, and in many cases much smaller. Peter of Dusburg states, for example, that five brothers and twenty-four *armigeri* attacked Sventopolk's stronghold of Sartowitz in 1242, and that a force of thirteen brothers and 250 mounted troops invaded Sudovia in 1281, while the *Livonian Rhymed Chronicle* mentions an expedition mounted by forty brothers and 500 Kurs against the Samogithians in 1257 and describes a camapign against the Lithuanians in 1290 in which the Christian forces comprised twelve brothers and a total force of 350 men, made up of *armigeri* and Kurs.

Losses of brethren in the Baltic region were also moderate in amount. The largest figure given in the chronicle sources refers to the year 1260, when, according to the *Livonian Rhymed Chronicle*, the provincial master and 150 brothers were killed in the heavy defeat then suffered by the Teutonic order. The same source reports that in 1279 the provincial master and seventy-one brothers were lost, while Peter of Dusburg states that fifty-four brothers were killed by the Prussians in 1249. Other figures are lower and always considerably smaller than the losses reported of other troops. Peter of Dusburg relates that when twelve brothers were killed in Pogesania in 1273, the numbers of other Christian troops lost totalled 500; and the *Livonian Rhymed Chronicle* similarly states that twenty brothers and 600 others lost their lives at the hands of the Semgallians in 1264. These figures cannot, of course, be taken as being altogether accurate, but the figure of fifty-four brothers killed in 1249 finds support in a contemporary papal letter which gives the number as fifty-three.

Even if these sources concerning the Baltic are not exact, they do give the consistent impression that the numbers of brethren were small by comparison with those of other troops; they also indicate that the forces based locally, whether brethren or others, often needed assistance if considerable gains were to be made. In the early years of the thirteenth century, despite the foundation of the Swordbrethren, the bishop of Riga regularly travelled back to Germany in order to obtain military assistance, and among crusaders who provided aid in Prussia was Henry, margrave of Meissen, whose arrival in 1236 enabled the Teutonic order to advance as far as Elbing, while conquests in Samland in 1255 were effected with the help of Ottokar II of Bohemia, the margrave of Brandenburg and what Peter of Dusburg called 'a huge multitude of crusaders'.[41]

Although, on all fronts, the numbers of brethren who could serve on campaigns were not large, at least in Syria they were held in high esteem by their opponents, and this reputation was presumably based primarily on their exploits in the field. Muslim views find expression, for example, in the writings of the early thirteenth-century chronicler Ibn al-Athir. He reports that when the Hospitaller Castellan of Crac des Chevaliers was killed in 1170 the Muslims rejoiced, because he had been 'a man who, through his bravery, occupied an eminent position, and who was like a bone in the gullet of the Muslims'.[42] The Hospitaller master Roger of Moulins, who was killed in the spring of 1187, was similarly described by Ibn al-Athir as 'one of the most famous Frankish knights, and he had inflicted the greatest ills on the Muslims'.[43] After the Christian defeat at Hattin later in the same year, Saladin was reported by Ibn al-Athir to have offered fifty dinars for every Templar and Hospitaller brought to him and to have ordered their execution because 'they were more vigorous in war than all the rest of the Franks'.[44] When describing the capture of two leading Hospitallers in the following year, Ibn al-Athir further asserts of Saladin that 'it was his custom to massacre the Templars and Hospitallers, because of the violent hatred which they bore against the Muslims and because of their bravery'.[45] Such comments are echoed in other Muslim sources reporting

warfare in the East, but, by contrast, little comment on the orders
was made by Muslim chroniclers describing the Spanish reconquest. This is probably a reflection, however, of the limited scale of
the order's contribution in the field in the Iberian peninsula rather
than an indication of military reputation. In the Baltic region,
thirteenth-century pagans left no written sources, while Russian
chronicles offer little comment on the fighting qualities of Westerners, who in any case are all referred to without distinction as
Nemsty.

The bravery and determination noted by Ibn al-Athir were not
the only qualities which distinguished the brethren of the military
orders. They probably also provided a more disciplined force than
many secular contingents, although they did, of course, themselves have some secular troops under their command. The
Templar customs include a set of detailed regulations – based
on experience and not on classical texts – concerning conduct in
camp and on the march, and most of these were later adopted by
the Teutonic order. When camp was being pitched, brothers were
not permitted to take up places around the chapel until the order
was given. Once the camp had been established, foraging and the
collecting of wood were strictly regulated: no one was to be sent
out for these purposes without permission, unless he remained
within earshot; those brethren who had two squires were to
dispatch only one of them to obtain supplies, and brothers were
always to remain within hearing. If the alarm sounded within the
camp, those nearest were to respond, equipped with lance and
shield; the remainder were to go to the chapel and await orders. If
the alarm sounded outside the camp, no one was to leave without
permission. When the Templars were about to set out on the
march, no one was to saddle or mount his horse until the
command was given; when the order to mount was issued, care
was to be taken to ensure that nothing was left behind. On the
march a proper order was to be maintained, and at night silence
was to be observed. No one was to leave the column to water his
horse without permission. If the alarm sounded on the march,
those nearest were to prepare themselves, but were to take no
action until ordered, while others were to assemble around the
marshal to await his commands. Most importantly, when brethren were drawn up in *eschieles* or squadrons, ready to fight, no
brother was to leave his position or attack without permission.

Brethren were, of course, bound by a vow of obedience, and this was reinforced by the threat of severe penalties for disobeying orders in the field. Templars who engaged the enemy without permission were to lose their habit for a period and might be placed in irons; and in all the leading orders the penalty for desertion in battle was expulsion, although to lessen the risk of such an occurrence the rule of Santiago included the compassionate provision that 'if anyone is so fearful as to be unfit for campaigning, he is to occupy himself in other tasks of the house according to the master's discretion, so that he is not idle'.[46] On the other hand, military discipline was at times enforced with an extraordinary rigour. One instance, admittedly not concerning service in the field, is recorded in a Catalan version of the Templar Customs. In 1268 the brethren garrisoning Baghras decided that it could no longer be held and therefore abandoned it. They had not received permission from their superiors as was normally required, although the master and convent had already, in fact, agreed that resistance could no longer be maintained, and had dispatched a messenger with orders to relinquish the stronghold. The case was later discussed at length, and even though in the end the brethren who had abandoned the stronghold were not expelled from the order – this was the penalty for surrendering a frontier castle without permission – they were subjected to a penance of a year and a day on the grounds that, despite doing as much as they could, they had not destroyed absolutely everything which had been left behind. Even more extreme was the punishment meted out a decade earlier to two brothers of the Teutonic order in Prussia, who had apostasised and gone over to the enemy: they were publicly burned. Yet harsh punishments could not eliminate acts of disobedience. In 1260, some Templars were reported to have fled during a raid in the Holy Land, but a more common fault was the launching of attacks without awaiting orders. The Templar Customs report the case of James of Ravane, who held office in Acre and who was deprived of his habit and put in irons for undertaking a raid in Syria without permission; and narrative sources describing the third crusade relate that the marshal of the Hospital launched a charge before the command was given, and they also mention another brother who was summoned before the master of the Hospital for attacking against orders.

Yet the Templar master James of Molay was not alone in arguing that, because of their vow of obedience, brethren of the military orders were superior to other troops. The same opinion is found in some crusading treatises composed in the late thirteenth and early fourteenth centuries. The author of the *Memoria Terre Sancte* had brethren of a military order in mind when he wrote that

> everyone should know that the business of war and military activity cannot be undertaken well, nor conducted successfully nor brought to a satisfactory conclusion, especially in this matter [the recovery of the Holy Land], except by men of obedience; and we can see and realise this from the crusade of the holy king Louis, since his army was defeated by the sultan through the disobedience of his men, and the king himself was captured at Mansourah, as everybody knows.[47]

No theorist, however, undertook a thorough and detailed comparison of the relative merits of all types of troops, and some were of the opinion that the problem of obedience could be solved by employing mercenaries.

In his reference to Louis IX's Egyptian crusade, the author of the *Memoria Terre Sancte* was no doubt alluding to the conduct of the king's brother Robert of Artois. The latter's actions were characterised by ignorance as well as by disobedience, and the writer of the treatise argued that brethren had the further advantage over other troops of being well-informed and experienced:

> it should be realised that brethren, who are bound by obedience, are engaged in war throughout their lives, while seculars want to return to their homeland after two or three years; and afterwards new men are sent out who know nothing of the nature of warfare in that region; and everyone is aware that the man who is constantly involved in war knows most about it.[48]

Raymond Lull similarly claimed that their constant experience of war made brethren of a military order preferable to other troops.

Brethren of the orders in Syria obviously knew more than most crusaders about Muslim tactics and the conditions of warfare in the East; but they did not, in fact, usually spend their whole careers on that front. Many brothers recruited in the West appear to have served in the East for only a short period, often at an early stage in their careers. Of the Templars arrested in 1308 in Cyprus, where the order's headquarters were then located, over seventy per cent had been recruited in 1300 or later. The pattern of service is illustrated by the testimonies of the French Templars Humbert of Germille and William of Torrage, who appeared before papal commissioners in Paris in 1311. The former, who was then about twenty-seven years old, said that he had been received into the Temple in France in 1303; he had been sent out to Cyprus almost at once, but was back in France again by the time that the Templars were arrested there in 1307. The latter, who had joined the Temple in Poitou, had been sent out to the East during his first year as a brother, and had stayed there for a year and a half before returning to the West.

Nor did experience always provide a guarantee against rash decisions. Santiago's defeat at Moclín in 1280 occurred because the master attacked without waiting for adequate support to arrive. In the Holy Land, heavy losses were sustained at Cresson in the spring of 1187 when the Templar master Gerard of Ridefort rejected the advice of the master of the Hospital and of his own marshal and committed his troops against a much larger Muslim force, and a few months later he was one of those who unwisely advised Guy of Lusignan to give battle to Saladin instead of using the available manpower to defend castles and strongholds. Yet it should be remembered that verdicts of this kind are made with the benefit of hindsight, and the foolhardiness of some decisions may not have been quite so obvious before the event.

Usually, however, the counsel given by leading brethren of the military orders on all fronts revealed a realistic assessment of the political and military situation, and often tended towards caution. During the conquest of the island of Mallorca, the prior of the Aragonese Hospitallers advised James I against attacking the Muslims in the hills near Inca because he considered it too dangerous, and a few years later the Aragonese provincial master of the Temple was opposed to an assault on the tower of Moncada because of its proximity to the Muslim city of Valencia. During the third crusade, the Templars and Hospitallers advised against besieging Jerusalem on the grounds that during a siege they would be exposed to Saladin's forces and that, even if the city were taken, it would be difficult to hold it because of the lack of settlers. And before Damietta was captured during the fifth crusade they advised against accepting a Muslim offer which would have restored Jerusalem to the Christians, because they felt that the city could not be held, especially as the walls had been dismantled. Brethren of the military orders in the frontier regions of western Christendom were not usually fanatics, and it was not only in the Holy Land that they were prepared, if necessary, to ally with, and fight alongside, infidels. In 1225, for example, the forces which the Castilian king, Fernando III, assigned to the Muslim ruler of Baeza, and which were to assist him in gaining castles and towns from the neighbouring Muslim state of Seville, included contingents from Santiago and Calatrava; and there were similar alliances between the Teutonic order and pagans in the Baltic region.

In practice, crusaders often benefited from the orders' experience and knowledge. Brethren were in the first place able to advise on the conditions of war and enemy tactics. Peter of Dusburg thus reports that in January 1262 the brothers of the Teutonic order in Prussia dissuaded the counts of Jülich and Mark from launching an attack too late in the day and that it was also on the order's advice that the count of Jülich later sent out scouts to warn of ambushes. During the second crusade, over a century earlier, the French king, Louis VII, had even gone so far as to place his army under the command of the Templars when it was being harassed by the Turks in Asia Minor:

> It was therefore agreed by common counsel that all should enter into mutual brotherhood with them in this time of danger, rich and poor alike swearing on oath that they would not flee from the field of battle and that in all matters they would obey the leaders assigned to them by the Templars.[49]

In the eastern Mediterranean, however, the orders' experience was more commonly utilised by placing contingents of brethren in the vanguard or rearguard of crusading forces. In his *Historia Damiatina*, for example, Oliver of Paderborn states that in February 1219 the Templars were in the van when the crusaders advanced on Damietta during the fifth crusade, and that they brought up the rear when the army attempted to retreat in August 1221. Joinville similarly relates that the Templars were the leading forces when Louis IX's crusade advanced south from Damietta in December 1249; that they covered the retreat of the crusaders when the latter became involved in a skirmish later in the month; and that the count of Artois was meant to be in the second line behind the Templars on the occasion when he broke ranks and pursued the Muslims to Mansourah. James of Molay's claim that in the East the Templars and Hospitallers always provided the vanguard and rearguard for crusading forces was certainly exaggerated, but they did fulfil this task on numerous occasions.

That a similar duty was undertaken by military orders in the Iberian peninsula might seem to be indicated by the statement that 'we have resolved to stand together in the army, both in the front, and in the last, line', which was included in an agreement made between the Temple, the Hospital and Santiago at Salamanca in 1178;[50] but accounts of twelfth- and thirteenth-century campaigns in Spain do not usually attribute such a role to the orders. On the approach to Las Navas de Tolosa in 1212, foreign contingents were led by the Castilian noble Diego López de Haro, not by the orders; and in the battle itself the orders' contingents were placed in the second line: Diego López was in the van, and the rear was brought up by Alfonso VIII. And surviving descriptions of mainland campaigns undertaken by the Aragonese king, James I, do not suggest that the orders normally provided the rearguard or vanguard: on the royal expedition into Murcia in 1265, the van was under the command of the king's sons, while James himself brought up the rear. But in Spain, of course, the foreign crusader element was of less importance than in the eastern Mediterranean and the Baltic: the bulk of the secular forces combating the Muslims in the peninsula were Spanish, and were themselves experienced in fighting the infidel.

In Spain, however, the orders were often important in helping to provide the nucleus of a force at the start of campaigns. As the Christian frontiers advanced and troops were drawn from an increasingly large area, it was often difficult to mobilise secular contingents rapidly, whereas the orders could usually put at least some of their forces into the field at short notice. According to one version of the *Primera crónica general*, some nobles did not arrive at

Alarcos in 1195 until after the battle was over, and the difficulty of
mobilising secular forces rapidly is also apparent in accounts of
James I's campaigns in Valencia; these also show that the military
orders helped to provide the nucleus of a campaigning army.
According to the *Chronicle of James I*, the forces for the assault on
Burriana in 1233 should have mustered at Teruel. On the
appointed day none of the barons (*ricoshombres*) appeared, but it
was reported to the king that the provincial masters of the Temple
and Hospital, together with the Calatravan commander of
Alcañiz and Santiago's commander of Montalbán, had been
waiting near Murviedro for two days. These then joined the
king, and the attack on Burriana appears to have been launched
by James, the military orders, the inhabitants of Teruel and the
men of the bishop of Zaragoza, who were only later joined by
other lay contingents. Similarly, when the Aragonese king set out
towards the city of Valencia in 1238, he was accompanied by his
own retainers, the provincial prior of the Hospital, a Templar
commander, the commander of Alcañiz and some *almogavares*, but
only three nobles are reported to have been present at that stage;
other contingents from Aragon and Catalonia did not arrive until
later.

Nor were the orders' military activities usually affected by the
limitations and restrictions which characterised the service provided by secular contingents. On all fronts most crusaders
campaigned for only a short period; and although in the Holy
Land there is no evidence of a time limit on the service given by
the feudal and general levy, the widespread limitations which
existed in Spain made it difficult to keep secular forces in the field
for long periods. A ruler might try to retain them by offering
payment, and they might be ready to waive their privileges in the
hope of gaining booty. Yet town militias had other concerns
besides fighting. During the siege of Burriana in 1233, James I
was told that the townsmen wanted to return home to harvest
their crops, and in the same year the inhabitants of Toro, Zamora
and several other towns abandoned the Castilian king, Fernando
III, at the siege of Ubeda when their term of service was
completed. Brothers of the military orders could, by contrast, be
expected to give prolonged service more readily. The *Crónica latina
de los reyes de Castilla* records that after Fernando III's expedition
in 1225 the brethren of Calatrava and Santiago were among those

who remained on the frontier; and when James I went to Montpellier after the capture of the city of Valencia in 1238, those left in charge of the new conquests included the provincial masters of the Temple and Hospital.

Yet, although brethren themselves might give unlimited service, in Spain the obligations of their vassals were, of course, subject to the same limitations as those of other secular forces. Men under the orders' authority could usually be called out only a certain number of times or for a limited period each year. In the Templar lordship of Cantavieja in southern Aragon, the inhabitants were obliged to take part in a raiding expedition (*cabalgada*) only once a year with the provincial master and twice with the commander of Cantavieja. In the *fuero* granted by the order of Mountjoy to those living at Alfambra, the latter were required to perform host service (*hueste*) and *cabalgada* twice a year, while according to the *fuero* of Ocaña, issued by the order of Santiago in 1281, mounted troops were obliged to serve for three months each year at their own expense. Some vassals even enjoyed complete exemption from service. By the terms of the *carta de población* drawn up by the Templars in 1224, settlers at Villalba in the lower valley of the Ebro were exempted from *hueste* and *cabalgada* for fifteen years, while the *fuero* of Uclés, which was under the lordship of Santiago, granted footsoldiers a permanent exemption from the obligation of *fonsado*, which denoted an offensive campaign.

The reliability of the orders' vassals was sometimes in doubt, even if they did serve. In Syria, the majority of those living on estates subject to the military orders were not Western Christians, and probably most were Muslims. Similarly, in the Baltic region in the thirteenth century the bulk of the population was made up of native peoples, and even in Spain, where the orders' vassals included a larger proportion of Western Christians, Muslims were still numerous in some districts. Doubts concerning the latter's reliability are revealed in the Templar charter granted to the Muslim inhabitants of Chivert in northern Valencia, for although these were expected to assist in the defence of Chivert itself if it was attacked, they were not required to take part in expeditions. Little is known of the service given in practice by non-Westerners in either Spain or the Holy Land, but in the Baltic region desertions by native troops were not uncommon, and were a contributory factor in some of the serious defeats suffered by the

Teutonic order. In 1259, some Kurs deserted when Kurland was
attacked by the Samogithians, and the same happened in the
following year, when the Teutonic order experienced one of its
severest setbacks. Native troops serving with the Teutonic order
again fled in 1286 when Riga was being attacked, and they did
the same in the next year, when Semgallian raiders were being
pursued: the Teutonic order was again defeated.

Nor in practice were brethren themselves always available to
fight against the infidel. Their arms were sometimes being turned
instead against fellow Christians in defence and pursuance of their
own interests. The military orders did, in fact, have papal permission to use force to protect their possessions against Christian
aggressors. This concession was justified partly by reference to
Roman law, which stated that all law codes allowed force to be
used in defence against force, and partly on the more practical
grounds that the orders' properties needed to be protected if these
institutions were to be able to fight against the infidel effectively
and carry out their other obligations. When Gregory IX in 1235
granted the Hospitallers permission to defend their properties, he
stressed that these were possessions which 'make a not insignifi-
cant contribution to the defence of the Holy Land', and Honorius
III had earlier expressed the same idea in a slightly different
manner in stating that when Hospitaller rights were attacked 'this
is not merely a private matter, but a common concern of the poor
and of Christ'.[51]

In all frontier regions, orders at times turned their weapons on
fellow Christians. In Livonia, for example, the Swordbrethren
were in 1233 engaged in armed conflict with the papal legate
Baldwin of Alna when the latter was trying to assert authority
there, and later in the century the Teutonic order was fighting in
this region against the archbishop and inhabitants of Riga, while
in Prussia there were conflicts between the Teutonic order and the
neighbouring rulers of Pomerelia. In Syria, the military orders not
only used force to further their own interests in private quarrels,
sometimes against each other, but also became involved in the
political conflicts which characterised the crusader states, particularly in the thirteenth century. The orders' wealth and military
strength inevitably gave them considerable political influence,
especially when the kingdom of Jerusalem was lacking an effective ruler, and in 1231 Gregory IX even wrote of the Templars

and Hospitallers – admittedly with some exaggeration – as those 'through whom that land has been governed up till now in many difficult times and without whom it is believed it could in no way be governed'.[52] In the early 1230s these orders were adopting a neutral stance in the dispute between the Ibelin and imperialist factions and sought to mediate between the parties – a role which they similarly assumed on a number of other occasions. But there were also times when they were protagonists, rather than conciliators, and took up arms against fellow Christians. Thus in the succession war in Antioch in the early thirteenth century the Templars sided with Bohemund, while the Hospitallers supported the claims of Raymond Roupen, and in the war of St Sabas in the later 1250s the Temple and the Teutonic order were among the allies of the Venetians, and the Genoese had the assistance of the Hospitallers.

In Castile, the orders likewise became embroiled in the political struggles which beset the kingdom in the later thirteenth century, although in Aragon they remained aloof in the conflict between the crown and the Aragonese Union in the 1280s. In Spain, the military orders were also ready to use force when their own rights or interests were directly threatened by fellow Christians. In 1242 the bishops of Cuenca and Sigüenza and the abbot of Monsalud reported that when they had ordered the master of Santiago to surrender property which had been adjudged to the archbishop of Toledo, the master had replied that 'although he was an old man, he would be the first to resist us by force and would not shrink from bloodshed'; they also stated that when they later went to the property in question 'we encountered the brothers of Uclés who arrayed their numerous armed knights and footsoldiers against us and our followers... they told us menacingly not to enter their land to enforce any judgement, and not to try to gain access to any of the places in question; otherwise they would use their lances on us and on any others entering, and would pierce our sides with their lances'.[53] The effect of such actions on the struggle against the infidel should not, however, be exaggerated, for on no front was war against non-Christians continuous; but the orders' conflicts with fellow Christians did use up resources which might otherwise have been employed against Muslims or pagans.

In Syria, the independence which the orders enjoyed also meant that they could, if they wished, refuse to give service when asked. This was already happening on occasion in the twelfth century. William of Tyre reports that in the later 1160s the Templars opposed plans for the invasion of Egypt on the grounds that it would be in breach of treaty agreements, and according to him they did not participate in the expedition launched in 1168; he also relates that when Saladin invaded the county of Tripoli in 1180, the Templars and Hospitallers preferred to remain in their castles and declined to assist the count.

In Spain, the orders did not possess the same degree of independence, but in the second half of the thirteenth century they were displaying an increasing reluctance to give service. The first clear indication of changing attitudes is provided by a papal letter issued in 1250, in which Innocent IV commanded the Templars and Hospitallers in Aragon to assist in the struggle against the Muslims in Spain. This followed a complaint voiced by James I. Fuller evidence is encountered in Aragonese royal registers later in the century. To enforce service at the end of 1286 and early in 1287, for example, Alfonso III had to issue repeated summonses and also found it necessary to threaten action against property. In April 1287 he wrote to the commanders of Alcañiz and Montalbán, who belonged to Calatrava and Santiago respectively,

> since the Zenetes were entering or preparing to enter and invade our kingdom of Valencia, you were warned and required both by us and by the noble lord P. Fernández, *procurador* of Valencia, to prepare yourselves and to maintain a force of both mounted and foot troops there for the defence of that kingdom. You have, as we understand, nevertheless done nothing, and we are not a little surprised by your conduct. Therefore by these present letters we again tell and order you to prepare yourselves to hold the frontier there for the defence of the aforesaid kingdom, together with your force of knights and footsoldiers, so that you are there throughout the month of April; otherwise you can be certain that the possessions which you hold in the kingdom of Valencia will be seized forthwith on our orders;[54]

and a fortnight later a further threat of confiscation was dispatched both to the commander of Alcañiz and to the Templars and Hospitallers. Most comments of this kind emanate from the registers of the Aragonese kings, but there is sufficent evidence to show that the problem was not limited to that kingdom.

Yet if there were occasions when the orders could not be relied upon, these failings should not be exaggerated, and particularly in Syria and the Baltic they made an important contribution to warfare in the field against the infidel. Amaury of Jerusalem was no doubt thinking partly of actions in the field when, in a letter to the French king, Louis VII, he wrote of the Templars that 'if we can achieve anything, it is through them that we are able to do it'.[55]

Naval and Other Activities

THE orders' military operations were undertaken mainly on land. For most of the twelfth and thirteenth centuries these institutions were of little importance in naval warfare. The order of Santa María de España was the only foundation which appears to have had this as its main function, and even that order did not devote itself exclusively to fighting at sea, for in 1279 Alfonso X gave its brethren the inland castle of Medina Sidonia, 'in which they are to establish the chief convent which that order is to keep on this frontier of the kingdom of Seville'.[56] Occasional references to ships belonging to the leading orders are encountered in twelfth- and thirteenth-century sources, but these usually concern transports. Participation in naval warfare was admittedly not altogether unknown: Oliver of Paderborn mentions a Templar ship which was damaged during the fifth crusade when the Christians were attacking a tower on an island near Damietta, and Henry of Livonia describes how in 1216 the Swordbrethren and the men of Riga fitted out and stationed a ship at the mouth of the Dvina in order to prevent the Oeselians from blocking the harbour. But these appear to have been isolated incidents.

Towards the end of the thirteenth century, however, when Western bases in Syria were being lost and the Templars and Hospitallers were transferring their headquarters to Cyprus, these orders appear to have been developing their fleets in the eastern Mediterranean. In 1291 the Hospital was reported to be sending armed galleys to the East on the orders of Nicholas IV, and in the following year the Pope was instructing the Temple and Hospital to use their galleys in defence of Armenia, while in 1300 a fleet comprising ships belonging to these two orders and to the king of Cyprus attacked the coasts of Syria and Egypt. Hospitaller statutes of that year also contain the first surviving regulations concerning the office of admiral. These define his functions, and the wording suggests that the post had only recently been created: the earliest extant reference to a Hospitaller admiral comes, in fact, from the year 1299. The growing importance of the orders' fleets was also reflected in the writings of crusader theorists of that time, who often assumed that naval assistance, particularly in blockading Egypt, could be provided by the military orders. In the last decade of the thirteenth century Charles of Naples maintained that the Templars and Hospitallers could each provide ten galleys, while in a memorandum addressed to Nicholas IV at about the same time, Raymond Lull advocated that a member of his proposed military order – created by an amalgamation of the existing ones – should be given the post of admiral and should be 'lord of the sea'.[57] Crusading proposals put forward by the orders themselves also indicate their ability to provide naval assistance: in a memorandum written in the first decade of the fourteenth century, the Hospitaller master Fulk of Villaret envisaged that the Templars and Hospitallers would assist in blockading Egypt, and although James of Molay, the last Templar master, was averse to having a blockading fleet under the command of the military orders, his reason was fear of reprisal by the Italians and not inability to fulfil the task.

The orders' military concerns were not restricted just to fighting on land or at sea. As has been seen, they also gave advice on military matters, and were of particular importance in this respect in Syria during the thirteenth century, when the defence of the Holy Land was coming to depend increasingly on them. At an early stage of the orders' history some rulers had, in fact, even placed themselves under an obligation to seek counsel from them on questions of war and peace. In 1143, the count of Barcelona promised not to make peace with the Muslims without the counsel of the Templars, and a similar undertaking was given in the following year to the Hospitallers by Raymond of Tripoli, although it is not known whether these promises were always observed.

Several orders were, of course, hospitaller as well as military foundations, and their duties sometimes included the care of those wounded in battle. In the rule of Santiago it was decreed that, when the Christian host entered Muslim territory, brethren in charge of infirmaries should make necessary preparations so that they could care not only for injured brothers but also for others who were wounded; and when property was given in 1205 to the order of Calatrava for a hospital in Santa Eulalia, the donors included the condition that

> the commander of that hospital is to enter Muslim territories and go against the Saracens in the company of royal armies, and is to provide, according to the hospital's resources, for both knights and footsoldiers – the poor and the needy and also the sick as well as the wounded; he is also to take with him both a chaplain, who is to give the last sacrament to the sick and the wounded, as required, and a master of surgery, who is to treat the wounded'.[58]

Nothing is known of the way in which these precepts were implemented, but in the East the Hospitaller master Roger of Moulins reported that his own order had in 1177 cared for 750 men wounded in the battle of Montgisard. These orders were thus combining one kind of charitable activity with fighting, which had come to be regarded as another.

4.   Resources and Manpower

Income

THE struggle against the infidel could not be sustained without extensive financial resources and reserves of manpower. The costs of building, extending and repairing castles, and of equipping and maintaining brethren and other troops were very considerable: it was estimated that when Safed was being rebuilt in the early 1240s the Templars expended 1,100,000 besants in two and a half years, and that subsequently annual expenditure there amounted to 40,000 besants: amongst other supplies, more than 12,000 mule loads of barley and wheat were consumed there each year. The Temple and Hospital were able, in fact, to assume a leading role in the defence of the Holy Land because – unlike the rulers and nobles of the crusader states who normally had to rely mainly on income obtained locally – these orders were able to draw regularly on sources of revenue, as well as reserves of manpower, from all regions of western Christendom. In the later twelfth century, William of Tyre wrote of the Templars that 'there is now not a region in the Christian world which has not conferred a portion of its wealth on these brothers'.[1] The Templars and Hospitallers were, however, exceptional in acquiring property in all parts of the West. Although other orders were not usually dependent entirely on the financial resources they derived from frontier regions, they drew the bulk of their income from a limited area. The Swordbrethren had to subsist primarily on what they possessed in Livonia. The Spanish orders relied mainly on revenues obtained within the Iberian peninsula, and sometimes only in certain parts of Spain: although Santiago gained rights throughout the peninsula, several others – such as Avis and San Jorge de Alfama – were more localised. It is true that Santiago also made some acquisitions in France and that Mountjoy had possessions in the Holy Land and Italy, but most of Mountjoy's estates lay in Aragon, and only a small part of Santiago's income was derived from lands outside the peninsula. The Teutonic order had a rather wider appeal than the Spanish ones, and obtained possessions in most Western countries, including England and Spain, but its main source of revenues in Western Europe was inevitably Germany.

In the first place, however, all orders were able to profit from warfare in frontier regions. All could expect to gain spoils from successful campaigns and raids. In 1154, for example, the Templars received a ransom of 60,000 dinars for Nasr, the captured son of the Egyptian vizir, Abbas; and nearly twenty years later brethren in Spain participated in a raiding expedition which reputedly seized 50,000 sheep, 1200 goats and 150 captives near Ecija, although on this occasion they were defeated before they could bring the plunder home. As has already been seen, in Syria the leading orders were also at times able to exact tribute from neighbouring Muslim powers: in the early 1170s the Templars were receiving 2000 dinars a year from the Assassins.

Yet only the Teutonic order in Prussia had from the outset an automatic claim on all lands taken from the infidel: on other frontiers orders were dependent on donations, which were the second means of acquiring wealth. In some districts, however, grants included a fixed share of conquests. Raymond Berenguer IV not only promised a fifth of all lands won from the Muslims to the Templars, but also in 1157 assigned to the Hospitallers a tenth of territory gained without foreign aid. In Portugal, the Templars were in 1169 promised a third of all lands conquered to the south of the Tagus, and a fifth of conquests was conceded to the order of Calatrava by the Castilian king, Alfonso VIII, in 1174. In Livonia in 1207 the Swordbrethren sought a third of all gains in the region, including those to be made in the future. Albert, bishop of Riga, offered a third only of existing conquests, and this was eventually accepted, although this agreement was just the first in a series of settlements concerning the division of conquered territories in that region. As has already been mentioned, orders in Spain were also sometimes allowed to retain land which they themselves conquered from the Muslims.

Rights in frontier regions were obviously granted to military orders in return for aid either already given or to be provided in future against the infidel. It has been seen that defensive obligations in the Holy Land and elsewhere were transferred to the orders through the donation of castles, while many charters made reference to past services. Thus during the siege of Seville in 1248,

the Castilian king, Fernando III, promised the order of Avis some
properties in the city

> for the many services which you have at all times performed for
> me and which you do for me every day, and especially for the
> service which you have done in the host at Seville, while I have
> been besieging it, and because you came to my assistance from
> Portugal.[2]

Those who patronised military orders in regions away from the
frontiers of western Christendom were usually not so directly
involved in the struggle against the infidel, but were giving rights
and possessions in order to provide resources for that conflict. In
the twelfth century, the concept of holy war was still fairly new
and influenced patterns of patronage at a time when the
popularity of older religious houses was waning. The English
family of Clare was not alone in favouring the Benedictines in the
eleventh and early twelfth centuries, and then diverting its
patronage to newer foundations, including the military orders.
These orders were, of course, by no means the sole new claimants
on patronage at this time: in the twelfth century the Clares were
also favouring the Augustinian canons and the Cistercians; but
the latter were among those who, at least in the beginning, sought
to limit their properties and were therefore not constant rivals for
patronage. The desire to preserve the Holy Land under Christian
rule and to further the struggle against the infidel both there and
on other fronts brought innumerable gifts to the military orders.
Most of the charters of donation which survive as parchments or
in cartularies are admittedly not very explicit on this point, and
stress the benefits to be obtained by the donor rather than the uses
to which the donation was to be put, but some are more specific.
When Emperor Rudolf of Habsburg, for example, issued a
confirmation of Hospitaller rights and privileges in 1274, he said
of the brethren that

> spurning worldly conflict, they fearlessly march against the
> forces of the pagan pestilence, staining the standards of Christ-
> ian victory and the banners of their own knighthood in the
> blood of the glorious martyr; they fight valiantly against the
> barbarian nations, and do not fear to give themselves up to a
> worthy death.[3]

For some patrons, such as the viscount of Béarn in 1224, a gift to a military order was a substitute for going on a crusade, but there were other Western patrons who had taken the cross and themselves seen the orders in action. The French king, Louis VII, rewarded the Templars on his return from the second crusade for the assistance they had given during his expedition, and a gift was made to the Teutonic order at Damietta in 1218 by the German crusader Sweder of Dingede 'when I had seen the heavy expenditure which the brethren of the Teutonic house in Jerusalem incur both in supporting the sick and in maintaining knights against the assaults of the Saracens'.[4] It was also during the fifth crusade that Andrew of Hungary made donations to the Hospitallers, explaining that 'when we came to the aid of the Holy Land, we saw how the sacred house of the Hospital of St John the Baptist of Jerusalem excels in divers good works to the profit and honour of the whole of Christendom, just as we had earlier heard by report'.[5]

Andrew of Hungary, like Sweder of Dingede, went on to mention care of the poor and sick, and it is clear that the orders' charitable, as well as their military, activities brought them support, in some cases from individuals who had themselves received assistance. Henry, count of Rodez, made a gift to the Hospitallers when he was lying ill at Acre in 1221, and in 1240 Geoffrey, lord of Preuilly, and Andrew of Vitré rewarded the same order for the services it had provided when they were on pilgrimage. Several years earlier the countess of Kybourg had favoured the Hospital because it had buried her brother at Jerusalem, and in 1215 Rosceline of La Ferté had promised the Hospitallers an annual rent if they managed to free her son who was held captive by the Muslims in Syria. Although the Hospital was usually prepared to assist in negotiating the release of captives, the orders of Mountjoy and Santiago had a more constant commitment to the ransoming of Christian prisoners. In the late twelfth and early thirteenth centuries, Santiago established some ten ransom hospitals in the kingdoms of Leon, Castile and Aragon, and some of the donations made to that order had the purpose of providing resources for the freeing of captives.

Although donations to military orders can usually be explained, at least in part, by a desire to promote the struggle against the infidel or to further the orders' charitable activities, secular rulers may in some cases have regarded patronage as a means of

obtaining military or political support against Christian enemies
and rivals. This was obviously happening in the Latin Empire of
Constantinople, but has also been postulated elsewhere. It has
been argued that the Templar march established in northern
Antioch was intended to be a defence against Greeks and Armenians as well as against infidels, and that, in the early thirteenth
century, Leo of Armenia was similarly seeking the support of the
Teutonic order against his Christian rivals. It has further been
maintained that the assistance which Spanish orders might give
against Christian opponents continued to influence royal patrons
in the Iberian peninsula. The Leonese kings are thought to have
tried to purchase the neutrality of the Castilian order of Calatrava
by making it an international institution, and the gift of Alcántara
by Alfonso IX in 1217 has been seen as marking the culmination
of this policy. Grants made to the Templars in England at the
time of the civil war between Stephen and Matilda have also been
explained as attempts to gain political support.

The persistent rivalries existing between Christian powers in
northern Syria give credence to arguments of this nature concerning Antioch and Armenia, but elsewhere the validity of claims
of this kind may be questioned. Spanish rulers did admittedly at
first envisage using local orders against Christian rivals; but as
these foundations quickly adopted a neutral stance in conflicts
between Christian kings, such considerations were probably of
little long-term significance. Morever, if the Leonese kings were
anxious to secure the neutrality of Calatrava, it is surprising that
they did not dispense more patronage to that order at an early
stage; and an agreement between the Leonese king, Alfonso IX,
and Calatrava in 1218 in fact made it less of an international
institution than it had been earlier, for after that date it retained
no lands in Leon directly under its control. It may also be
doubted whether in England before the middle of the twelfth
century the Templars were of sufficient importance to be courted
by rival claimants, and – as in other areas away from the frontiers
of Christendom – they could not have provided any significant
military aid: some benefactions to the Church in England at this
time are more easily explained as atonements for misdeeds
perpetrated during the anarchy.

In deciding to favour military orders, however, patrons were
frequently influenced not merely by a desire to further the

military and charitable activities of these institutions: personal and family ties, bonds of lordship, and geographical factors were also of significance. Many gifts were made either by individuals who were entering a military order or by their families. Donations made on such occasions are encountered in the records of almost all orders. Examples drawn from the Teutonic order include donations made by Henry of Hohenlohe, later *Deutschmeister* of the Teutonic order, and by his brother Frederick when they made their profession in 1219, and in 1277 by an inhabitant of Fritzlar called Conrad and his wife, Walpurgis, when their son Engelbert entered the house of Marburg. Some families developed a tradition of favouring a particular order. The cartulary compiled for the Templars of Sandford in Oxfordshire during the later thirteenth century includes transcripts of a series of donations made by the Sandford family, starting in the middle of the twelfth century with a gift of four acres of land made by Robert of Sandford, who was a knight of the abbey of Abingdon and who had founded Littlemore priory, and continuing into the second half of the thirteenth century. While some patrons were carrying on a family tradition, others were imitating their lords, vassals or neighbours. Some of these influences are illustrated in a document which was copied into a cartulary of the Templar house of Douzens, east of Carcassonne, and which records gifts of rights in Pieusse made by nearly twenty men in 1137, for it is clear that in many cases those named were either vassals or lords of other donors listed. Military orders were also sometimes favoured by their own vassals, as the Hospital was in 1275 by a widow called Christine Prudhomme, who gave to it all the land which she had been holding of it at Little Maplestead in Essex. Benefactors also often patronised an order which had a house in their neighbourhood: thus Templar possessions in the district of Huesca in northern Aragon increased most rapidly in the decades following the establishment of a Templar convent in the city of Huesca

Although patrons might have particular reasons for favouring a military order, they also expected to receive the spiritual, and sometimes material, benefits which a donation to any religious foundation could bring. They were in the first place seeking divine favour, to be shown in this world and even more in the next. An individual going on a journey might hope to ensure his safety through a gift, as Pons Calveira did when setting out for

Jerusalem shortly before the middle of the twelfth century: he gave rights to the Templars of the French convent of Roaix 'so that God may grant me a safe return home'.[6] A desire for more wide-ranging favours in the present life was expressed by the Aragonese king, James I, in 1235, when he gave the castle of Peñalba to the Hospitaller house of Sigena 'so that Jesus Christ may aid and strengthen us and enhance and increase our standing'.[7] Concern was more frequently expressed for the salvation of a benefactor's soul. Almost all charters of donation included phrases such as 'for the salvation of my soul', and sometimes a more explicit comment was made about fearing the agonies of hell and wishing to gain the joys of paradise. Occasionally, specific grounds for fear were stated: in 1301, Gerard of Beckingen explained that in making a gift to the Teutonic order he was mindful of the harm which he had caused in the past through pillaging and plundering and for which he could not easily make recompense.

Convents of the military orders, like other religious foundations, were expected to include the names of patrons in their prayers. Those, for example, who entered into bonds of confraternity with an order had their names recorded in lists, some of which have survived and which could be used at the altar. Patrons were also regarded as participating in the good works undertaken by an order, which might in addition promise to bury a benefactor in one of its cemeteries. A gift was thus made to the Hospitallers by Henry II, duke of Mecklenburg, in 1302

> so that they may remember in their prayers all of us who have been mentioned, and so that we may be regarded by God as participants in the prayers, fasts, masses, almsgiving, punishments and all holy works which the brothers of the aforesaid order perform or carry out throughout the world for all time'.[8]

Yet patrons did not usually seek to found convents of military orders in the way in which monasteries were commonly endowed by wealthy benefactors. Although a large gift might lead to the setting up of a convent, charters of donation to military orders were not normally foundation charters: they merely recorded gifts and contained no provision about the building of a house. The exceptions mostly concern hospitals, and convents founded for sisters or clerics. Alfonso VIII of Castile was among those who established ransom hospitals subject to the order of Santiago, and in 1219 García Gutiérrez and his wife Mary gave property for the founding of a convent in which sisters of Calatrava could reside, while in 1260, Beatrice, the widow of Raymond Berenguer IV of Provence, made provision for establishing a house at Echelles, in the diocese of Grenoble, in which the Hospital was to maintain eighteen clerics. But, in most orders, such foundations were few: donors normally expected the income from their benefactions to be added to general funds used for fighting the infidel or for charitable work; and although in modern studies patrons of military orders are often regarded as the founders of convents, benefactors did not usually see themselves in this light. A changing emphasis is, however, apparent in the thirteenth century, for it was then becoming increasingly common for patrons to make gifts specifically for the endowment of chantry priests, or for masses and anniversaries, or for lamps which were to burn before altars in orders' chapels. In 1224, for example, Philip Augustus's widow, Ingeborg, gave rents to the Hospital for the maintenance of thirteen priests in its house at Corbeil, with the provision that every day three of them should say three masses for the dead; and, in 1275, a benefactor who established two chantries in the Templar house of Valencia specified that

> the clerics who serve the said chantries in the said church are to celebrate daily a requiem mass for my soul and for those of all my benefactors, and are to be present by day and night at offices which are said and celebrated in the said church every day and night, and are to go every day to my grave and absolve me and say prayers.[9]

Among the more material benefits which patrons could obtain from military orders, as from other religious foundations, was maintenance. This might take the form of a daily allowance of food, or comprise a single annual payment in money or in kind. A donation could, therefore, be a way of making provision for the elderly or for others who could not easily support themselves. In the early years of the thirteenth century Robert of Talavera and his wife made a gift to Santiago's convent of Uclés on the condition that 'if, which God forbid, it should happen that we fall into dire poverty and are in great need of their help, they are mercifully to provide us with necessities'.[10] In many instances, however, orders entered into more immediate undertakings. Details of numerous annual payments made by the English Templars are found in Edward II's Close Rolls, where they were recorded after the seizure of Templar property: among the recipients was Agnes, widow of Richard of Weston, whose pension consisted of ten quarters of wheat, ten of barley, two oxen, four pigs, six sheep, five hundred faggots and also cash, all of which had been promised to her in return for a gift to the Temple of a hundred marks, a wood and eighty acres of land. Some other donors received a single cash payment at the time when a gift was made: many documents were worded as charters of donation and mentioned the spiritual benefits to be obtained by the benefactor, but also referred to a payment made by the recipients 'out of charity'. Thus a twelfth-century charter recorded that Robert, son of Mengy of Willingale, gave seven acres and other rights in Essex to the Hospitallers for the souls of himself, his wife and other members of his family, and that, because of his 'very great need', the Hospital gave him 'out of charity' three marks of silver and six shillings.[11] In some transactions of this kind the initiative may have come not from the donor but from an order which was anxious to secure a particular piece of land. A donation to a military order could also be a means of obtaining release from a debt: property which was in the hands of creditors was granted, and it became the recipient's obligation to recover it by paying off the debt.

Some acquisitions by military orders were made in return for promises of protection. In Catalonia, this practice was so frequent that a gloss on the code of customs known as the *Usages of Barcelona* made the comment: 'What of the Hospitallers and Templars, who daily receive custodies of this nature ?'[12] The protection envisaged was not of a military nature, and, in fact, many who placed themselves under an order's protection were really seeking to gain the benefit of its privileges and immunities. In the 1285 statute of Westminster, the complaint was made that 'to the detriment of their lords, many tenants erect crosses on their holdings, or allow them to be erected, so that they can protect themselves against capital lords of fees through the privileges of the Templars and Hospitallers'.[13] It was presumably also to gain such privileges that some individuals sought to free themselves from the lordship of others and to subject their holdings to the authority of a military order. In the closing years of the twelfth century, Baldwin Tyrell gave land in Essex to the Hospitallers at the request of the tenants of the property, who were willing to buy out their lord's rights so that they could enjoy more long-term benefits as vassals of the Hospital.

Other patrons of military orders were seeking by their gifts to ensure that land was brought under cultivation and worked. This was obviously a consideration in frontier districts, where there was much waste and underpopulated territory, but a similar purpose could occasion gifts remote from the borders of Christendom. In 1168, for example, the prior of Saint-Etienne du Mas gave property to the Templars of Douzens 'for breaking'.[14] In this instance the donor was to receive a portion of the produce, and on some occasions a donation constituted merely a lease of land. Acquisitions made from ecclesiastical lords were commonly of this kind, but few lay donors sought rents from the orders they patronised.

While patrons' motives can to some extent be discerned, it is not always easy to ascertain the social standing of the orders' benefactors. It seems, however, that in most regions military orders were favoured by all ranks of lay society. Although in the district of La Selve, in Rouergue, the most important families favoured the Cistercians while the lesser nobility supported the Templars, this was not the usual pattern. In the county of Comminges, on the northern slopes of the Pyrenees, the Templar commandery of Montsaunès received gifts from the count and from all the leading noble families; many of the Teutonic order's houses in Germany had their origins in donations made by the higher nobility; and although in some parts of England the majority of donations to the Hospitallers were made by middling and lesser landholders, the order was also receiving important grants from leading nobles. A recent study of the possessions of Santiago's commandery and priory of Uclés in Castile has shown that seven grants were made by the king and members of the royal family, twenty by those categorised as landowners (*terratenientes*), and twenty by donors defined as small proprietors. Templar confraternity lists from Aragon also demonstrate that favour was received from all ranks of lay society. The

Aragonese and Navarrese *confratres* named in a parchment roll which covered the period up to 1225 were mostly of sufficient standing to possess a horse and arms, and included some leading Aragonese and Navarrese nobles, such as Peter Taresa and Blasco Romeu, while the fifty-two confraternity agreements in a list which was copied into a twelfth-century cartulary of the convent of Novillas concerned individuals of lesser rank. In Spain there were, however, some regional variations in the patterns of patronage. Royal grants were concentrated in frontier regions: the Templars in Aragon received few gifts from the Crown in areas remote from the Muslim border, and, similarly, none of the surviving donations of land to Santiago's convent of Vilar de Donas, which was situated in Galicia in north-western Spain, was of royal property. In Aragon and Catalonia the Templars were also more frequently patronised by noble families who had extensive rights in more southerly districts, such as the counts of Urgel, the Torrojas and the Moncadas, than by the Cardonas or the counts of Ampurias, whose power was centred further north. In Spain, as in some other countries, there were also a number of corporate donors: annual benefactions for the ransoming of captives were, for example, made to Santiago by several towns, including Cuenca, Huete and Moya. The one group which did not patronise military orders to any extent was the clergy. Although some rights were acquired from bishops, only one out of nearly fifty gifts to the priory and commandery of Uclés was made by a cleric, and very few clergy were listed among the Aragonese and Navarrese *confratres* of the Temple. The papacy, on the other hand, was always a leading supporter of these orders.

Although not all donations were gratuitous and while it is often difficult to draw a clear-cut distinction between gifts and sales, in some areas military orders gained a considerable amount of property through transactions which were described straightfor-wardly as sales. Of ninety charters recording acquisitions by Santiago's convent of San Marcos between 1170 and 1284, thirty-four were worded as instruments of sale; and between the years 1174 and 1310, thirty-three purchases of property were made by Santiago's commandery and priory of Uclés, compared with forty-nine acquisitions through gift. Purchases were numerically even more significant on some Templar estates in Aragon. Sales to the Temple in and around the city of Huesca occurred almost twice as frequently as gifts, and while some twenty grants of landed property in the city of Zaragoza to that order are recorded, nearly fifty instruments of the sale of rights to the Templars there have survived. It should not be assumed, however, that the value of acquisitions was necessarily in proportion to their number. Most purchases by the Templars in Aragon were of minor significance.

In purchasing property, military orders were obviously investing surplus revenues in a way which would bring long-term profit. But purchases also enabled orders to consolidate and concentrate possessions – an end which could also be achieved through exchanges. Purchase was often used as a means of gaining full rights over a particular piece of property. The Templars' acquisition of a mill at Cascajo, just north of Zaragoza, illustrates this process. In 1162, García of Albero and his wife Mary sold to the Temple the rent of eighty shillings which they received for the mill from Duranda, the widow of a certain Folquer, and from her children. In the years following this initial sale, the order gradually bought out the rights of the tenants. In 1168, four of the children sold their half share in the mill, and three years later a further eighth was purchased from one of Duranda's sons. In 1173 the Templars bought the rights of another son, who was a canon of Zaragoza, and finally, in 1178, the portion belonging to Arnold, a son of Duranda by Alamán of Atrosillo, was purchased. On other occasions, orders were buying out the rights of overlords, to whom rent or other obligations were owed. Some documents, however, which appear to register the purchase of further rights in properties in fact record the settlement of disputes, with claimants being bought off by an order. In many other instances, property bought by military orders was adjacent to lands they already held. Thus a sale to the prior of Uclés at Torreluengua, to the south of Uclés, in 1218, was followed by a further thirteen purchases there by the order of Santiago; and twelve out of seventeen sales to the Temple in the parish of St Mary in the city of Zaragoza were of properties adjoining existing possessions of that order. Purchases also allowed orders to achieve a concentration of property in the vicinity of a convent. While grants to the Templar convent of Palau in Catalonia were scattered over a fairly wide area, purchases made by that house were concentrated in the nearby city of Barcelona and in the district of Vallés, just to the north – in Palau itself and in the neighbouring villages of Parets del Vallés and Sta Perpetua de Mogodá.

Opportunities for buying property were frequently furnished by landholders' financial difficulties. It has been seen that strongholds in Syria were purchased by the Templars and Hospitallers from nobles who could no longer afford to maintain them – although these particular acquisitions were scarcely investments – and it is easy to find references to the financial problems of sellers elsewhere. In 1163, a certain Saurina sold property to the Temple in Barcelona because she was in need of money to ransom her son from captivity, and in 1303 the noble William of Anglesola sold the castle of Culla in Valencia to the same order because

> we are liable for so many debts and injuries that we do not think that all the landed property we have in the kingdom of Valencia is sufficient for satisfying and emending them.[15]

But sales were not necessarily indicative of financial hardship. In 1224, the prioress of the nunnery of San Julián de Sierra Javalera sold to Santiago her convent's rights at La Armuña, on the left bank of the Tagus, so that she could purchase vineyards close to the nunnery; and as marriage portions were often expressed in money terms, some lands were sold in order to make payments due to widows.

The acquisitions made by military orders through gift and purchase were very varied in kind. Since warfare was costly, these orders could not, like some monastic foundations, place restrictions on the types of property which were considered acceptable. Whereas the Cistercians sought to ensure that they did not obtain rights which would bring them into contact with the world, the second clause of the rule of the Teutonic order stated:

> Since very great expenses are incurred because of the numbers of people, the needs of hospitals and the costs of knights and of the sick and poor, the brothers can have both movable and immovable property, which is to be held in common in the name of the order and of the chapter – namely, lands and fields,

vineyards, townships, mills, fortifications, parish churches, chapels, tithes and the like.[16]

Acquisitions consisted most commonly of rights over land or over those who occupied land. Income from these often included not only rents but also other profits, such as those derived from monopoly rights and powers of justice. Possessions comprised mainly rural properties, but military orders did acquire considerable urban rights. In England, the Temple gained numerous holdings in London, where the order's English headquarters were situated, and also obtained rights in other cities such as Oxford, Bristol and Lincoln. In the Aragonese city of Zaragoza, the same order received rents from many houses and shops in the neighbourhood of the Cineja gate – the southern gate in the Roman wall – and near the western gate, the Puerta de Toledo. In southern Spain, however, the Castilian kings sought to ensure that military orders did not obtain too large an interest in conquered cities, which were under royal lordship.

Acquisitions also frequently included ecclesiastical properties and rights. Gifts of churches and tithes were often made – some lay donors of these were perhaps influenced by the Church's efforts to limit lay control of ecclesiastical property – and many orders were assigned existing religious foundations, such as hospitals and monasteries. The Teutonic order, for example, received numerous gifts of hospitals in Germany. When a patron was seeking to ensure the future of his foundation by associating it with a well-established military order, the latter probably gained little in financial terms, for obligations as well as income were being transferred: thus the Hospitallers presumably profited little from Guibert of Thémines's gift in 1259 of a hospital at Beaulieu in the diocese of Cahors, for the donor wanted a religious community to be maintained there. But some donations were of decaying or collapsing foundations, and had the purpose of conferring revenues on a military order. When Alexander IV gave the Hospitallers the monastery of Mount Tabor, near Nazareth, which had recently been destroyed by the Muslims, the intention was that the abbot and surviving monks should be absorbed into other monasteries and that the Hospital should receive all of Mount Thabor's lands, which included extensive holdings between Nazareth and the Sea of Galilee.

Acquisitions were not always, however, in the form of land or rights over land. Many nobles sought to enhance the orders' military capabilities by making bequests of horses and arms: confraternity lists record many donations in this form. Lesser *confratres*, on the other hand, often promised a cash legacy. Cash grants were, in fact, not uncommon, and may have been more frequent than the surviving evidence suggests, since records would not always have been preserved if single payments were involved. The bequests of money made by *confratres* often amounted to only a few shillings, but some cash grants were very considerable. In his will drawn up in 1222, the French king, Philip Augustus, left 2000 marks each to the Templars and Hospitallers, and he also allocated a further 150,000 marks to the two orders and to the king of Jerusalem for the maintenance of 300 knights for three years in the Holy Land. Among papal subsidies was one of 10,000 marks to the Hospital in 1302, paid out of monies which had come into the Church's hands from legacies and other sources. Important long-term assignments of cash included the tenth of royal revenues which Raymond Berenguer IV gave to the Aragonese Templars in 1143, together with a thousand shillings annually from royal dues both in Zaragoza and in Huesca.

Acquisitions of landed property similarly varied considerably in importance. It was usually in the frontier regions of Christendom that the largest territorial gains were made, for extensive tracts of land were obtained when border castles were assigned to an order. Away from the frontier, individual acquisitions were usually of less significance. There is thus a contrast in the gains made by the Templars in different parts of the kingdom of Aragon. Whereas in areas which were near the Muslim frontier they obtained large blocks of territory, in the more northerly parts of Aragon and Catalonia acquisitions consisted mostly of small gifts and purchases, whose total value was less than that of the order's more southerly estates. Most acquisitions made by military orders in western kingdoms which were remote from the frontiers of Christendom were likewise of limited individual value. Cartularies of the orders in these regions are filled with records of predominantly small donations and sales. Of 135 twelfth-century grants to the Hospitallers in Essex recorded in a fifteenth-century cartulary, more than half were of no more than nine acres of land or one shilling in rent, and many of the thirty-two grants which provide no indication of value were probably also of minor significance. Only sixteen donations were of more than twenty-one acres or seven shillings in rent, and even the largest gifts were usually of less than a hide in extent. The territorial expansion of the military orders thus paralleled both that of contemporary Cistercians, who acquired considerable properties in marginal areas, and that of the Augustinian canons in the twelfth and thirteenth centuries, whose endowments usually consisted of smaller properties in the more populated parts of the West.

In addition to acquisitions which provided a direct income, orders also received privileges whose purpose was to encourage donations or to furnish other opportunities for increasing income. The Hospital obtained from Innocent II a privilege which remitted a seventh of penance to anyone who became a lay associate of the order and made an annual benefaction to it. The further incentives were added that such people – provided that they were not excommunicate – were not to be denied a Christian burial, and that when the Hospitallers came to collect these benefactions they could once a year open churches and hold services in places under interdict. This privilege was later extended to other orders. Remissions were also offered by popes and prelates in return for assistance on particular projects. In 1184, the bishop of Cuenca in Castile promised a relaxation of forty days' penance to those who patronised Santiago's ransom hospital at Cuenca, and, three years later, Urban III sought in the same way to encourage donations for the same order's ransom hospital at Toledo. In the thirteenth century, Gregory IX offered a remission of a seventh of penance to those providing funds for the construction of the Teutonic order's stronghold of Montfort in the Holy Land, just as the archbishop of Toledo gave an indulgence to those who contributed to the costs of building Santiago's castle of Aliaguilla in Castile. Gifts were further encouraged by privileges which permitted military orders to bury outsiders. Even the minor order of St Thomas of Acre obtained this right: when the bishop of London issued a licence for the order's cemetery in the city in 1248, he stated that anyone could be buried there, and a more general burial privilege was received by the order from Alexander IV. Among the concessions made by secular rulers which enabled orders to increase their income was the right to hold markets and fairs in places under their authority.

In England, the earliest concession of this kind was made by Stephen, who allowed the Templars to hold a weekly market at Witham in Essex, while the annual fairs which the Templars were entitled to hold in England included those at Baldock in Hertfordshire and Wetherby in Yorkshire.

Other privileges provided exemptions from dues and taxes and thus allowed military orders to retain for their own purposes a larger proportion of their income. In the ecclesiastical sphere the most important exemption in the twelfth century concerned the payment of tithes. Already, before the middle of the century, the Templars and Hospitallers had been freed by the papacy from the obligation of paying tithes on the produce of their demesne lands. This was a privilege enjoyed by many monasteries, although when Innocent II exempted the Templars in 1139 he justified his action by arguing that 'those who are defenders of the church should live and be sustained from the goods of the church', rather than by alluding to the commonly expressed claim that those who had taken vows of poverty should receive and not pay tithes.[17] Amongst the most extensive exemptions given by secular rulers were those granted by Aragonese kings to the Templars and Hospitallers, who in the late twelfth and early thirteenth centuries received charters which freed them from all royal exactions.

Besides gaining new properties and privileges, orders could benefit by increasing the value of their existing rights. It has been seen that colonisation was being undertaken in some frontier regions, where land was often unprofitable until it was settled. But assarting and the creation of new settlements were also occurring elsewhere. In the twelfth and thirteenth centuries, lands were being newly cultivated in many parts of the West, although the opportunities for doing this varied from one district to another. In Herefordshire, the Templar commandery of Garway had its origins in a privilege from Henry II which allowed the assarting of 2000 acres of woodland at Archenfield, and in the thirteenth century the Templars similarly reclaimed large tracts of land around Temple Brewer in Lincolnshire and Temple Newsham in Yorkshire. By contrast, there is little evidence in Hospitaller records of assarting in Essex. And while the Templars and Hospitallers founded some sixty new settlements in Aquitaine during the twelfth century, in some parts of northern France they arrived too late to play a significant role in reclamation. In some districts, such as the slopes of the Pyrenees, pastoral farming was developed, and in Southern Europe the value of lands could be enhanced by irrigation. On some estates in Aragon the Templars were receiving four times as much rent from irrigated as from non-irrigated land, and they are known to have extended canals and to have created new irrigation systems in various places, although in some instances the initiative appears to have come from tenants rather than from the order itself, which seems at times to have been reluctant to invest considerable sums of capital for a return which would only slowly be realised.

While these were legitimate ways of increasing income, military orders were often accused of profiting by abusing their rights and privileges. The secular clergy, for example, frequently claimed that the orders were seeking to extend their ecclesiastical privileges unlawfully. In 1154, the patriarch of Jerusalem voiced a series of grievances against the Hospitallers, who, among other charges, were accused of refusing to pay tithes and of loudly ringing the bells of their churches during interdict in order to divert to the Hospital the benefactions of the faithful. A quarter of a century later more widespread protests were made at the Third Lateran Council, when complaints included the claim that when Templars and Hospitallers were seeking alms they did not limit themselves to opening churches under interdict only once a year. In 1207, Innocent III was again reproving the Templars after receiving further complaints, and protests continued throughout the thirteenth century. Conflict with the secular clergy was not, of course, peculiar to military orders, and prelates were inevitably hostile to exemptions which reduced their own wealth and authority; but there is little doubt that many of the clergy's protests were justified, as was admitted by some Templars at their trial.

Although the revenues of the military orders were derived mainly from the property given or sold to them, income was also obtained from banking and moneylending. The Temple was the most important military order in this field but it was by no means the only one which engaged in such activities. Templars and others provided a variety of services. Convents of military orders were often used as places of deposit for money, jewels and documents. It has sometimes been stressed that the orders' military and religious character made them particularly suited to this task, though it would be wrong to assume that all convents throughout western Christendom were located in strongly fortified castles, garrisoned by warrior brethren. Possessions were sometimes deposited merely for safekeeping, but on other occasions depositors were arranging to have goods transferred from one place to another. When the English king, Henry III, for example, promised an annual pension of 800 *livres* to the count of La Marche in 1235, it was agreed that Henry would assign this sum each year to the Templars in London and that the count would obtain payment from the Temple in Paris; and, in 1270, a Catalan knight received from the convent of Palau near Barcelona money which he had deposited with the Templars in the East. In some instances, the money itself was transported, but this was not always necessary; and, whatever form transfers took, the network of convents which the leading orders had throughout western Christendom facilitated operations of this kind. Many deposits were of an occasional nature, but it was also possible to have a current account with the Temple, which would regularly receive a client's revenues and make payments on his behalf. In France a number of nobles, including several of Louis IX's brothers, employed the Templars in this capacity. More importantly, the Temple in Paris acted as a treasury for the French Crown at least from the time of Philip Augustus until the reign of Philip IV: in this period the Capetian monarchy had no treasury of its own.

The military orders – especially the Templars – also advanced money to clients. In Aragon, the Templars were already engaging in moneylending activities in the 1130s, and in the following decade the French king, Louis VII, was borrowing from them during the second crusade. In the twelfth century, loans were usually made in order to provide for some special need, such as the costs of a crusade, but in the following century borrowing was becoming a more regular feature of government financing. The cash obligations of rulers were increasing, and in order to make necessary payments kings and princes were commonly anticipating their revenues by resorting to loans. Most borrowing was, therefore, a short-term measure and was not an indication of long-term difficulties, although debts were not always, in fact, repaid. To obtain loans, rulers turned to those whose capital was sufficient to provide considerable sums, such as Italian firms and the Templars. Thus in the thirteenth century, the Templars were frequently advancing money to the Aragonese kings, with arrangements being made for repayment out of future royal revenues. On some occasions, however, the order did not in fact possess adequate funds and was itself obliged to borrow before it could meet royal demands; but it could presumably not afford to reject royal requests for loans.

Although the nature of the orders' financial operations is fairly clear, it is not easy to ascertain how they were reimbursed for their services. These no doubt helped to encourage patronage in the long term, but little information survives about more immediate returns. Despite the fact that the French kings were regularly using the Temple in Paris as a treasury, little is known of the benefit gained by the order, although an account from the year 1288 did make reference to a pension of 600 *livres* paid by the king to the treasurer of the Temple. It has, however, sometimes been suggested that military orders commonly invested money which had been deposited with them. This is possible, but it is difficult to find positive evidence, and the information which does exist tends to contradict the theory. In Aragon, Templar sources usually refer to 'demand' rather than to 'time' deposits, such as are encountered in Genoese and other records: and it was 'time' deposits, which could not be withdrawn without notice, that were normally used for investment purposes. There were also occasions when deposits held by the Templars were confiscated, indicating that deposited goods were retained in their own hands: in 1258, money left at the Temple in London by Henry III's half-brothers was seized, and five years later the future Edward I was said to have broken open a number of coffers in the London Temple and taken possession of some £10,000 belonging to merchants and magnates. The Aragonese chronicler Desclot similarly reported that later in the thirteenth century the Aragonese king, Pedro III, seized the treasure which James of Mallorca had deposited with the Templars in Roussillon. It was also not uncommon for a client to keep the key to one of the locks on a coffer so that it could not be opened without his knowledge. Even if orders did at times use deposits, there would still be the problem of discovering to what extent the order, rather than the client, profited.

The sources are also usually silent about the profits made from moneylending. Many records of loans were no doubt destroyed when debts had been repaid, and the instruments of debt which do survive usually mention only the repayment of the capital sum lent. This does not, however, necessarily imply that no additional payments were made. In the first half of the twelfth century, profit could lawfully be gained through the mortgaging of property. Lands were surrendered by the debtor, and the creditor received the revenues from these until repayment of the capital was made by the debtor. If the latter was unable to pay, the lands passed permanently under the creditor's control. Except in cases where the debtor was the tenant of the creditor and was released from his obligations to his lord, the mortgaging of property became illegal in the mid-twelfth century, and from that time onwards revenues from pledged property were normally to be set against the capital owed. But the mortgaging of land did not altogether cease: in 1189 a woman and her son pledged four vineyards to the Aragonese Templars, stating that the order should receive the produce from them 'for the souls of our forebears' until a debt of fifty shillings to the Temple was repaid.[18] From the later twelfth century onwards, however, revenues from pledged lands were commonly received in repayment of the capital advanced. When in such cases the acknowledgement of debt made no provision for any additional payment to the creditor, interest may sometimes have been deducted from the loan at the time when the money was lent, so that the amount mentioned in the instrument of debt represented the sum to be repaid, but not the amount actually received by the borrower. It should not be assumed, however, that there was always a concealed cash return: the benefit could be in other forms. Thus, on 3 July 1202, a document was drawn up on behalf of Pedro II of Aragon, in which he acknowledged that the Templars had lent him a thousand *morabetinos*, and on the same day, in another charter, the king restored to the order its rights of lordship over the city of Tortosa, which it had lost in 1196 following claims made by the queen mother, Sancha, after her husband's death. In this instance, the profit was in the form of rights rather than money. There are nevertheless also a few documents which explicitly state that the Templars received a monetary profit from loans. When, in 1232, the bishop of Zaragoza assigned to the Templars his dues from their churches in his diocese for a year, he said that he was doing this to repay a debt of 550 *morabetinos*, 'namely five hundred as capital and fifty as usury annually on the said five hundred *morabetinos*'.[19] This rate of ten per cent – two per cent less than the maximum allowed to Christian moneylenders in Aragon and half of the rate normally charged by Jewish moneylenders there – was also mentioned in a number of other documents from James I's reign, and in some of them it was referred to as the 'rate and custom of the Temple', implying that this was the charge usually made by the Aragonese Templars. Whether Templars elsewhere gained a similar return is not known, but as moneylending was not just an occasional or peripheral activity for the Templars, and as in the thirteenth century it was becoming easier to justify repayments beyond the capital sum lent, it may be doubted whether many Templar loans were as gratuitous as the Church would have wished.

A less important source of revenue was provided by trade, in which at least some orders participated, both through investment and by engaging in the carrying trade themselves. An example of investment is provided by a document from the year 1307, in which the Aragonese Templars made arrangements to recover from an inhabitant of the Valencian town of Peñiscola not only the sum of 2000 shillings which they had deposited with him but also 'the share due to us of the profit which he made with the aforesaid money on the journeys which he undertook by sea and elsewhere with his ships.'[20] But this is an isolated example. Here the Templars were not themselves trading; but that the Templars and Hospitallers shipped people and goods across the Mediterranean is apparent from an agreement made between the citizens of Marseilles and the masters of the two orders in 1233, for this allowed the latter to load two ships in that port for each of the two passages every year with merchandise and pilgrims as well as with the orders' own possessions. From licences issued by English kings it is also apparent that in the thirteenth century Templar ships were carrying wine from La Rochelle to Portsmouth and other English ports, and that brethren of the same order were transporting to Flanders wool produced on their estates in England: it is not known, however, to what extent on these routes Templars were shipping produce other than their own.

Although most military orders had various means of acquiring wealth, not all of these retained their importance throughout the twelfth and thirteenth centuries. Opportunities for profiting from Christian advances against the infidel often dwindled or disappeared. This clearly happened in Spain. The grant of a fifth of conquered lands made by Raymond Berenguer IV to the Templars was revoked when James I issued a confirmation of Templar privileges in 1233; the fifth assigned to Calatrava by Alfonso VIII in 1174 was reduced to a tenth in 1185; and the promise made to the Portuguese Templars in 1169 of a third of territories gained to the south of the Tagus was not implemented. Clearly rulers felt that over-generous promises had been made, and they sought to reduce the concessions which had earlier been granted. In any case, after the middle of the thirteenth century few conquests were being made in the Iberian peninsula. Advances in the Baltic region did not come to a halt as early as this, but after the end of the thirteenth century frontiers in that area changed little. In the Holy Land, opportunities for gains by conquest were at all times limited, but it has been seen that some acquisitions were made – by treaty rather than by force – in the first half of the thirteenth century, from which the orders did benefit. But the lands obtained by Theobald of Champagne and Richard of Cornwall were the last significant gains in Syria.

The chronology of acquisitions in districts away from the frontiers of western Christendom cannot always be precisely defined. For some orders – particularly the smaller ones – the surviving sources are sparse, and further investigations are needed before conclusions can be drawn concerning several others. It should also be remembered that at the end of the thirteenth century some military orders were still comparatively recent foundations. Yet it is clear that in many parts of the West little new property was being acquired by the Temple and Hospital during the later thirteenth century. In many areas these orders gained the bulk of their possessions in the second half of the twelfth century and early decades of the thirteenth. The numbers of donations to the Templar house of Provins, in Champagne, declined after the first quarter of the thirteenth century: in the last half-century of its existence this convent received fewer than ten gifts. Similar trends can be perceived in Templar commanderies in Aragon: in Boquiñeni and the neighbouring places of Pradilla and Tauste, situated near the Ebro above Zaragoza, only three dated grants occurred after 1200, compared with nineteen in the previous half century. Templar evidence also reveals a decline in acquisitions by purchase. Thirty-six out of forty-six sales to the order of landed property in the city of Zaragoza were made in the years between 1161 and 1220; and more than three-quarters of the money spent by the Templars in acquiring property in Zaragoza was expended in the sixty years up to 1220. In and around Zaragoza donations to the Hospital were also declining in the second half of the thirteenth century, while of the grants made to that order in the English county of Essex during the thirteenth century, nearly eighty per cent occurred between c.1220 and c.1260; after 1260 the number of gifts rapidly dwindled. A fall in acquisitions by gift and sale was not, however, peculiar to the Templars and Hospitallers. Santiago's commandery and priory of Uclés made few gains in the later thirteenth century: of forty-nine gifts of property received by the year 1311, only five occurred after 1250, and thirty-two out of thirty-three purchases had been made by the latter date.

It has sometimes been suggested that this decline in acquisitions was occasioned in part by the mortmain legislation enacted in various Western countries during the thirteenth century. Yet it may be doubted whether these laws exercised a significant influence. Restrictions on alienation to the Church had often been imposed at earlier times; and, even after mortmain legislation had been passed, alienation under licence was often allowed. Gains could also be made illicitly: in 1294 and again in 1300, the English Hospitallers were receiving pardons from Edward I for acquiring property in contravention of the 1279 statute. The slump in acquisitions, moreover, did not usually coincide in time with the enactment of mortmain laws.

Other reasons may be adduced for the dwindling number of donations. Religious houses normally gained the bulk of their property within a limited period of their foundation, after which their popularity waned. It is not therefore surprising that patronage of military orders declined, especially in the changing circumstances of the thirteenth century. The success of the Spanish reconquest must have led to the belief that it was no longer necessary to lend large-scale support to military orders in the Iberian peninsula. Lack of success in Syria, on the other hand, may also have discouraged patrons. The failure of Gregory X's crusading plans in the mid-1270s shows that it was becoming increasingly difficult to arouse enthusiasm for the cause of the Holy Land. Some, though no doubt only a minority, went so far as to question the validity of crusading, and advocated its replacement by peaceful missionary activity. Some potential patrons were, no doubt, also deterred by claims that the orders based in the Holy Land were not making the best use of the resources they did possess.

The decline in purchases is to be related to the orders' financial situation. In the thirteenth century, many foundations were not only ceasing to increase their wealth to any extent: they were also experiencing difficulty in maintaining their existing sources of income.

In some districts revenues were permanently lost. Although in Spain and the Baltic region infidel counter-offensives were of only temporary significance, in Syria the situation was rather different. The Christian gains made there in the first half of the thirteenth century hardly compensated for the losses sustained in the later part of the twelfth; and in the second half of the thirteenth century the Mamluks were gradually taking over what remained of the crusader states. In a letter sent to a French subordinate in 1268, the Hospitaller master, Hugh Revel, assumed that his colleague would know

> how, for the last eight years, in the whole kingdom of Jerusalem we have received no revenues, and whatever we held outside the gates of Acre has been subjected to enemy control; since although Château Pèlerin, Tyre and the city of Sidon are still in Christian hands, outside the walls the Christians receive nothing.[21]

The instructions given to Hospitaller envoys to the Council of Lyon six years later again stressed that although in the past the Hospitallers had obtained a large part of their income from properties in the East, these had now almost all been lost. Besides the lost income from land, the military orders in the Holy Land were, of course, in the thirteenth century also being deprived of tributes paid by neighbouring Muslim rulers.

Yet it was not only in Syria that sources of income were lost. The frequency of papal threats against those who harmed the possessions of the military orders shows that the retention of rights anywhere in western Christendom required constant vigilance. Nor were losses incurred only through the seizure of landed property. The secular clergy was often anxious to increase its own income by reducing the privileges of military and other religious orders. The right to bury outsiders possessed by most military orders was, for example, restricted by diocesans in various ways. In 1192, after a series of disputes, the bishop of Lérida limited the Templars' right of burial to only three places in his diocese, and also in Catalonia at about the same time the bishop of Tortosa ruled that the Templars in the city of Tortosa 'are to receive none of our parishioners for burial unless they can ascend to the castle of the Zuda on their own feet or on horseback without the aid of man or woman'.[22] Following a Templar complaint a few years later, Innocent III was even obliged to rule more generally that no one was to remove by force the bodies of those who had chosen burial in the Temple. Losses of income were also frequently caused by the activities of impostors, who claimed to be collecting alms on behalf of a military order.

Even if landed property was not permanently lost, its profitability was sometimes reduced through devastation caused by raiding and other disturbances. This obviously frequently occurred in the frontier districts of Christendom: after rebellions in Prussia in the year 1260, for example, many lands there were lying waste. But this was a problem which affected not only the frontier regions of Christendom. At several times in the thirteenth century the income of military orders in the kingdom of south Italy and Sicily was reduced by disorder and conflict there. In 1201, during the minority of Frederick II, the master of the Hospitallers complained of the destruction wrought by Germans and Lombards; the Hospital's lands again suffered in the 1260s, when Charles of Anjou was seeking to establish himself at the expense of the last Hohenstaufen claimants; and the conflict provoked by the Sicilian Vespers occasioned further devastation in the closing decades of the century. Gascony, which was a frequent source of contention between England and France, was another area where the orders' interests were harmed by war: in 1299, for example, the Hospitallers reported to the Pope that some of their houses in the district of Bordeaux had been burnt and numerous other losses sustained. Yet it was not only wars between states or royal claimants which reduced income: local feuds and petty violence also caused damage, and examples of this kind of disturbance can be found in almost any part of western Christendom. The scale of the losses which might be suffered through war and disorder is illustrated by a survey of Hospitaller lands in the British Isles in 1338: at Chibburn, in Northumberland, rents which in times of peace amounted to twenty marks a year (£13. 6s. 8d.) were worth scarcely £5. 10s. 0d. because of war with the Scots, while at Thornton, in the same county, land which was worth annually sixpence an acre in peacetime was valued at hardly threepence an acre.

The value of rents was also affected by the inflation which characterised much of the West during the twelfth and thirteenth centuries: if dues could not be quickly adjusted, their purchasing power was diminished. Returns from land also depended on climatic conditions. In the eastern Mediteranean region there were many years when the harvest was affected by drought. A complaint by the Hospitaller master in the 1240s was echoed by Hugh Revel in 1268, when he wrote of drought in Armenia, and further Hospitaller comments about the lack of rain and the sterility of the land in Syria and elsewhere in the eastern Mediterranean have survived from the years 1274, 1279 and 1282. In 1279 the brethren of St Thomas of Acre similarly complained to the English king, Edward I, that 'at the present time the land of Cyprus and Syria has remained unproductive of earthly produce'.[23] It has also, of course, been argued that, although there were few major crop failures in western Europe during the twelfth and thirteenth centuries, some lands there were being overworked and were suffering from soil exhaustion by the later years of the thirteenth century. Evidence of corn yields is lacking for orders' properties in the West for this period, but the Hospitaller survey of the year 1338 includes a number of comments about the poverty and sterility of land in various parts of England. It was reported, for example, that at Bothemescomb in Devon only 150 out of 240 acres were being cultivated 'because of sterility', and at Temple Combe in Somerset there were sixty 'feeble and sterile' acres, of an annual value of only one penny each.[24]

By no means all of the revenues which the orders did receive could be devoted to maintaining troops and strongholds on the borders of western Christendom or to further investment in property. Much of Templar and Hospitaller income from countries in the West was used for the support of brethren there, for it was in Western Europe that the majority of Templars and

Hospitallers resided. There were also numerous other calls on income. Houses of the military orders throughout western Christendom usually contained considerable numbers of laymen and sometimes also laywomen, who were in the employ or service of an order. Religious obligations to patrons constituted a further drain on resources. In 1280, the bishop of Valencia considered that an income of twenty pounds in Valencian currency was necessary to maintain a chantry priest and his assistant and to provide for lamps and candles. In England, it was stated in a royal inquest undertaken in 1309 that the cost of maintaining a chantry priest and a lamp at Witham in Essex was £4. 6s. 8d. a year, while three other priests who celebrated in the Templar chapel at Cressing together cost annually ten pounds. A further twenty shillings was expended every year at Cressing on lamps. The order's obligations for priests and lamps there took more than a quarter of its income from Cressing. There were also payments to be made to individuals who were in receipt of corrodies and to those whose favour and help an order needed. In 1338, the English Hospitallers were paying pensions to various members of the royal court, including sums totalling seventeen pounds to barons of the exchequer.

A considerable amount of income was also expended on the more general charitable work undertaken by the orders. Mountjoy assumed the task of ransoming captives when it was amalgamated with the ransom hospital of the Holy Redeemer in 1188, and it was then decreed that a quarter of its revenues should be devoted to this activity. According to the rule of Santiago, booty taken from Muslims was to be used for the ransoming of captives, and presumably all the surplus revenues from Santiago's ransom hospitals were used in this way. Mountjoy and Santiago were the only two orders which regularly undertook the freeing of captives, but a Hospitaller statute issued in 1182 ruled that twelve pence were to be given to every freed captive, and in the early thirteenth century the order of Avis had a hospital at Evora, whose functions included the receiving of 'captives freed from the servitude of the Saracens'.[25]

The Hospital of St John and the Teutonic order had been founded for the care of the poor and sick, and considerable resources were still devoted to these tasks after the two foundations had become military orders. John of Würzburg, who visited the Holy Land in the 1160s, reported of the Hospital that a great number of sick – both men and women – is gathered in various buildings, and is daily supported and restored to health at great expense. When I was there, I learned from the report of the servitors themselves that the sick totalled up to two thousand. Of these, sometimes more than fifty were carried out dead in the space of a day and night, but again and again there were more new arrivals.[26]

Despite clauses about the care of the sick in the Hospitaller rule and in statutes compiled in 1182, it is not known what proportion of Hospitaller revenues was used for this purpose. There was obviously the danger that once the Hospital and the Teutonic order had assumed military functions, less would be spent on charitable activities; and, around the year 1180, Alexander III did express concern because the Hospitallers' military duties were having an adverse effect on their work for the poor and sick. But the two orders did not abandon their charitable activities. Although the Hospital and Teutonic order led in the provision of hospitality and care for the sick, there were also several other military orders which maintained hospitals; but, as was frequently pointed out during the trial of the Templars, the Temple had no obligations of this kind.

Nevertheless, the Temple, like other military orders, was expected to dispense alms. Its rule stated that a tenth of bread used in every house was to be assigned to the poor. This regulation was mentioned by many Templars when they were interrogated in the early fourteenth century, and they also frequently referred to the practice of dispensing alms three times a week. The rule of the Teutonic order similarly decreed that a tenth of bread baked in the order's houses should be given in alms or that alms should be dispensed three times a week, while the rule of Santiago required sustenance to be given to the poor every day. The royal inquest of Templar rights at Cressing in 1309 again gives an indication of expenditure, for it was then estimated that the cost of providing for the poor there three days a week amounted to fifty-two shillings a year, and this sum comprised about a sixteenth of total income.

The orders' disposable income was further reduced by the dues and taxes which had to be paid to outsiders. Although lay patrons did not usually retain any rights in properties given to a military order, and although overlords' claims were often surrendered or bought out, some income was inevitably used in paying rents; and exemptions did not usually free orders completely from other dues and taxation. The exemptions which military orders enjoyed were, in fact, often reduced during the course of the twelfth and thirteenth centuries. Tithe exemptions were opposed by the secular clergy, who lost income through them. Shortly after the middle of the twelfth century, therefore, Adrian IV restricted the tithe privileges enjoyed by religious houses and decreed that they should apply only to newly-cultivated lands (*novales*) and, although Alexander III restored the exemption formerly possessed by the Templars and Hospitallers, Innocent III in 1215 decreed that these orders should be exempt from paying tithes only on old demesne land (*labores*) acquired before that date and on demesne *novales*. Military orders were also often obliged to make local agreements with bishops which further reduced their tithe privileges: in some cases a limit was placed on the amount of demesne land which was to be exempt, and on other occasions orders were obliged to pay a portion of the tithes from which they had been freed by papal privilege. Exemptions from secular dues and taxes were similarly reduced by rulers anxious to increase their revenues in order to meet growing financial needs. Despite the royal charters of exemption granted to the Aragonese Templars and Hospitallers, by the later thirteenth century most of their convents were subject to a hospitality tax (*cena*), their freedom from royal tolls and customs had been reduced and they were paying half of the *monedaje*, which was a tax given in return for a royal undertaking not to manipulate the coinage. In England, royal encroachments appear to have been more intermittent, but brethren of the military orders there, like their colleagues elsewhere, were expected to contribute to extraordinary royal taxation, which was becoming increasingly frequent in the later thirteenth century. At that time military orders were also expected to contribute to some of the general taxes which the papacy was then demanding of the Church. Although they were not asked to pay taxes of this kind levied in aid of the Holy Land, in the 1280s they were instructed to pay the tenths imposed by Martin IV and Nicholas IV for the support of the Angevins in the years following the Sicilian Vespers, and Martin IV similarly demanded contributions to the tenth which was to finance the French crusade against Aragon.

Nor could the surplus wealth which the leading orders did possess in the West always be easily transferred to the Holy Land. A responsion of a third of revenues from the lands belonging to the Templars, Hospitallers and the Teutonic order in Western Europe was meant to be dispatched to the East, but fear of dearth, the needs of war or merely the desire to profit from the issue of export licences occasioned frequent royal prohibitions on the export of the kinds of goods – such as arms, grain, meat and animals – which normally made up shipments to the East. The orders, admittedly, often did receive export licences, but these were by no means always forthcoming. In 1306, the Hospitallers turned to the Pope in an attempt to persuade Charles of Naples to allow the export of goods which they needed in Cyprus, and one of the proposals advanced by the Hospitaller master Fulk of Villaret, in a crusading memorandum early in the fourteenth century, was that the Pope should instruct rulers not to impede the export of arms, money or other goods by the Templars, Hospitallers and the Teutonic order. Some rulers appear to have gone further and seized goods which orders were intending to dispatch, for in 1295 Boniface VIII was protesting to the English and Portuguese kings about the appropriation of Hospitaller responsions. That the papacy was itself not blameless in this respect, however, is indicated by a letter from Boniface in 1297, in which he sought to justify his request for a subsidy from the military orders by reminding them that for the preceding two years no demands had been made on their responsions by the papacy; but at least on some occasions popes were devoting the sums obtained in this way to crusading purposes.

In assessing the adequacy of the military orders' financial resources, it is necessary to distinguish between different orders and between different periods. Some of the smaller orders never possessed sufficient revenues to become viable. Monfragüe's poverty led the Castilian king, Fernando III, to amalgamate it with Calatrava in 1221, and it was apparently the weak financial situation of the order of St Thomas of Acre which prompted proposals in the later thirteenth century for an amalgamation with the Temple: already, in 1257, Alexander IV had written to the brethren that 'you have to bear a very great burden of expense, and your resources are not sufficient for this'.[27] But Monfragüe was merely the remnant of an order, trying to secure a footing where others were already firmly entrenched, and St Thomas of Acre was similarly seeking to compete in the Holy Land with long-established institutions.

Yet even well-established orders often lacked the necessary resources to take on additional obligations or to overcome serious reverses in war. In the Holy Land, the Hospital overreached itself financially by giving over-enthusiastic support to proposals for conquering Egypt in the later 1160s: according to William of Tyre it then incurred debts totalling 100,000 besants. It was, in fact, often necessary to subsidise orders which assumed new responsibilities or suffered military setbacks. When the count of Barcelona assigned the castle of Amposta to the Hospitallers in the mid-twelfth century he also gave them 2000 *morabetinos* for the needs of the stronghold, together with an annual subsidy of a thousand *morabetinos*. The gift of a series of castles to Trujillo by Alfonso VIII in 1195 was similarly accompanied by the grant of rents worth annually 3000 *aureos* 'for the fortification and perpetual maintenance of the aforesaid castles'.[28] When the Templars undertook the building of Château Pèlerin in 1218 they received financial assistance from the Flemish noble Walter of Avesnes, and after Safed had been returned to them in 1240 the initiative in restoring the castle seems to have emanated from the bishop of Marseilles, who sought help from Westerners then in the Holy Land, because the Templars did not possess adequate resources. The effects of setbacks in war are illustrated by the need to subsidise the order of Calatrava after it had lost a number of strongholds following the defeat at Alarcos in 1195: Alfonso VIII provided financial assistance, 'taking into account the poverty of your order resulting from the loss of your chief house of Calatrava and of almost all your possessions following the misfortune at Alarcos, where you campaigned with me'.[29]

Yet during the course of the thirteenth century there is growing evidence of more long-term financial difficulties experienced by leading orders. References to debts become more frequent, and these were by no means all short-term debts: although very few financial accounts survive from the thirteenth century, it is evident that obligations could not always be quickly met from incoming revenues. In 1273, the Hospitallers in Aragon were reduced to using the responsions they owed to their superiors in the East for paying off local debts, and a few years later they were

taking out new loans to clear old debts. Santiago was doing the
same in 1263. This was during the mastership of Pelayo Pérez
Correa, who already, in 1258, had been excommunicated for non-
payment of debts; and loans taken out during his period of office,
which ended in 1275, were still being repaid in 1287. Templar
obligations in Aragon totalling more than 100,000 shillings, which
were listed in an account drawn up in 1277, were similarly not all
recent debts. It is, of course, true that in Aragon as elsewhere the
Templars themselves were still lending money; but, as has been
seen, it is not clear to what extent the order's own resources were
being used for this purpose; nor were the Templars always able
easily to provide the required sums.

In an attempt to solve serious financial problems in Germany at
the beginning of the fourteenth century, the Hospital placed
severe limitations on the recruitment of new brethren – just as
some impoverished monasteries did – and also banned any new
building operations. A more common solution to financial problems was to alienate property, which might provide relief in the
short-term, but at the expense of long-term income. In 1253,
Innocent IV allowed the Templars to reduce their burden of debt
by disposing of property in Provence to the value of 2000 marks,
and there were numerous further alienations in the second half of
the thirteenth century. In 1285, for example, the master of the
Hospitallers was selling houses at Blois to the monastery of
Marmoutier 'because of the necessity of subsidising the Holy
Land',[30] and in the following year his subordinates in Hungary
were granting away rights to an individual because they could not
pay a debt owed to him. Even if property was not permanently
alienated, it was sometimes leased on generous terms so that an
order could obtain cash immediately. In 1233, Margaret, the wife
of Humbert of Beaujeu, received the Hospitaller house of Cossieu
in Burgundy for an annual rent of thirty shillings, on the
condition that she paid off the debts of that house; and this was
clearly not an isolated incident, for at the general chapter of 1262
complaint was made about the granting away of property in the
West for large sums of cash and small rents; and the prohibition
enacted in that year had to be repeated in 1303.

Both the charitable and the military activities of the orders were
affected by these financial problems. In the middle of the
thirteenth century Santiago abandoned the ransoming of cap-

tives, ostensibly on the grounds that its services were no longer needed. Yet this was hardly a convincing explanation, and it seems more likely that the change was occasioned by financial pressures. During the Templar trial it was reported that in the mid-1290s the master of the Temple had forbidden excessive almsgiving because of heavy expenditure in the East and elsewhere, and in 1306 the Hospitaller master, Fulk of Villaret, was claiming that his order did not have the resources 'for maintaining our lords the sick'.[31]

The consequences for the defence of the Holy Land are apparent from numerous complaints and appeals voiced by leading officials of the orders in the East. A common grievance was that resources which they expected to receive from Western Europe were not being dispatched. In 1268, the Hospitaller master was bewailing that nothing was being sent from Italy and parts of France and very little from England and Spain; and in both 1301 and 1302 the general chapter of the Hospital was obliged to issue decrees insisting that responsions should be paid in full each year. Masters were at times reduced to making desperate appeals for aid. In 1260, the Templar master told his deputy in England that the order's expenses were so great that, unless help was forthcoming from the West, the Temple would be forced either to abandon the defence of the Holy Land or to alienate much of its property in the West. In 1275, a later master was similarly telling the English king, Edward I, that the state of the order was so poor that it might be necessary to stop defending the Holy Land, and in the preceding year Hospitaller envoys at the Council of Lyon had elaborated on the poverty of their own order. Difficulties were still encountered in the eastern Mediterranean even after the last Western footholds in Syria had been lost. In 1300, the head of the Templars in Aragon was passing on urgent appeals from his superior in Cyprus, and statutes issued by the Hospitaller general chapter in the following year referred to 'the great distress and poverty in which our house finds itself'.[32]

The eastern Mediterranean was not the only frontier region where problems arose. In 1233, the master of Santiago was dispatching requests for help to kings and princes throughout the West, pointing out that his order's resources were scarcely sufficient for the task of defending its strongholds; and the orders' reluctance to give service in Spain during the later thirteenth and early fourteenth centuries was seemingly occasioned at least in part by financial problems. In the early months of 1304, Calatrava claimed that it did not have enough land to maintain the number of knights which the Aragonese king was then demanding of it, and when the Templar provincial master sought to excuse his order from further military service in May of the same year, he asserted that the Templars had already incurred heavy expenses on the frontier and that it had been necessary to contract loans to cover these. And although the Templar provincial master told a subordinate in the autumn of the same year that he was then intending to furnish troops, he also claimed that he would have been justified in excusing the order because of the large sums which had been expended on frontier service in that year.

Although, as will be seen, some expressed scepticism about the orders' financial problems, others realised that, despite the numerous properties and widespread rights which the leading orders possessed throughout western Christendom, the surplus revenues which could be devoted to military or charitable obligations were hardly adequate. It was thus to relieve financial difficulties that numerous grants were made to military orders by the papacy in the thirteenth century. The heavy costs of defending Santiago's strongholds led Gregory IX to make financial concessions to that order in 1234, and its limited resources were again stressed by Innocent IV when he gave further assistance. The Hospital's heavy burden of debt similarly prompted a papal subsidy in 1255, and Clement IV referred to that order's 'great need' when giving additional aid in 1267.[33] Yet such concessions were not enough to solve the orders' problems.

Recruitment

MOST military orders gained the majority of their recruits, like the bulk of their income, from a limited geographical area. Brothers' names show that the Spanish orders drew support mainly from the Iberian peninsula, and that the order of St Thomas of Acre mainly comprised Englishmen. The Teutonic order attracted recruits largely from German-speaking regions, as did the Swordbrethren. Yet postulants were never drawn exclusively from a particular area. Some members of the Spanish order of Mountjoy, for example, appear to have been of Italian origin, and the Teutonic order did include some brethren who were not from German-speaking districts. But the Temple and Hospital were the only military orders which regularly attracted recruits from all parts of western Christendom. Even these two orders, however, appear to have looked to France as their chief recruiting ground. Of seventy-five Templars from the central convent in Cyprus who were interrogated in the early fourteenth century, forty had joined the order in France or Provence; and of the seven tongues into which the Hospital was divided by the later thirteenth century, three were French territories, while in 1302 it was decreed that forty-one of the eighty brethren making up the Hospital's military establishment in Cyprus were to come from the French tongues. Since there was little competition in France from other military orders, its importance as a recruiting ground for Templars and Hospitallers is scarcely surprising.

Not all of those who sought admission were accepted, for the military orders adopted the established monastic custom of imposing restrictions on membership. Entry into these orders, as into other religious foundations, was in the first place limited to freemen. Although in the thirteenth century knightly descent was required of those seeking admission to the rank of knight in a military order, the qualification for entry to other ranks was merely freedom from serfdom. Thus in the Hospitallers' admission ceremony it was said to a postulant: 'we also want to know from you if you are the serf of any lord',[34] and similar questions were asked of recruits to other orders. The significance in practice of this limitation depended in part on the extent to which serfdom survived in different regions of the West, and on the readiness of lords to emancipate serfs who wished to adopt the religious life: in 1313, the abbess of Wetter was willing to free Gerard of Oberwetter when he wanted to join the Teutonic order, but this would not be the reaction of all lords. Some recruits, on the other hand, may just have concealed their unfree status: it is recorded that at the time of Louis IX's Egyptian crusade a Templar sergeant who had been a serf was reclaimed by his lord. Yet such entrants were probably few. Although former serfs who left their own districts ran little risk of discovery, the records of the trial of the Templars show that a large proportion of recruits resided in the vicinity of the convent which received them. And for those seeking emancipation there were other ways of securing freedom.

Yet, if most recruits were freemen, it is difficult to discover from which groups of free society brethren were mostly drawn. A number of attempts have been made to trace the family backgrounds of individual brothers, and the conclusion has usually been reached that comparatively few postulants came from the ranks of the upper nobility. The importance of recruitment from the lesser nobility – from the knightly and *ministerialis* classes – has been stressed. It has been shown that the majority of Templar masters were drawn from families belonging to the middle and lesser nobility, and an examination of the origins of members of the Teutonic order in Thuringia during the thirteenth century has revealed that, of 105 brethren, nine came from comital families and eleven from the free nobility (*Edelfreie*); eighteen were *reichsministeriales* and fifty-six *ministeriales*; one came from a family of free knights and ten belonged to patrician and burgess families. Yet those whose origins can be traced with certainty comprise only a minority of the total membership of an order, and it is usually easier to discover the antecedents of brothers who belonged to families of some standing. This approach may therefore lead to an underestimate of recruitment among families of modest status.

A different approach is provided by trying to calculate the relative numbers of knights and sergeants in the leading orders during the later thirteenth and early fourteenth centuries, for this should indicate what proportion were of at least knightly descent and how many were merely of free status. Unfortunately, most documents do not specify the ranks of individual lay brethren, but information is provided by the records of the Templar trial. These show that in Cyprus the majority of lay brethren were knights. But in Western Europe, where most Templars resided, knights comprised only a small minority. Of 193 lay brethren who testified before papal commissioners in Paris in 1310–11 and whose rank is definitely known, 177 were sergeants and only sixteen were knights. Even in Spain, where the Temple had been engaged in the *reconquista*, knights appear to have formed a minority, for of twenty-eight lay brethren questioned at Lérida in 1310, nineteen were sergeants, and the majority of Templars receiving pensions in Aragon in 1319 also appear to have been sergeants. A Hospitaller survey undertaken in the British Isles in 1338 also reveals a preponderance of sergeants: at that date there were seventy-eight lay brethren of the Hospital in England, Wales and Scotland whose ranks are known, and these comprised thirty-one knights and forty-seven sergeants.

Although in the early fourteenth century sergeants were more numerous than knights in the Temple and Hospital, it might nevertheless be questioned whether rank in an order always provided a true reflection of social background. It could be pointed out that in the Teutonic order the master was given discretion to accept as knights men who were not of knightly origin, just as secular rulers reserved the right to create new knights; and some recruits to the rank of knight may have hidden their non-knightly origins, for there is no evidence that any proofs of descent were required. One who did so and was discovered was a Templar called Oliver, whose case was mentioned in the order's Customs. There is also the possibility that some members of knightly families were admitted as sergeants. Since in the later thirteenth century nobles were – apparently for economic reasons – becoming increasingly reluctant to knight their male offspring, a growing number from knightly families may have been seeking admission as sergeants. The records of the Templar trial certainly include comments which imply that some sergeants were of noble origin: the sergeant Amaury Cambellani, for example, said that 'he had often begged his kinsmen – noble men, for he himself was noble – to transfer him to another order'.[35] Yet, if most admissions took place in a recruit's own locality, such cases may have been few; and the functions performed by many sergeants in military orders suggest that their origins are to be sought among peasants and craftsmen, for an early-thirteenth-century Hospitaller regulation implies that it was the norm for brethren to continue in the occupations which they had pursued while still in the world. Although the evidence is not free from ambiguity, it would seem that in the early fourteenth century the Temple and Hospital did not recruit mainly from the nobility.

In the thirteenth century, those admitted to the rank of knight in the Hospital and Temple were required to be not only of knightly descent but also of legitimate birth. A Hospitaller statute issued in 1270 imposed this restriction, although it did make an exception for the bastards of princes and greater lords. In

Santiago, however, legitimate birth appears to have been expected only of those who held castles or were members of the order's council, and it was not until the fourteenth century that the question of legitimacy was raised in the surviving statutes of Calatrava.

In the early Middle Ages there had been no age restriction on recruitment to the religious life: children were commonly offered as oblates by their parents. But by the twelfth century this practice was being called into question, and the military orders – like other new religious foundations of the period – sought to check the acceptance of children in this way. Calatrava and other orders which adopted Cistercian usages were governed by Cistercian regulations, which imposed a minimum age for the admission of novices. No minimum was set in the Templar rule, but those admitted as novices were expected to be old enough to bear arms and to make a final decision for themselves:

> Anyone who wishes to give his son or kinsman for ever to the military order should bring him up until he reaches an age when he can manfully and with armed might drive out the enemies of Christ from the Holy Land . . . For it is better not to take vows in boyhood than to commit the enormity of retracting when one has reached manhood.[36]

Such regulations did not, in practice, mean that children could not be reared in houses of the military orders: it appears, in fact, not to have been uncommon for sons of nobles to be sent to an order's convent instead of being placed in a noble household. But it was usually made clear that such children were under no obligation to become brethren. In the Teutonic order, where no one under fourteen was allowed to take vows, boys living in convents made their profession on reaching that age only 'if it seemed right to the boys themselves and if they were acceptable to the brothers',[37] and a similar provision was included in the rule of Santiago, where the minimum age for taking vows was apparently fifteen. These conditions were also frequently echoed in agreements which were made about individual children. This did not mean that military orders admitted no very young recruits at all. Some Templars interrogated in the early fourteenth century admitted that they had made their profession before they had reached their teens: one Templar questioned at Cahors in 1307 said that he had been received into the order at the age of nine or ten, and Guy Dauphin told papal commissioners in Paris that he had been about eleven years old when he made his profession. Yet the records of the Templar trial show that these were exceptions: of 224 brethren appearing before the papal commissioners in Paris in 1310–11, only thirty-three had joined the order when they were below the age of twenty, and the average age on entry of this group was twenty-seven and a half. These figures cannot, of course, be taken as being absolutely accurate, as it is clear that some brothers had only an approximate notion of their own ages, but brethren would have known at what stage in their lives they had joined the Temple, and their testimony can be taken as a general indication of recruitment patterns.

If most recruits to military orders were adults, marriage was likely to be a more common impediment to entry – except to the order of Santiago – than it had been in the monastic world of the earlier Middle Ages. Marriage did not in itself preclude entry, but if a wife or betrothed was still living, her consent had to be obtained. Recruits were therefore questioned about their marital status. The warnings which accompanied this inquiry were not, however, always effective. One Templar interrogated in 1311 reported that the brethren present at his reception had included James of Vaucelles, who was later returned to the wife he had espoused before joining the Temple. There were also occasions when recruits coerced reluctant wives. When in the course of a dowry dispute in England in 1233 it was argued that Alice, the wife of William Fitzmuriel, could assert no claim because she and her husband had entered the Hospital at Buckland, she maintained that 'she had been placed in that house on the orders of her husband and against her own will'.[38]

Recruits were also questioned about their health. In the past, parents had commonly regarded religious houses as suitable places of refuge for their deformed or handicapped offspring. Such recruits were even less welcome in military orders, which needed men who could fight, than in contemplative foundations. But the Templar Customs include clauses detailing the fate of those who were found to have concealed an infirmity, and this suggests that not all recruits were as healthy as they maintained, while it is also clear that those who admitted recruits were sometimes prepared –

no doubt under pressures of various kinds – to accept men who confessed that their health was poor.

Since individuals who had entered religious houses were not allowed to leave at will, military orders could not freely accept apostates from other religious foundations. This is made apparent both in papal letters and in decriptions of admission ceremonies. Despite the questioning of recruits, however, some postulants were, in fact, refugees from other orders. On one occasion it was even necessary for the visitor of the order of Avis to command that all mendicant friars who had been admitted to Avis without the permission of the Pope or of their superiors should return to their own orders within two months. Transfers from one order to another could be made with permission, but it was envisaged that a stricter, not a less austere, way of life would normally be adopted. As Innocent III pointed out in a letter concerning a canon of Arrouaise who had later joined the Hospital, 'one should ascend from a laxer to a stricter order; on no account should there be a descent from a stricter order to a more lax one'.[39] Few transfers to military orders would therefore be expected. Some were nevertheless permitted, particularly from one military order to another, and especially when individuals found themselves at odds with their colleagues. Innocent IV thus allowed a brother of Santiago to transfer to the Temple since 'on account of the fierce hostility he has incurred, he cannot remain in that order without danger to his life'.[40]

As well as being asked about ties with other religious foundations, recruits were also questioned about debts, for orders were obviously anxious not to incur any liability for obligations which postulants had earlier contracted. Up to the twelfth century those embarking on the religious life were, on the other hand, commonly expected to make a gift on entry. By the time that the military orders were emerging, however, canonists were beginning to question the propriety of demanding donations from recruits. Yet such views spread only slowly and many religious institutions – including military orders – continued to expect gifts from postulants. The order of Santiago seems to have remained deaf to current views throughout the thirteenth century, for between 1271 and 1274 its general chapter enacted a statute which declared that if the master or commanders gave the habit to anyone other than a knight 'they should give it to him as a sergeant, provided he gives of his possessions from which the order can profit'.[41] A change of attitude is discernible elsewhere in the thirteenth century – simoniacal entry was classified in the Teutonic order, for example, as one of the most serious offences – but the practice was by no means stamped out. In 1278, it was admitted that many Hospitallers belonging to the convent of Fürstenfeld in Styria had been received simoniacally, and a number of Templars interrogated in the early fourteenth century testified that simony was common in their order.

The reasons which led men who could satisfy entry requirements – or who could conceal their shortcomings – to abandon the world and enter a military order were inevitably complex, and are not fully described in the surviving sources. Recruits themselves may not always have analysed their own motivation very clearly, and no doubt there was room for self-deception. It is therefore difficult to explain the motives of particular individuals. Some of the influences commonly at work can be discerned, but the significance of particular motives cannot be quantified.

In the early Middle Ages the decision to enter a religious house had often been made by the parents of a recruit rather than by the postulant himself, and it is obvious from the wording of the clause forbidding the admission of children that the compilers of the Templar rule had no intention of depriving parents of all say in the choice of their sons' careers. The surviving description of the Hospitaller admission ceremony in fact indicates that many parents sought to place their offspring in military orders:

> Good friends, you seek the company of the house, and you have good reason, for many noble men offer up earnest prayers and greatly rejoice when they can place any of their children or friends in this religious order.[42]

This is also apparent from particular documents in which parents made provision for their children. When William VII of Montpellier compiled his will in 1172 he decreed that one of his sons should become a Templar, and similarly in 1288, Manfred of Lonnig, a citizen of Coblenz, dedicated two sons to Christ and the Virgin Mary in the local house of the Teutonic order. Even when children placed in the custody of a military order were given the choice of staying or leaving once they had reached years of discretion, they were sometimes left in no doubt of what was

expected of them: when Walter of Nordeck offered his son to the
brethren of the Teutonic order at Marburg in 1267, the document
then drawn up made it clear that the father wanted him to take
the habit, for it included a sentence beginning: 'If indeed, which
God forbid, he refuses to remain with the brethren in that house,
when he reaches years of discretion....'.[43] Yet if some parents –
anxious to avoid the splitting of family estates, or to be rid of a
child who was infirm, or to offer a son to God in return for
spiritual benefits – were instrumental in persuading their children
to join military orders, the evidence concerning the ages of
Templar recruits suggests that parental pressure was not as
important a factor in providing postulants for the military orders
as it had earlier been in producing entrants for monasteries. But
even if only a limited number of children and adolescents took the
habit in a military order because of parental wishes, they might be
subject to family and outside pressures of other kinds. When, as
sometimes happened, several members of the same family entered
an order at one time, it may be doubted whether all were equally
enthusiastic recruits. Doubt may also be expressed about the
commitment of those who made their profession alongside, or at
the behest of, their lords. Peter of Dusburg reports, for example,
that Conrad of Thuringia entered the Teutonic order 'with a
large following of knights', and that when Theoderich, margrave
of Meissen, was in Prussia in 1272 'he caused twenty-four noble
men from his household, strenuous in arms, to be given the habit
of the house of the Teutonic order'.[44]

Furthermore, although the practice of child oblation had been
rejected, younger sons – who comprised a considerable proportion
of postulants – were often still in need of a livelihood; and as the
custom of primogeniture spread, and families possibly increased in
size, growing numbers found themselves in this category. To such
men, and also to others, the military orders may have seemed to
offer a more comfortable existence than the alternatives available
in the secular world. The words addressed to postulants at
admission ceremonies show that the orders were themselves
aware of this danger and sought to stress the rigours of the
religious life. In the Hospital a recruit was told that

> although it may be that you see us well-clothed and with fine
> horses, and think that we have every comfort, you would be

mistaken, for when you would like to eat, it will be necessary to fast, and when you would like to fast, it will be necessary to eat. And when you want to sleep, it will be necessary to keep watch.[45]

That such warnings were not always effective is apparent from James of Vitry's criticism of those who expected a higher standard of living than they had enjoyed in the world:

Indeed many, after they have joined an order, want to have the things which they were unable to enjoy in the world...I have heard of one man, who during the whole of his life in the world had never rested his head on a pillow but who, after joining an order, disturbed the whole convent by his grumbling and complaints, when he was lacking a pillow for just one night, because the linen pillow case was being washed.[46]

To some recruits, membership of an order offered not only an improved standard of living but also enhanced status. Some may have thought merely of escaping from serfdom, but there were also other possibilities. Those historians who have drawn attention to the influx of *ministeriales* into the Teutonic order have argued that the taking of vows often led to a marked change in social standing. It has been pointed out that the *ministeriales* of the abbey of Reichenau and of other lords who became members of the convent at Mainau not only acquired control of considerable property rights at the abbey's expense but also in standing came to equal the aristocratic inmates of the monastery. The creation of the order's state in Prussia by the former *ministerialis*, Hermann of Salza, has also been discussed in this context; and it has been demonstrated that, throughout the Teutonic order, men of *ministerialis* origin commonly held posts of authority and power.

While those seeking a career might be drawn to a military order by considerations of these kinds, for the elderly a religious house could be a place of refuge for old age; and possibly some elderly parents were even coerced into taking the habit by heirs anxious to secure control of family property. For some recruits, entry was a means of escape from financial difficulties or the consequences of crime. In 1311, the Templar Bertrand Guasc stated that he had joined the order twenty years earlier when he had been on a pilgrimage and run out of money, while in 1236 the English king, Henry III, had allowed Geoffrey Bauzan, who was then a prisoner in the Tower of London, to become a Hospitaller, provided that he left the kingdom and did not return without permission. Yet it is only rarely that secular motives are mentioned in documents relating to individual brethren.

Both in these sources and in others of a more general nature, greater stress was placed on spiritual matters. No doubt the formulae employed did not necessarily reflect the real feelings of a postulant: that material considerations were commonly of importance is suggested by the testimony of the Templar knight Guy Dauphin, who reported that when he took the habit 'they asked him why he wanted to do this, since he was noble and rich and had enough land'.[47] Yet for many recruits there was little material advantage to be gained by entering a military order, and it is not difficult to provide examples of men who abandoned considerable wealth on taking the habit. Spiritual concerns should not be discounted too quickly. What was regarded as the proper motivation for entering a military order was explained to Templar recruits at their admission ceremony:

> You ought not to request the company of the house in order to have lordships or wealth, nor to gain bodily comfort or honour. You should seek it for three reasons: the first is to abandon and leave behind the evils of this world; the second is to serve our Lord; the third is to be poor and to do penance in this life, for the salvation of the soul.[48]

These motives find expression in numerous documents of a more particular nature. In many, the abandonment of the vanity and evils – also described as the delights – of the world was emphasised, as in the case of the founders of Santiago, who were said in the prologue of the order's rule to have been called away from worldly pomp and the works of Satan. The more positive aspect – the adoption of a life of poverty and penance as a means of salvation – was also stressed. Some took the habit to atone for a particular offence, and some sinners were apparently goaded into joining an order by what were interpreted as displays of divine disfavour. Peter of Dusburg tells the story of a certain Gerard who entered the Teutonic order after four men bearing lighted candles had appeared before him when he was lying in his bed behind closed doors; they accused him of numerous failings and warned him to amend his way of life. Several Spanish documents of the later twelfth century further speak of brethren as vowing to shed their blood and to die; like friars going into Muslim lands, some recruits to military orders may have been seeking martyrdom, although this attitude would hardly have been welcomed by their superiors, who would have agreed with Aquinas that these orders were founded 'to shed the blood of the enemy rather than for the shedding of their own blood'.[49] In whatever form it was expressed, concern for the salvation of the soul was mentioned much more frequently than the service to be given against the enemies of the Church and of Christianity. The Catalan noble Bernard William of Entenza, who joined the Hospital at the beginning of the fourteenth century, was unusual in stating that

> the purity of undefiled devotion, which has long been known to inspire our feelings towards the Holy Land, and to which we have been unable until now to give full expression, has caused and persuaded us to come to the Holy Land.[50]

Yet, since entrants to any religious foundation might hope for salvation and sometimes material benefits as well, there must obviously be further factors which help to explain recruitment to military orders. Although it was sometimes maintained that membership of a military order was of less spiritual merit than the contemplative life, to many men – especially in the early crusading period – participation in the struggle against the infidel was probably a more comprehensible way of serving God than enclosure in a monastery, and also more demanding and therefore of greater spiritual value. They would have echoed the words of the hero of the *Moniage Guillaume*, who claimed:

> There is greater worth in the orders of knighthood, which fight against the Saracen race, conquer their lands, capture their towns and convert the pagans to our law. Monks have no concern but to live in a monastery, to eat and to drink decanted wine, and to sleep when they have said compline.[51]

Yet in the thirteenth century such notions were probably of diminishing significance. The factors which caused a decline in donations to military orders presumably also led to a reduction in the numbers of recruits motivated by an enthusiasm to assist in the struggle against the infidel.

But there were other reasons for joining a military order which did retain their importance. For those whose motivation was mundane, a military order had the advantage that a recruit did not have to abandon the world as completely as the monk did: the occupations of secular life, including fighting, could still be pursued. Nor, despite the warnings given to postulants, was life in a military order marked by the austerity and asceticism which characterised some monasteries.

Whether recruits had any sense of vocation or not, military orders had the further attraction that they were not as exclusive as many monasteries. They did not impose any educational qualifications: those who could gain admittance to monasteries only as *conversi* could become full members of a military order. And whereas noble descent was in practice required for entry into many religious foundations, military orders were usually open to all who were of free status.

Yet in many cases the choice of order was no doubt determined not merely by the perceived merits of an institution but also by personal, family or neighbourhood ties. Many boys reared in a convent belonging to a military order probably took the habit of that order later, as did individuals who had earlier been *donati* or employees. Peter of Neuilly told papal commissioners during the Templar trial that he had spent six years in the service of a Templar knight in the East before making his profession, and another Templar witness had been a *donatus* in the order for ten years before taking the habit at Chambereau in the Limousin. Many joined orders which already contained members of their own family: numerous Templars questioned in the early fourteenth century stated that they had been admitted by, or in the presence of, a member of the order who was a relation. It was also not uncommon for an individual to enter an order which had already been patronised by his family.

These last factors were obviously of no significance in an order's earliest years, and it was then that difficulties were most often encountered in attracting recruits. For almost a decade after its foundation the Temple expanded little: it was not until the order began to become known in the West in the later 1120s that it started to gain widespread support. Mountjoy appears to have found itself in similar difficulties, for in 1180 – only a few years after its foundation – it asked the Pope to allow the recruitment of Brabanzon, Aragonese and Basque mercenaries, against whom decrees had been passed at the Lateran Council in the preceding year.

While Mountjoy may never have overcome the problem of attracting sufficient recruits of any kind, the international orders seem to have experienced long-term difficulties in finding enough clerics who wanted to take the habit. It is true that in 1179 the master of the Hospital claimed to have 14,130 priests available, but he is unlikely to have had precise information, and he was probably including priests who were not members of his order. A different impression is conveyed by the records of the Templar trial: of the sixty-six Templars interrogated in Cyprus whose ranks are known, only three were chaplains, and only eight clerics have been identified among the 144 Templars traced in the British Isles at the time of the trial. Many convents of the leading orders in fact lacked a resident chaplain who was a professed brother. Thirteenth-century statutes of the Hospital and of the Teutonic order indicate that some houses had no resident priest at all, and in 1338 only eleven out of thirty-four Hospitaller houses in England and Wales had chaplains who were members of the order. On the other hand, the frequency of decrees limiting numbers in convents of sisters implies that there was often a superfluity of female recruits, which is partly to be explained by the small numbers and exclusiveness of Western nunneries.

Of greater importance to the orders, however, was the supply of lay male recruits. Warfare inevitably led to a higher mortality rate than was usual in religious houses, and losses had to be replaced. Although evidence is fragmentary, various sources suggest that in most parts of Western Europe the Temple and Hospital usually had little difficulty in attracting enough laymen. It is apparent in the first place that postulants did not always find it easy to secure a place in one of these orders, and needed the assistance of influential patrons. During the trial of the Templars, Guiscard of Marsac said that it had been at the insistence of himself and of William Flote that the son of a Lyon citizen had been admitted to the Temple; and a Templar sergeant who had made his profession about the year 1276 claimed that he had been received only after he and his friends had pressed for two years for him to be admitted; while another, who had taken the habit some twenty years later, asserted that his petition to enter had been supported by the archbishop of Béziers. Most of the examples drawn from the records of the Templar trial concern the recruitment of sergeants, but the section of the Hospitaller admission ceremony which has already been quoted seems to imply that it was not only these who encountered difficulty in securing admission. It may also be pointed out that in the later thirteenth and early fourteenth centuries it was necessary on more than one occasion for the Hospitallers to restrict recruitment in order to relieve pressure on declining resources. At times when heavy losses were suffered in Syria, the orders appear, in fact, to have had little difficulty in obtaining replacements, especially as only a small proportion of Templars and Hospitallers were stationed in the Holy Land. Thus when the Hospitallers lost forty brethren at the Siege of Tripoli in 1289, the master quickly obtained reinforcements from the West: 'we have ordered that some of our brethren should be summoned to these parts from each province, so that the convent may be brought up to strength'.[52] Brothers transferred to the East had in turn to be replaced, but the orders seem to have been able to recruit quickly when necessary: Matthew Paris, in his *Flores historiarum*, reported that after the battle of La Forbie in 1244 'to make good the loss of brothers, the Templars and Hospitallers admitted to their orders many selected laymen, and sent assistance to the Holy Land'.[53] From such comments it may be inferred that the frequent employment of auxiliaries in the Holy Land was occasioned not by recruiting problems, but by the desirability of using troops of various kinds.

In contrast to this evidence about recruitment in Western Europe in general by the two leading orders, there are some twelfth- and thirteenth-century Spanish sources which can be interpreted as indicating recruiting difficulties, although some of the evidence in question does admit of other explanations. The Aragonese records of the Templars and Hospitallers show that at various times individuals were entering into agreements whereby they promised to receive the habit within a fixed period of time. Peter of Barbastro, for example, in 1221 undertook to enter the Hospital at Sigena within three years. It may also be noted that in the later thirteenth century the number of Templars who can be traced in some Aragonese convents declines; and when, at the turn of the thirteenth and fourteenth centuries, the Templar commander of Mallorca asked the provincial master to send some brothers needed on the island, none could be sent. In 1250, it was apparently also becoming necessary for the order of Santiago to look further afield for recruits, for in that year the master dispatched brethren to Germany with powers to admit new members. Obviously in Spain there were a number of orders competing for manpower, and even the Templars and Hospitallers there had to rely on recruits drawn from the peninsula: despite their involvement in the reconquest, they did not receive assistance from other parts of Western Europe.

One other area which experienced recruiting problems in the thirteenth century was the Baltic region. The amalgamation which took place between the Teutonic order and the Sword-brethren was partly occasioned by the Livonian order's lack of members: it did not possess widespread property or numerous convents outside that district, and it must have found it difficult to compete for recruits in Germany with the rapidly expanding Teutonic order.

Whatever the fighting qualities of their brethren, military orders could not maintain the struggle against the infidel without the necessary supplies of money and manpower. In Spain, their reserves of both seem to have been limited, but there they did not constitute the major Christian force. In the Holy Land, however, the defence of Christian territories was increasingly dependent on the military orders, and, although the Templars and Hospitallers were apparently able to recruit sufficiently, the inadequacy of their financial resources was an important factor in the loss of the crusader states.

5. Structures and Regulations

Organisation

IN their early years, when military orders usually consisted of just a small group of brothers under the leadership of a master, little administrative or governmental machinery was needed. As more property came to be acquired, however, and recruits attracted, it became the normal practice to establish subordinate convents, which housed a group of members and which assumed responsibility for the administration of properties in the surrounding area. Unlike the possessions of many monasteries, which were scattered over a wide area, the lands subject to a convent of a military order were usually fairly compact. Although some of Santiago's convents in southern Spain appear to have drawn part of their revenues from possessions much further north, acquisitions made by military orders were normally administered by the nearest house. A convent and the lands attached to it came to be known as a commandery, preceptory or bailiwick, while in Spain the term *encomienda* was employed. Although Santiago had some *encomiendas* in France, the subordinate foundations of most of the lesser orders were concentrated in particular areas of western Christendom, and only the Templars and Hospitallers established convents throughout the West.

Once orders had begun to expand in this way, very often an intermediate stage of organisation was soon needed. It became difficult for masters to undertake the supervision of all their subject houses, and arrangements commonly had to be made for the dispatch of resources and manpower to frontier districts from numerous convents which were remote from the borders of Christendom. Military leadership also had to be provided on several fronts, for the leading orders were fighting in Spain or the Baltic as well as in the Holy Land; and in Syria and the Iberian peninsula they had to provide separate contingents in each of the Christian states. The administrative models provided by existing religious orders did not serve the purposes of the military orders. The Cistercian system of filiation, for example, would have involved too many stages in the transmission of supplies and too many levels of command, and it did not produce regional groupings of houses. The military orders therefore initiated the practice of grouping the convents within a district into what the Templars called provinces and the Hospitallers priories, whose limits were often determined by political boundaries and which to some extent foreshadowed the provincial organisation of the orders of friars in the thirteenth century. The Temple and Hospital were already beginning to establish a provincial administration before the middle of the twelfth century: the Hospitallers had a priory of St Gilles by about 1120, when the order was still a charitable institution, while the equivalent Templar province, that of 'Provence and certain parts of Spain' was first mentioned by name in 1143. By the early fourteenth century the number of Hospitaller priories exceeded twenty. The system elaborated by the Hospitallers and Templars was imitated by the Teutonic order, which was beginning to establish provinces in Western Europe in the early decades of the thirteenth century, while the Spanish orders created regional groupings by establishing *encomiendas mayores*. In the thirteenth century, the order of Santiago had five – one in each of the kingdoms of Leon, Castile, Portugal and Aragon, and the fifth in Gascony – and Aragon similarly formed an *encomienda mayor* of the order of Calatrava. Even St Thomas of Acre to some extent copied the leading orders, for the head of its London house had authority over subordinate establishments in England and Ireland. In the records of Mountjoy, on the other hand, there is no evidence of any intermediate level of administration between the master and individual houses.

It should not, however, be assumed that the administrative organisation of the leading orders everywhere fitted neatly into a three-tier pattern. Administration evolved as needs required and there was never any attempt to achieve total uniformity; and in institutions which had establishments scattered over most of western Christendom there was ample scope for local variation. In some cases, intermediate officials existed between the convent and the province, and in Germany the term *provincialis* was used of two levels of administration in the Teutonic order. German houses of that order were grouped into bailiwicks, and the heads of these were sometimes termed *provinciales*; but these were in turn subject to the *Deutschmeister*, to whom the word *provincialis* was also applied. In some respects the *Deutschmeister* was comparable with the heads of provinces in other orders, but the surviving evidence does not permit an exact definition of the functions and powers of the *Deutschmeister* and of the heads of bailiwicks in Germany. The marital status of some of Santiago's members also necessitated special arrangements. Nevertheless, the basic pattern was of three levels of administration.

In frontier regions of western Christendom, convents were often housed in castles, and some elsewhere were similarly located in fortified strongholds. This is particularly true of Spain, where many castles which had at one time been in marcher areas were by the mid-thirteenth century remote from the Muslim border. But in districts away from the frontiers of Christendom, convents were administrative centres rather than military bases, and were usually created as an order's growing property rights required the establishment of further administrative units. They were sited in cities, towns and villages and had no military function. Typical of such houses was Templehurst in Yorkshire, which according to an inventory drawn up after the Templars' arrest in 1308 comprised a chapel, hall, dormitory, kitchen, larder, bakehouse and brewery, together with adjacent farm buildings.

Convents housed a group of members, usually mainly lay brethren, although some orders – especially Santiago – had a number of separate convents of clerics; and the Hospitallers, Santiago, Calatrava and the order of the Faith and Peace also possessed houses for sisters. Santiago's clerical convents are to be explained by the incorporation of several existing religious communities into that order at an early stage, while the establishment of houses for sisters was sometimes prompted by a desire to group together women who had sought to adopt a religious life by attaching themselves to male houses: thus, in 1220, Calatrava was given permission 'to bring together the dispersed sisters and to enclose them in a suitable place, two or three days' journey from Calatrava'.[1]

Convents varied considerably in size. The largest communities were in frontier regions. It has been seen that some castles in Syria had garrisons of sixty or eighty brothers, although on other Christian frontiers numbers appear to have been smaller. Convents remote from frontier regions were, however, almost always small, and usually housed fewer than thirteen members, which was regarded in the rule of the Teutonic order as the normal complement for a convent. Although there were at least fifteen brothers resident in the Teutonic order's house of Altenburg in Thuringia in 1296, at Nägelstedt in the same region the highest figure recorded in the thirteenth century is three, and in most of that order's houses in Thuringia the largest number of brothers mentioned in thirteenth-century documents is less than ten. And although, in the early fourteenth century, twenty-five Templars were arrested at Mas-Deu in Roussillon, the house of Boquiñeni was more typical of convents away from the frontier in the Templars' Aragonese province: in the twelfth and thirteenth centuries the largest number of brothers who can be traced there at any one time is five. In 1338, the biggest communities of Hospitaller brethren in England were at Chippenham, Clerkenwell and Buckland, where ten, seven and six brothers respectively resided, but most English Hospitaller houses at that time contained no more than two or three brothers. In Western Europe, some of the largest convents were those housing sisters: in 1298 an upper limit of thirty-nine was placed on the Hospital's convent at Beaulieu, in the diocese of Cahors, and there were at least thirty-five sisters resident there in that year, while in 1338 it was reported that the female house at Buckland usually contained fifty sisters.

In many houses members of an order were far outnumbered by outsiders who lived or worked there. An inventory of the Templar house of Baugy in Normandy reveals that, although there were apparently only three resident brothers in 1307, twenty-seven non-Templars were attached to the house. Outsiders commonly included individuals who were in receipt of corrodies, *donati* who were living a semi-religious life and assisting in the work of a convent, and paid employees. Among the latter were secular priests who assisted in chapels, and laymen who performed agricultural or household tasks. In hospitaller orders, outsiders were also employed to care for the sick, although this was an activity which characterised only a minority of convents. In Mediterranean districts there was often a further group made up of slaves: surviving inventories show that thirteen Templar commanderies in Aragon had an average of twenty slaves each in 1289, and the house of Monzón possessed nearly fifty.

The head of a convent was in most orders called a commander or preceptor, although the terms prior and prioress were used in houses of clerics and of sisters. These officials were usually imposed from above, as convents did not normally enjoy the right of electing their superior. Some commanders were appointed for life, but this was not the usual practice. In many orders, heads of convents commonly held office for only short terms, and were then often given charge of another convent; and in the Teutonic order, and possibly in some others, offices at this level had to be surrendered each year, although tenure could be renewed. Rapid changes of personnel no doubt in some cases hampered efficiency but – like those who held the office of *podestà* in one Italian city after another – many officials must have possesssed an accumulated fund of administrative experience; and short terms of office probably served to emphasise that posts were meant to be a responsibility rather than a reward, and possibly helped to prevent the growth of tension which could easily occur when a small community was subject to the same individual for a long period.

The head of a convent was in the first place responsible for discipline and the observance of the rule in his house; he could admit recruits, though his powers in this respect were sometimes subject to limitations; and in frontier districts he led the members of his convent in the field. He was also responsible for the administration of the properties subject to his house, although he did not usually enjoy complete freedom of action: alienations of rights, for example, normally required permission from superiors. In many orders, heads of convents were expected to submit annual reports on the state of their houses, although the form of these statements varied. It is apparent, from a group of reports which survive for the year 1289, that Templar commanders in Aragon did not submit accounts: they merely listed all movables, including slaves, equipment and stock as well as provisions, thus indicating whether a convent's movable property was being maintained. In the Teutonic order, on the other hand, commanders were to produce 'accounts of debts and rents' as well.[2] Heads of convents were also commonly obliged to surrender a portion of the income of their houses each year to their superiors. The rule of the Hospital states that subordinate establishments were to pay a third of their revenues as a responsion, but a statute issued in 1262 ordered heads of priories to exact responsions of fixed amount from the houses subject to them. By 1338, however, English houses of the Hospital were expected to surrender all surplus revenues. A list of responsions for the year 1307 shows that Templar convents in Aragon then paid fixed sums each year, although it is clear that payments did not represent a uniform imposition: the amounts were obviously related to the means and needs of each house. The heads of many houses were also, of course, expected to supply manpower, if required, for use in frontier regions.

The head of a convent was in some cases the only administrative official in a house. If he was assisted by others, they were few in number. Some convents had sub-commanders, but this was not a universal custom, and there was usually no more than one further administrative post. In the Temple, this often went under the title of *claviger* or *camerarius*, while in the Teutonic order the equivalent office was sometimes that of cellarer. The functions of this official are nowhere defined, but it may be presumed that the post corresponded to that of cellarer in Cistercian monasteries. Other offices are occasionally encountered – the importance of the Templars' financial operations led them to establish treasurers in their Paris and London houses – but the administrative organisation within convents of the military orders was usually simple. There was no decentralisation of control and no obedientiary system of the kind found in older monasteries. Brothers were, however, sometimes delegated to supervise a group of conventual properties, and lived – often by themselves – on granges within a commandery. Yet their powers were limited, and decisions concerning the acquisition and exploitation of property remained the preserve of the head of a house. These delegated brothers were nevertheless often given the title of preceptor or commander. Besides administrative officials, convents which housed mainly lay brothers were expected to have a chaplain, although he was not necessarily a professed brother.

The remaining members of a house participated in government and administration only through the conventual chapter. Although brethren might meet together briefly every day, the chapter was usually held once a week. According to the Templar Customs, a chapter was to be convened every Sunday and on the eves of certain festivals in all places where there were four or more brothers, and the statutes of the Teutonic order rule that 'brothers are, if possible, to hold a chapter every Sunday in their houses and their castles'.[3]

Heads of provinces were known by various titles: in the Temple they were usually called masters, and in the Hospital priors, while the term *comendador mayor* was used in Santiago and Calatrava; but there was no attempt to achieve uniformity in nomenclature. Like most conventual superiors, these officials were not elected by their subordinates; their terms of office tended, however, to be longer than those of commanders, although they were not usually appointed for life. There is some evidence to suggest that in the thirteenth century the post of provincial master in the Temple was granted for terms of four years, and in the Hospital towards the end of that century, priors were recalled every five years. It was also not uncommon for former heads of provinces to occupy more subordinate posts: there was little concept of a career structure in the military orders. The head of a province, like that of a house, was responsible both for the properties under his authority and for the brothers who were subject to him. In frontier regions he was also a military leader. He normally reported on the state of his province when he was recalled, and he had to ensure that his province's obligations to the master of his order were fulfilled. In the leading military orders, heads of western provinces were usually expected to send a third of their revenues to the East, although by the early fourteenth century the obligation had apparently sometimes been commuted into a fixed payment: thus, in 1304, the Aragonese Templars were negotiating with a Barcelona merchant for the transfer of a responsion of exactly 1000 marks. On this occasion payment was made in money, but – because of the scarcity and high price of many goods in the East – responsions were more frequently sent in kind, at least from Mediterranean countries. By the later part of the thirteenth century, however, when the orders had lost most of their income in Syria, the normal responsions were not sufficient to meet needs in the East, and western provinces were frequently being required to send subsidies in addition to their usual payments.

Heads of provinces did not usually have a large staff of subordinate officials. Although the Templar Customs suggest that the post of quartermaster (*drapier*) existed in the provinces of Antioch and Tripoli, and that there might also be provincial marshals in the East, these were frontier provinces and not typical. Brothers in charge of provinces were accompanied by a household rather than by a body of administrators. The Templar Customs allowed provincial masters in the East a *familia* of a knight companion, a sergeant, a deacon, a Saracen scribe and a boy, and in practice the entourage of the Aragonese provincial master in the later thirteenth century usually consisted of a knight companion, a sergeant, a chaplain, a scribe and two or three squires. Nevertheless, some provincial heads normally resided in a particular house and could use whatever administrative resources it had. Santiago's *comendador mayor* of Castile was based at the convent of Uclés until 1245 and then at Segura, and the head-quarters of the *encomienda mayor* of Portugal were located success-ively at Palmela, Alcácer and Mértola. The English prior of the Hospital similarly resided for most of the year at Clerkenwell. But not all provinces had a physical centre where provincial heads normally lived. Although by the later thirteenth century the Aragonese Templars apparently had a central archive and treasury at Miravet, the provincial master remained an itinerant official.

All provincial heads, however, spent a certain amount of time travelling around their provinces, and these journeys provided an opportunity to obtain counsel. It is known, for example, that when the Templar provincial master in Aragon arrived at a convent he was often joined by commanders from neighbouring houses. An alternative method of seeking advice was to summon a small meeting of leading brothers in a province, and an early fourteenth-century document which states that 'the council is being recalled to Miravet to discuss important business' shows that among the Aragonese Templars this practice became insti-tutionalised.[4] Yet the most important consultative body at this level was always the provincial chapter, which was attended by all heads of houses. In the Hospital, such assemblies can be traced back as far as 1123, and in most orders provincial chapters were normally held annually: the statutes of the Teutonic order, for example, decree that 'chapters general will be celebrated each year by the preceptors of Livonia, Germany, Prussia, Austria, Apulia, Romania and Armenia'.[5] In many provinces, chapters assembled on the same day each year – in Prussia the Teutonic order's chapter was held on 14 September, and the French province of the Temple usually held its chapter on the feast of St John the Baptist, in June – but in Aragon the Templar chapter met at various dates in April or May, although it always assembled on a Sunday. In the later thirteenth century the Templar chapter in Aragon was held at several different locations, including Miravet, Gardeny, Monzón and Tortosa, but some provincial assemblies always met at the same place: in 1250 it was ruled that the Prussian chapter of the Teutonic order should always meet at Elbing, and a document from the year 1283 refers to the Hospitaller house of St Gilles as the one 'in which the general chapter of the said priory was accustomed to assemble'.[6]

Heads of provinces were usually directly responsible to the headquarters of their orders. The central convents of the Temple and Hospital were located in Jerusalem until 1187, soon after which they were transferred to Acre, while the Teutonic order was also centred at Acre, at least in its early years and after its stronghold of Montfort had been lost in 1271. At the headquarters of an order, the most important official was, of course, the master, who in the three leading military orders was chosen by a specially constituted committee of thirteen, and who normally held office for life. Masters had their own attendants or household, but in the more important orders many duties were undertaken by other central officials. In the Hospital and the Teutonic order the grand commander took charge of the central convent in the master's absence. He also had control of supplies and domestic administration, and in the Hospital he was responsible for properties in the East. In the Temple, in the twelfth century, some of these responsibilities were assigned to the seneschal, who acted as the master's deputy, while others fell to the commander of the kingdom of Jerusalem. Towards the end of the twelfth century, however, the office of seneschal disappeared, and a grand commander took over both the seneschal's functions and those of the commander of the kingdom of Jerusalem. In all three orders, the leading military official was the marshal, who had authority over the brethren-at-arms. He was also responsible for distributing arms and mounts, and he led forces in the field in the master's absence. Officials of lesser standing included the *drapier*, who had charge of clothing, and also the treasurer, although in the twelfth century the commander of the kingdom of Jerusalem occupied that role in the Temple. In the Hospital and the Teutonic order, the sick were in the charge of the hospitaller, and in the former order the conventual prior was the leading ecclesiastical official. These officers each had their own household, but they often also had subordinate officials and sub-departments under their control. Among the minor officials subject to the grand commander in the Temple and Hospital was the commander of the Vault, where stores were kept (the equivalent in the Teutonic order was apparently the *preceptor expensarum*), while lesser military posts commonly included those of sub-marshal, *turcoplier, gonfanonier* (standard bearer) and master squire; and, as has been seen, in the Hospital the office of admiral emerged at the end of the thirteenth century. The saddlery and forge were also usually under the marshal's control, although a rigid separation of functions was never achieved, for some weapon stores were commonly under the authority of the grand commander.

In these orders, the influence of lay administration can to some extent be discerned, for offices such as those of seneschal and marshal existed in most royal and princely courts of the time. In the military and financial spheres, the orders' administrative needs were, of course, not very different from those of secular powers. Calatrava's central administration was, however, influenced by its Cistercian origins, rather than by secular models. Apart from the master, the leading lay officials were the *clavero* and *obrero*. The former's duties included the provision of food and clothing, and he corresponded to the cellarer in Cistercian houses, while the latter may be likened to the master of works encountered in some monasteries. The main clerical officials in Calatrava were the prior and sacristan. In the order of Santiago, on the other hand, there is no evidence of the emergence of important central offices other than that of the master. This is possibly because its activities were not restricted mainly to one region of Spain, and it was therefore more decentralised: unlike Calatrava, which was chiefly involved in the Castilian reconquest, Santiago was fighting against the infidel throughout the peninsula. In the orders of Mountjoy and St Thomas of Acre there is similarly no record of central officials other than the master, but the limited scale of their operations obviously made such posts unnecessary.

Little detailed evidence survives of the day-to-day workings of central administration, even in the leading orders. Statutes and customs usually provide little more than definitions of officials' rights and powers, although the need to state these – sometimes at a fairly late date – suggests either rivalry between officials or a rather haphazard administrative system. These sources do, however, give a certain amount of information about accounting procedures. It was decreed in 1283 that the accounts of the

Hospital's treasury were to be audited each month by the master and some of the brethren, and a similar custom was followed in the Teutonic order, although the Templar Customs state merely that the treasurer should render account when required to do so by the master or by the *prudhommes*. In the Teutonic order, all central officials who allocated goods or disbursed money – with the exception of the hospitaller – were also expected to render accounts each month, while Hospitaller statutes issued in 1301 ruled that minor officials who received goods from the store or Vault were to give a receipt, and the brother in charge of the store was to take these receipts each month to the treasury, where the brothers who had received the goods were to render account of what had been done with them. Most of the Hospitaller rulings on accounting are, however, fairly late, and imply either an earlier lack of a regularised accounting system or the need to improve the effectiveness of existing procedures.

Central convents, like lesser establishments, housed both brethren and outsiders. In that of the Hospital, the brothers were by the later thirteenth century grouped into seven *langues* or tongues, according to their district of origin. This practice does not appear to have been imitated by the Templars but, given the language differences among brethren in the central convent, it is likely that some informal groupings existed. In the Hospital and the Teutonic order, outsiders at the central convent included those who cared for the sick. Hospitaller statutes issued in 1182 ruled that four doctors were to be employed, who should be capable of examining urine, diagnosing diseases and prescribing medicines. The rule of the Teutonic order decreed rather less precisely that 'in the principal house, which is the head of the order, doctors are to be employed as the resources of the house allow and the numbers of the sick demand'.[7]

In 1164 and 1187, it was decreed that the convent of Calatrava should meet in chapter every day, as was the common monastic practice, but presumably, in most military orders, the chapter meeting of the central convent, like that of minor establishments, took place every week. Here masters could receive counsel, although the head of Santiago appears to have depended for advice mainly on the council of thirteen known as the *Trece*, which was made up mostly of leading commanders. Probably all military orders of any size, however, adopted the practice of holding periodic general chapters, which were attended by some brethren from provinces. Few rulings have survived concerning the frequency of these assemblies, but in the Teutonic order and Santiago they were to be held annually, as was already the norm in some non-military religious orders. Yet it seems that this was not always done, for the requirement to hold annual general chapters in the order of Santiago was reiterated on several occasions in the second half of the thirteenth century.

At each level of government within military orders, officials were thus counterbalanced by chapters. The taking of counsel by those in authority was, of course, a long-established practice in both secular and ecclesiastical circles, and it was seen to rest on biblical precedents. The Customs of the Teutonic order warned all those in positions of power 'diligently to seek advice and patiently to acquiesce in good counsels, since it is said in Proverbs: *there is safety where there is much counsel*', and allusion was also made to the precedents set by Moses and by the apostles.[8]

On some issues there was, in fact, a requirement that decisions should be taken in a chapter meeting, and it also became the norm for several other types of business to be transacted there. Decisions about the admission of postulants were, in most orders, to be made at chapters: according to the Templar Customs, for example, in normal circumstances the master 'ought not to admit brothers without a chapter'.[9] The dispensing of justice was also usually the preserve of chapters, which – as in monasteries – acted as chapters of faults. In practice this activity probably took up a considerable portion of the time of local chapter meetings. New legislation was normally enacted in the general chapter of an order. Although the master of the Teutonic order was allowed to grant dispensations from regulations in particular instances, 'he cannot and ought not to revoke them permanently without the consent of the chapter';[10] and it is clear from the wording of most surviving sets of statutes that they were issued at general chapters. Codes of customs were, admittedly, not necessarily promulgated by chapters, but they did not – at least in theory – constitute new law. Of the Hospital's *Usances* it was stated that 'although these usages have not been decreed by chapter, the *prudhommes* of the house wanted to set them down as the usage and custom of our house'.[11] In the Temple the master was not allowed to make war or peace without the counsel of his convent, and, in many orders, officials were not allowed to act alone in alienating property: decisions on this issue usually had to be made at a meeting either of the central convent or of a general chapter. A decree stating that the approval of the general chapter must be obtained for alienations was issued by Santiago in 1265, and the statutes of the Teutonic order rule that 'possessions of the house ought not to be sold by the master or by commanders acting on his behalf or by ordinary brethren without the consent of the principal chapter.'[12] Similar regulations in the Temple led the castellan of Monzón in 1284 to inform the Aragonese Union that it was illegal to subject the men or possessions of the Temple to anyone except by the special order of the master and central convent; and when, eight years later, the Aragonese Templars were seeking to sell or exchange the lordships of La Zaida and Puigreig, they first obtained permission from the master and central convent.

General and provincial chapters were also the occasions when dues were normally paid and accounts rendered. Thus surviving summonses to the Aragonese provincial chapter of the Temple required commanders to bring their responsions to that assembly. Extraordinary financial demands could, however, be made at other times. Although a Hospitaller decree, issued in 1265, stated that a prior could impose extra taxes provided that he sought counsel from his annual chapter, this ruling was hardly enforceable if an order's financial situation demanded immediate action. Heads of provinces were likely to find themselves in the position of an Aragonese provincial master of the Temple who, at the turn of the thirteenth and fourteenth centuries, commanded one of his subordinates to

> bring to the commander of Gardeny as soon as you have received this letter all the money in your possession, whatever it is for, and any that you can lay hands on, as we have great need of it for a payment which we have to make.[13]

Summonses to Templar provincial chapters in Aragon also instructed commanders to bring to the chapter statements giving details of movable goods in their convents, and the statutes of the Teutonic order similarly required heads of houses to present accounts at the provincial chapter, while according to Hospitaller regulations, all leading officials present at a general chapter were to report on their terms of office. It was at provincial or general chapters that officials normally had their performance assessed.

In some orders the submission of reports was linked with the periodic surrender of offices. The statutes of the Teutonic order show that the annual resignation of offices was to occur at provincial or general chapters, and the Hospitaller Customs mention the delivering up of seals by leading office-holders at the general chapter. Chapter meetings were therefore also occasions when appointments were commonly made. Leading central officials and heads of provinces were named either in a general chapter of an order or at meetings of the central convent. The Customs of the Teutonic order, for example, rule that

> the master and convent will together nominate and change the grand commander, the marshal, the hospitaller, the *drapier*, the treasurer and the castellan of Montfort . . . Provincial preceptors of Armenia, Achaea, Sicily, Apulia, Germany, Austria, Prussia, Livonia and Spain are to be appointed and removed by the master with the consent of the principal chapter.[14]

Among those nominated in the general chapter of Santiago were members of the *Trece*, and some appointments to *encomiendas* also appear to have been made there. It was more common for heads of convents to be chosen at provincial chapters, although this was clearly not a fixed requirement. Although the Templar Customs refer to the appointing of commanders at these assemblies, and although some Templar commanders took up or laid down office when their provincial chapter was in session, it is not difficult to find examples of Templar appointments at this level which were made by provincial masters outside chapter meetings. And that not all commanders in the Teutonic order were selected in provincial chapters is apparent from a mid-thirteenth-century decree which states that the master of Prussia could appoint commanders with the counsel of the convent of Elbing, the chief house in the province.

Although commanders were not necessarily appointed at provincial chapters, at all levels assemblies had an important role to play. On some issues, such as the judging of faults and the admission of recruits, those presiding at chapter meetings were commonly obliged to accept a majority decision. The customs of the Temple even instructed the master to be obedient to his chapter, and in early thirteenth-century Hospitaller statutes it was decreed that, at the general chapter, nominations to posts were to be decided by a committee on which the master did not sit.

The relationship between officials and chapters was not, of course, a completely static one. On some occasions the former were apparently having their powers curtailed. Attention may be drawn in this context to differences between the Latin rule of the Templars and the later French version. In the Latin rule, the length of the probationary term for recruits was left to 'the judgement and wisdom of the master', which in the French version becomes 'the wisdom of the master and brothers'; and while, according to the Latin rule, a brother who committed a serious offence was to be subject to 'the mercy and judgement of the master', this is changed in the French version to 'the mercy and judgement of the master and brethren'.[15] Differences may also be noted between the Templar rule and the later Customs of the order. It is clear from the latter that a chapter was to be consulted about the admission of recruits and the alienation of property, but in the rule the summoning of all brothers to discuss these matters was left to the master's discretion. Yet the significance of such changes should not be exaggerated. They may not represent a deliberate attempt to restrict the powers of officials and may be stating merely what had usually happened in practice. And in the earliest surviving sources for most orders, officials were already subject to considerable restrictions.

There were, however, occasions when officials did clash with their subordinates, although less is known of conflicts within provinces than of disputes involving masters of orders and central convents or general chapters. Certainly most documents issued by heads of houses or of provinces were said to have been drawn up with the counsel or consent of other brothers, and they often bear the *signa* of these brethren. But *signa* were not usually made by brothers themselves, and statements about counsel may in some instances have been no more than repetitions of customary formulae. That some provincial officials omitted to seek counsel is suggested by a Hospitaller ruling, issued in 1270, which decreed that in every priory there is to be a seal, which is to bear the name of the prior, and it is to be placed in a box or chest, to which there are to be four keys; the prior is to hold one, and the other three are to be in the keeping of three *prudhommes* of the priory, each of them having one, so that the prior cannot seal anything with the said seal without the counsel of the *prudhommes* of the priory.[16]

Conflicts involving masters are recorded most fully in Hospitaller sources, although there was also dissension in the order of Santiago during the mastership of Pelayo Pérez Correa in the middle decades of the thirteenth century, and at the beginning of the next century, Godfrey of Hohenlohe, the master of the Teutonic order, was forced to resign. In the Hospital, as in other orders, conflicts seem to have been marked not so much by attempts to impose new restrictions on the master's theoretical powers as by efforts to ensure that he did not rule arbitrarily and that he pursued acceptable policies. In some instances it was felt – even if only in the short term – that these ends were to be achieved by obliging masters to take counsel. The crisis which led to the resignation around the year 1170 of the Hospitaller master Gilbert of Assailly appears to have been occasioned by the serious financial situation in which the order found itself, partly as a result of Gilbert's enthusiastic support for plans to conquer Egypt. At one stage the convent declared that it was prepared to accept him back provided that

he amended his conduct in numerous respects: he should not accept castles and strongholds on the frontiers with the Turks; he should not burden the house with superfluous and needless expense; and he should not undertake important business without the knowledge of the brethren and chapter.[17]

During the same crisis, Alexander III also expressed opposition to arbitrary action when he ruled in 1172 that the master who was then to be elected should promise to observe the ancient customs and statutes of the Hospital and should not make important decisions without the counsel of his chapter. The issue of counsel was raised again a century later, when the general chapter decreed in 1278 that a new seal should be made in the name of both the master and the convent. This seal was to be used to authenticate documents recording transactions and decisions in which the convent was supposed to participate, and it was to be kept by the treasurer under the seals of the master and several leading officials. The use of the master's own seal was being restricted, and although the detailed background to the decree is not known, the purpose of the enactment was clearly to ensure that counsel was taken before documents were issued on important matters. As a Hospitaller commentator explained a few decades later, the statute was drawn up 'so that nothing should be sealed which was not agreed with the counsel and by the advice of the *prudhommes*'.[18] Criticism of the Hospitaller master was, however, again being voiced less than twenty years later. In 1295, it was claimed that

> the good usages and beneficial statutes, through which the order used in the past to be illuminated and made resplendent, have become so corrupted and weakened that they are maintained not as they ought to be but only at pleasure

and in the same year Boniface VIII informed the master Odo of Pins that he had received complaints that the latter had acted 'too inappropriately and profitlessly, by not observing the praiseworthy customs, the honourable statutes and the fitting and proper decrees of your religion and your order'.[19] To ensure that the master did not rule arbitrarily, it was proposed that the government of the order should be entrusted to a group of diffinitors, which would include the master. Yet this plan was not implemented, and a few years later the continued residence in the West of the new master, William of Villaret, provoked fresh conflict with the convent in the East.

Yet, although a number of Hospitaller masters who were thought to have abused their authority were called to account, the need to do this implies that in practice these officials usually enjoyed a considerable freedom of action. The central convent seems, in fact, to have been slow in checking misconduct: thus a letter, which it sent to William of Villaret in 1296, lists a series of abuses perpetrated not only by his immediate predecessor, Odo of Pins, but also by other recent masters.

It might, of course, be argued that recalcitrant officials could not always be easily restrained. Some chapters had no seals of their own: an agreement in 1248, for example, concerning Hospitaller rights over certain churches in Portugal was sealed with the prior's seal 'because we brothers have no common seal'.[20] The majority of surviving seals are, in fact, personal, not corporate ones. Provincial and general chapters in any case met infrequently and lacked continuity of membership. There was also a common absence of established procedures for the disciplining of officials by their subordinates. The right of the *Trece* in Santiago not only to elect the master but also to remove him, if he was found to be pernicious or useless, was unusual. And some regulations did allow leading officials considerable latitude: in the rule of the Teutonic order, the master and other officials were instructed to accept the view of the wiser part of the brethren, 'but which is to be reckoned the wiser part, when there is a difference of opinion, is to be left to the judgement of the master or his deputy'.[21] Yet even when checks existed they were not always utilised. The Hospitaller statute enacted in 1278 was clearly not used to keep an effective check on the master, for in 1302 the general chapter had to decree that documents to be sealed with the conventual seal should be read, examined and sealed in the presence of the grand commander, marshal, hospitaller and treasurer, and it was at the same time thought necessary to state that these officials should not absent themselves unless they were sick. There appears in practice to have been a reluctance to subject officials to constant supervision.

In adopting this stance, brethren were probably influenced both by their monastic inheritance and by the example of the secular world. The vow of obedience exacted from every recruit must have exercised a restraining influence, especially when severe penalties were threatened for disobedience. Those holding authority in military orders were, moreover, assigned the paternal role traditionally ascribed to abbots: in 1299, the Hospitaller central convent, despite its differences with William of Villaret, could still address him as their spiritual father and refer to themselves as his children. In the secular world there was commonly a reluctance to impose permanent restraints on rulers. The demands which gave rise to concessions such as the Provisions of Oxford in 1258 in England, or the *Privilegio de la Unión* in Aragon in 1287, were short-lived responses to unpopular or unsuccessful policies, and were of little lasting significance. A monarchical form of government was the accepted norm. It is, therefore, not surprising that, until the situation became serious, those holding office in military orders enjoyed a considerable freedom of action.

These officials in turn, however, could not always exercise close supervision over their subordinates. Heads of provinces and masters of orders both faced difficulties, although the problems confronting the latter were the greater. Whereas provinces were relatively small and compact, masters of the leading orders were trying to exercise authority throughout western Christendom, and the situation was made worse by the fact that the headquarters of these orders were not situated centrally but at the eastern extremity of western Christendom. It should also be remembered that brethren were usually natives of the provinces in which they resided, and there was the danger that local loyalties would conflict with those to a master, especially when provinces were coterminous with kingdoms or principalities. At all levels, efficient government was also endangered by ignorance on the part of those in authority. This often resulted from the common medieval failure to keep adequate records: a decree issued by the Hospitaller general chapter in 1262, for example, indicates that not all priors had registers of properties and rents in their priories. Nevertheless, the main problem concerned the means of control and supervision.

One solution was to oblige subordinate officials to refer decisions to the centre, as often happened concerning the alienation of property. But, given the distances involved, this could not become a general requirement: subordinate officials had to be allowed a considerable freedom of action. In the later thirteenth century, however, it was not unknown for the central authorities of an order to appoint to commanderies within provinces, while subordinate offices were also at times retained in the hands of leading officials: in 1296, it was claimed that Hospitaller masters had kept some priories under their direct control, although it was more commonly commanderies which were held in this way by either masters or heads of provinces. But the purpose of the first practice seems to have been the rewarding of favourites, and a financial motive lay behind the second. Other means were used to maintain control and exercise supervision.

No doubt those in authority sought in the first place to ensure that trustworthy brothers were appointed to subordinate posts.

But, when making their choices, they were sometimes subjected to outside pressures, and in some instances local opinion within an order was taken into account when positions were filled: in 1307, the Templar master informed the Aragonese king that

> it is an established custom that when any preceptor of a province dies the brothers of the province, after informing the master of what has happened, advise according to their knowledge and opinion about the appointment of a new ruler for the province.[22]

In fact, most Templar provincial masters in Aragon had their origins in that province and therefore had local ties and loyalties. But the appointment of outsiders would itself have created difficulties, not least because of language differences; and there was a case for nominating brothers who were known to be acceptable to their future subordinates. Those in authority also sought to maintain control by keeping terms of office relatively short and by obliging office-holders to account regularly. Again, because of distance, however, the heads of many provinces in the leading orders could not be summoned out to the East very frequently.

A third means was visitation, undertaken both by heads of provinces and by – or on behalf of – masters of orders. Although no visitation records survive from the period under discussion, visitation was clearly an established practice in all the leading orders. A Hospitaller survey compiled in 1338, for example, shows that in that year the English prior spent 121 days visiting houses in his priory, spending up to three days at each. It was not so easy for masters of the leading orders to undertake comprehensive visitations. Although Templar and Hospitaller masters occasionally journeyed to the West, and although masters of the Teutonic order spent a considerable amount of time there, the heads of these orders were obviously unable to carry out a regular visitation of all their provinces in person. The task was therefore usually delegated. In the Temple up to the middle of the thirteenth century, visitation of western provinces seems to have been a function of the master *deça mer*, who is mentioned intermittently in the surviving sources: the post does not seem to have been in continuous existence. His authority presumably embraced all the European provinces. After 1250, however, he was replaced by visitors with rather more limited responsibilities. Thus one visitor exercised authority in the Iberian peninsula and was, in fact, often the head of one of the Spanish provinces. At the turn of the thirteenth and fourteenth centuries the post was held by the Aragonese provincial master Berenguer of Cardona, and the master of the order gave him complete authority

> over all our houses, namely the power to visit our houses and brothers in all the five kingdoms of Spain, to sell, alienate and exchange our property, and to enter into and carry out obligations, placing the same brother Berenguer of Cardona, the aforementioned visitor, in our place in all and each of the aforesaid matters, and granting him the power to undertake each and all of the things which we, the master and convent, could undertake in each and all of the aforesaid matters.[23]

Berenguer was clearly acting as the master's deputy in Spain, and his powers went beyond those merely of visitation; but, although in all his work he could be regarded as maintaining the authority of the master and central convent, the appointment of a local man could also be seen as marking in practice a decentralisation of power. In the Hospital, the equivalent post in Western Europe was that of grand commander. Some who held this position were called grand commander 'beyond the sea' or 'in overseas parts', while others were linked in their titles with a particular region; but it is difficult to perceive any clear-cut pattern of development, such as occurred in the Temple. The situation in the order of Santiago is a little clearer, for the rule states that at the general chapter 'visitors are to be chosen who are to visit the houses of brothers throughout the year; they are to return to the chapter on the appointed day and are to see that they inform the master and chapter of the state of the brethren and of the houses';[24] and the records of some thirteenth-century chapters name the visitors who, in groups of two or three, were to undertake the visitation of houses in various regions of the peninsula. Since, however, the obligation to appoint visitors in the chapter each year was reiterated in capitular decrees on more than one occasion in the 1270s, it is possible that the system of visitation in Santiago was then breaking down.

This is not the only example of the apparent collapse of systems of control. It was said of William of Villaret in 1299 that although he should have reported to the Hospital's headquarters six times during his thirty years as prior of St Gilles, he had, in fact, journeyed out to the East only twice; and that the system of recalling Hospitaller priors was not working effectively is further suggested by a decree issued in 1301, which stated that two or more priors should be recalled each year, and particularly those who had been away longest. Yet if those in authority had difficulty in maintaining close supervision of subordinates, attempts to assert local independence seem to have been few. Although in the first decade of the fourteenth century it was agreed in the Teutonic order that two local nominations should be made for the posts of master in Prussia, Livonia and Germany, those put forward were to be presented to the order's master and general chapter, and the final decision still rested with these. The most serious difficulties appear to have been encountered by the order of Santiago in Portugal. Problems there came to a head in the reign of Dinis, during which the *comendador mayor* of Portugal proclaimed himself master in the kingdom: the authority of the head of the whole order was to be limited in Portugal to the right of visitation. The justification advanced for this step was that Portuguese *encomiendas* had been despoiled for the benefit of those in Castile. With the support of the Crown, the *comendador mayor* gained his objectives, and from 1330 the Portuguese branch of Santiago was independent of the rest of the order. But this development was exceptional.

The intervention by Dinis is, however, by no means the only example of outside interference in the internal affairs of a military order. Influence was exerted from various quarters, both lay and ecclesiastical. Least significant in this respect was the role of the episcopate. The leading military orders, like many monasteries, gained exemption from episcopal jurisdiction, and although bishops not infrequently sought to pass sentence on brethren of these orders, they did not normally try to interfere in matters of internal administration. Lesser orders were not always so independent. St Thomas of Acre claimed exemption from episcopal jurisdiction, but in 1279 Archbishop Pecham of Canterbury was taking action against its London house for refusing to submit itself to visitation, and throughout the fourteenth century the London house was included in diocesan visitations.

All orders, of course, remained subject to the papacy, although there appear to have been no decisions which had to be referred to the Pope. At times, the papacy admittedly gave rulings on proposed changes in regulations, as Boniface VIII did in 1295 when the Hospitallers wanted to amend rules on food and silence, but papal assent does not seem to have been essential, for changes were also made without reference to the Pope. The papacy did intervene, however, when it considered that there were matters which needed correction. Numerous letters have survived from the second half of the thirteenth century in which popes ordered the recovery of rights which had been alienated or granted away on terms which were unfavourable to the orders, and there was inevitably concern to ensure that standards within convents were maintained and abuses remedied. Gregory IX, for example, reprimanded the Hospitallers in 1238 after receiving reports that they were keeping prostitutes in their houses and neglecting the vow of chastity. Attempts were also made to remove officials who were thought unfit for office. In 1262, Urban IV ordered that Stephen of Sissy should be deprived of his post as Templar marshal because of his unworthiness; and although Stephen argued that the Pope had no right to meddle in Templar appointments, and maintained his resistance up till Urban's death, Clement IV did achieve his dismissal. Clement IV's pontificate also provides examples of interference in appointments for other reasons. In 1268, he wrote to the master of the Hospital, seeking a post in that order for a papal chamberlain who was a Hospitaller: on this occasion a favour was being asked for a protégé. Two years earlier, political considerations had been uppermost in Clement's mind when he had sought to secure the appointment of the Templar Amaury of Roche and the Hospitaller Philip of Egly as heads of provinces in south Italy and Sicily: these were candidates supported by Charles of Anjou, who was then establishing his authority in the south at the expense of the last Hohenstaufen claimants; and two years later the Pope thwarted the Hospital's attempts to remove Philip of Egly from his post in the southern kingdom. But there was nothing very exceptional in the papal attitude to the military orders: popes intervened in similar ways in the affairs of other religious establishments.

Some Spanish military orders were subject not only to the papacy but also to other religious foundations, and formed part of the Cistercian family. Several had direct ties with the Cistercians.

The order of Calatrava sprang from the monastery of Fitero and in 1164 received approval from the Cistercian general chapter. In the 1170s, Mountjoy also established ties with Cîteaux, and Trujillo was mentioned in Cistercian statutes issued in 1190, while in 1273 the chapter accepted the affiliation of Santa María de España at the request of the Castilian king, Alfonso X. In the case of Calatrava the establishment of ties can be explained by the circumstances of the order's foundation, and Trujillo may have been seeking to achieve independence of Pereiro. In other instances affiliation may have been seen as a means of securing the future of a newly-created order. If this was so, hopes were not fulfilled, and Calatrava was, in fact, the only military order which had lasting direct ties with the Cistercians.

Orders which had links with the Cistercians were subject to the general chapter of Cîteaux, which exercised legislative, administrative and judicial powers. The chapter used its legislative authority mainly in the early stages of a relationship: it was in the 1170s, for example, that Mountjoy was allowed by the chapter to depart to a certain extent from normal Cistercian observances. But the records of the Cistercian chapter show that on judicial and administrative matters it took a continuing interest in the affairs of Calatrava, at times devoting a considerable amount of attention to what might seem trivial issues. In 1216, the master of Calatrava was ordered by the chapter to give satisfaction to the viscount of Fronsac concerning a horse which some of his knights were alleged to have stolen. The matter was raised again in the chapter of 1217, and in the following year the master was threatened with a penance of bread and water if he did not comply within a certain time; finally, in 1219, the master was instructed to pay the value of the horse. Yet while this case illustrates the vigilance of the chapter, it also indicates that the master of Calatrava was not always an obedient servant.

Military orders linked to the Cistercians were also the daughters – though adopted rather than natural ones – of Cistercian monasteries. In 1187, Calatrava was affiliated to the abbey of Morimond, and three years later Trujillo was made subject to Moreruela, while in 1273 Sta María de España became a daughter of Grandselve. The relationship established in this way was similar to that which obtained between Cistercian monasteries. Thus the Cistercian general chapter ruled that the brothers of Calatrava should be sons of Morimond, and that the abbot and the aforesaid house should have the right of filiation over them, just as Cîteaux is known to have over Morimond, namely authority to carry out annual visitations, to set up a master who is to be in the place of an abbot, to remove him, to correct faults which occur, to punish excesses and the like.[25]

Little information has survived of visitations up to the end of the thirteenth century, although Guy of Morimond is known to have visited Calatrava in 1195, when he granted the Cistercian abbot of San Pedro de Gomiel the right to carry out visitations in his place, and one set of regulations (*difiniciones*) for Calatrava – issued presumably during a visitation – has survived from the period 1196–1213. From these it is clear that visitors were concerned with economic administration as well as with the quality of conventual life, for officials – including the master of Calatrava – were ordered to render accounts during visitations. The maintenance of Calatrava's property was the purpose of a further ruling in this set of *difiniciones* which stated that no possessions were to be alienated without the counsel of the visitor as well as of the chapter; and that later visitors sought to enforce this regulation is apparent from a Cistercian decree issued in 1260, which reports that the abbot of Morimond had intervened when the master of Calatrava proposed to alienate several castles to the Castilian king, Alfonso X.

Whereas the powers listed in the ruling concerning Morimond and Calatrava corresponded to those which Cistercian abbots normally exercised over daughter houses, in the case of military orders the abbot of a mother house also had the right to appoint a prior who was responsible for the spiritual welfare of brethren in the daughter foundation and who acted as a permanent representative of the abbot. Yet the authority of priors, who were often foreign monks, was not always readily accepted. About the year 1234 it was claimed that the prior named by the abbot of Morimond was causing dissension in the order of Calatrava because of his ignorance of the country's customs; and thirty years later some chaplains were refusing to make their profession to the prior of Calatrava, whom they did not regard as a member of their order. The abbot of Morimond nevertheless retained his right of nomination.

The links between some military orders and Cistercian monasteries were paralleled by the affiliation of the orders of Avis and Alcántara to Calatrava itself. Ties between these two foundations and Calatrava had apparently been established by 1187, when Gregory VIII included the places of Evora and Pereiro – where the two orders were then based – among the possessions of Calatrava. The authority which the head of Calatrava enjoyed included in the first place the right – it was also, however, an obligation – of annual visitation. Thus, when the master of Calatrava was visiting Avis in 1238, he decreed that 'the master of Calatrava is to visit the house of Avis each year in person or through a deputy according to the custom of the order'.[26] He also then ruled that no master of Avis was to be elected unless the head of Calatrava or his representative was present, and that during a vacancy in the mastership of Avis its members were to be subject to the master of Calatrava. An agreement drawn up in 1218 similarly mentioned Calatrava's right to visit Alcántara, though according to that document the brethren of the latter order were to be allowed to appoint their own prior.

Lastly, military orders were subject to interference from secular powers, especially kings. It has already been seen that the transport of supplies to the East from western provinces was sometimes impeded by European monarchs, and they also at times restricted the movement of brethren. In 1275, the English king, Edward I, ordered the Hospitaller prior of Ireland not to go out to the East, even though he had been summoned by the master of the order. The king wanted him in Ireland and sought to enforce his will by the threatened seizure of Hospitaller lands there. Secular rulers, like popes, also interested themselves in appointments, and for some of the same reasons. In 1299, Edward I was seeking a post for a Hospitaller whose kinsman had rendered service to the king, while in the aftermath of the Sicilian Vespers, the Aragonese king was attempting to secure the appointment of a Templar provincial master who could be relied upon to support the Crown. Royal protégés were clearly not automatically accepted, for in 1290 and 1307 the candidates put forward by Aragonese kings for the post of Templar provincial master were not appointed; but the Templars, who could not afford to forfeit royal favour, did on both occasions nominate a provincial master who was known to be acceptable to the

Aragonese crown. There is no evidence to suggest, however, that royal interference in appointments was a regular occurrence, as it was with regard to some other posts in the Church. Secular influence in the internal affairs of military orders was usually of only minor significance, although in Spain several attempts were made by kings to have the headquarters of Spanish orders located in their own kingdoms; but their objective appears to have been merely to ensure that resources and manpower were not diverted to other regions of the peninsula.

Ranks

IT has already been seen that members of military orders were grouped into several ranks. Yet, although all of these orders had clerical as well as lay brethren, the lay groupings were not everywhere the same. The threefold division of knights, sergeants-at-arms and non-military sergeants – these were called *frères des mestiers* in the Temple and *frères d'office* in the Hospital – is encountered only in the three leading orders. Sergeants are mentioned in documents of the order of Santiago, but there is no evidence to indicate that they comprised two groups; and there are no references at all to sergeants in the sources for Calatrava. This foundation appears to have been influenced by its links with the Cistercians, for in statutes drawn up at the turn of the twelfth and thirteenth centuries a distinction was made between brother knights (*fratres milites*) and *conversi*, and it is possible that these groupings also existed in other orders which had ties with the Cistercians. Military orders were, perhaps surprisingly, more uniform in their acceptance of women. Although the Templar rule, claiming that 'the ancient enemy has driven many from the straight path to paradise through their consorting with women',[27] forbade the admission of sisters, references occur during the twelfth and thirteenth centuries to women who in various Western countries adopted a religious way of life by associating themselves with a Templar convent. Sisters were also admitted to the Teutonic order, as well as to the Hospital, Calatrava, Santiago and the order of the Faith and Peace.

In their early years, however, orders usually comprised a small body of brethren among whom no distinctions were made. Ranks were introduced as membership grew. While in some orders references to sisters occur at a relatively early stage, among brethren it is usually the distinction between lay and clerical members that is first apparent. Groupings among lay brethren become discernible more slowly, partly because chaplains were the only brothers whose rank was commonly noted in charters and other documents. The distinction between lay and clerical brethren in the order of Santiago is found in Alexander III's confirmation of the foundation issued in 1175, only five years after the order was established, but sergeants are not mentioned in surviving sources until the thirteenth century. In the order of Calatrava, brothers' spiritual needs were at first attended to by monks from Fitero, but in 1164 – only six years after the order's foundation – the Cistercian general chapter referred to 'chaplains who have made their profession in your house'.[28] The distinction between knights and *conversi*, on the other hand, is not found until the turn of the twelfth and thirteenth centuries. There were clerics in the Hospital long before it became a military order, even though the right to admit them was not formally conceded by the papacy until 1154, but groupings among lay brethren only slowly become apparent. Although the term *miles* may have been used in one document in 1148 to signify a rank in the order, and although brethren-at-arms are mentioned in statutes issued in 1182, the threefold grouping of lay brethren is first explicitly mentioned in capitular decrees issued in the first decade of the thirteenth century.

In the thirteenth century, distinctions of rank in part reflected social differences. As has been seen, knights were expected to be of knightly descent, while sergeants and chaplains had to be free-men. Knightly recruits to the Temple were asked: 'Are you a knight and the son of a knight, or are you descended from knights on your father's side, so that you can and ought to be a knight?'[29] The same restriction was implied by a Hospitaller statute of 1262, which stated that no one was to be received as a knight of the order unless his parentage made him worthy of the rank, and a Santiago decree issued between 1271 and 1274 stated more explicitly that a knightly recruit must be of noble rank (*omne fidalgo*).

Knightly descent does not, however, appear to have been demanded of those seeking admission as knights before the thirteenth century. Freedom from serfdom is the only social requirement mentioned in twelfth-century sources. In this context it may be pointed out that, although by the twelfth century the term *miles* was becoming an indication of rank as well as of function in the secular world, secular laws restricting knighthood to those of knightly descent belong to the thirteenth rather than to the twelfth century. No doubt many of those who became knights in a military order in the twelfth century belonged to families which could be described as knightly, but knightly descent was apparently not an essential qualification for admission to the rank of knight at that time.

When distinctions of rank began to be made in military orders, they were at first based on function rather than family origins. Chaplains were mainly concerned with spiritual matters, while non-military sergeants were employed in various tasks within convents or on the land. Knights and sergeants-at-arms did not, of course, differ in function, but here the orders were apparently adopting a distinction made in the secular world, which at that time probably had its basis in wealth. The group to which a fighting brother was assigned in the twelfth century presumably depended on his earlier military status, which was in turn determined by his material standing.

One witness at the Templar trial asserted that sergeants had originally been paid employees, and that it was financial hardship which had led the Temple to accept them as brethren. The rank of brother sergeant emerged, however, at a time when the Temple was rapidly increasing its possessions. The creation of new ranks in military orders probably occurred when the needs of expanding institutions justified them and also when a wider range of applicants sought to join what had originally been a small coherent group. When Innocent II confirmed the Temple's right to admit clerics he explained that he was doing this so that 'you shall lack nothing for the fulness of salvation and the care of your souls':[30] it was thought advantageous to have chaplains who were members of the order rather than to rely exclusively on secular priests. The rule of the Teutonic order explains the acceptance of women by stating that 'some work with the sick in hospitals and with animals is more suited to the female sex',[31] although it should not be assumed that all sisters were engaged in work of these kinds or were admitted for these reasons. Elsewhere their acceptance seems to have been a response to external pressure, for it was not uncommon for women to adopt a life of piety and devotion in the vicinity of a church or beside a male religious house. It was not, however, thought appropriate that squires – the personal atten- dants of knights – should be admitted as brethren: these were always seculars.

It has been seen that, in the early fourteenth century, sergeants formed the largest group in the Temple and Hospital; but they were also the least privileged brethren in military orders. In the Temple, for example, only knights were allowed to wear white clothing. This colour was originally adopted not as the mark of a particular rank – at the time there were none – but so that 'those who have abandoned a tenebrous life may be reminded by their pure white habit that they have been reconciled with their creator'.[32] The white habit was not, however, allowed to other ranks when these were established, except in the case of chaplains who rose to the episcopate; and when the Teutonic order adopted Templar customs, white was said to be 'a symbol of knight- hood'.[33] In the order of Santiago no distinctions of colour were made in dress, but in 1259 it was decreed that only knightly and clerical brethren should be allowed to wear the sign of the scallop, which was the emblem of Santiago pilgrims.

The chapter of Santiago at the same time ruled that priests and knights should take precedence over other brethren in processions, in chapel, in chapter and at table. In the Temple there was similarly a ruling that knights and chaplains should be seated first at table, while sergeants were to wait for a second bell before sitting. It was usually assumed, however, that all brethren would receive the same food.

In some orders, special consideration was shown to chaplains who erred. In the Temple and the Teutonic order, clerics who were being punished were not expected to work alongside the slaves, as lay brethren were, and they were to be beaten in private; while in the Teutonic order, chaplains undergoing penance also fasted in private. Rules and codes of customs also often include more general injunctions commanding that clerical brethren should be honoured, and in some documents issued by military orders respect was shown to clerics by listing them before lay brothers.

It was commonly envisaged, however, that the government and administration of a military order would be in the hands of lay brethren and that clerical members would normally restrict themselves to spiritual matters. When Innocent II confirmed the Templars' right to admit clerics in 1139, he stated that 'they are not to be allowed to intrude themselves rashly into your chapter and into the government of your house, but only to the extent that they are commanded by you';[34] and similar statements were included in later papal bulls to the Hospital and the Teutonic order. Yet, if lay brethren were expected to predominate, it is necessary to assess the relative importance of knights and sergeants in government, and to consider whether in practice ordained brothers were concerned only with spiritual affairs, and also what powers were allowed to sisters.

The ranks of those who held office provide a first indication of the significance of each group. Leading posts in central administration were usually in the hands of knights. Already, in 1139, Innocent II had decreed that the master of the Temple should be a *militaris* person and, since by this time there were both knights and sergeants in the order, he was presumably using the term in the sense of a knight. The same word was employed in 1220, in a similar letter issued by Honorius III concerning the Teutonic order; while in 1231, Gregory IX decreed that the master of the order of the Faith and Peace should likewise be a knight. It was not until 1262 that the Hospitallers issued a statute requiring their master to be of knightly rank, but this ruling was, no doubt, merely confirming existing practice. Yet, although the office of master became the preserve of knights, the rule of Santiago decreed that during magisterial vacancies, authority should rest with the leading prior, who was a cleric. No explicit rulings have survived concerning other leading central offices: it has been claimed that, in the Hospital, by 1270 such posts could be held only by knights, but the statutes of that year ruled merely that capitular bailiffs should be of legitimate birth. It may be presumed, however, that the main offices of central government were normally held by knights. This is implied by a clause in the Templar Customs which states that:

There are five brother sergeants who each ought to have two mounts, namely the sub-marshal, the standardbearer, the brother cook of the convent, the farrier of the convent and the commander of the Vault of the sea at Acre. And each of these five can have two mounts and one squire: no other brother sergeant should have more than one mount.[35]

These were the posts which were usually held by sergeants. The more important officials – such as the seneschal, marshal and *drapier* – were expected to be knights, although records of the Templar trial in Cyprus reveal that the lesser offices of infirmarer and almoner were at least on some occasions also occupied by sergeants.

The clause which has been quoted from the Templar Customs also implies that sergeants were not expected to be heads of provinces, and studies of the social origins of provincial masters in various areas confirm that provinces were usually in the charge of knightly brethren. But visitations of provinces were sometimes carried out by clerical brothers. The conventual prior of the Hospital was acting as grand commander in Spain in 1308, and thirteenth-century decrees issued by the general chapter of Santiago reveal that the visitors appointed for the various kingdoms of the Iberian peninsula often – though not always – included a clerical brother. That there was a role for clerics in this task is apparent from a ruling of the Santiago chapter in the early 1270s that

in each general chapter visitors – both brother knights and clerics – are to be chosen, who are to carry out a visitation of the whole order faithfully and properly with regard to spiritual as well as to temporal matters.[36]

A number of rulings have survived from the thirteenth century concerning the holding of lesser offices within provinces, and these tended to favour knights. Santiago decreed on several occasions that only brothers who were *fidalgos* could hold castles; the Templar Customs ruled that sergeants could not be commanders of knights or hold chapters in places where there were knights; and a restriction on Hospitaller chaplains was imposed in 1283, when it decreed that clerical brothers could not hold bailiwicks where the order had the right to inflict a death sentence.

In practice, convents which housed only clerics were normally under the control of an ordained brother, and sisters' houses were subject to a prioress. This meant that brethren were sometimes

under the authority of a sister, for brothers were often seconded to
female houses to carry out necessary tasks, and at Sigena in
Aragon there were adjacent Hospitaller communities of brethren
and sisters which formed a single convent under the authority of
the prioress. It is more difficult to discover the ranks of those in
charge of convents which mainly housed lay brethren. Although
the repetition of the Santiago decree about the holding of castles
suggests that it was not fully implemented, for more· precise
information it is necessary to rely on Templar and Hospitaller
sources from the early fourteenth century. In Aragon at that time,
most heads of Templar convents were knights: of twenty-four
commanders holding office between 1300 and 1307 whose ranks
can be traced from sources concerning the Templar trial, twenty
were knights and four were sergeants: no chaplains are known to
have had charge of convents. At the beginning of the fourteenth
century, the Aragonese Templars still had a military role; and in
other areas where orders were engaged in fighting, local administration was probably also dominated by knights. Yet evidence
from Western kingdoms in which orders had no military responsibilities suggests that in these the knightly element was less
important than in the Iberian peninsula. Although the records
of the Templar trial in France show that the proportion of
knightly commanders was higher than that of knightly brethren,
the majority of commanders were sergeants, and a small number
of posts in local administration were held by chaplains. This
French evidence is, admittedly, fragmentary, and not all of those
who bore the title of commander or preceptor were heads of
convents. Yet it does not seem to have been the normal Templar
practice to reserve certain posts within French provinces for
knights. Knights and sergeants often succeeded each other in
the same office: about the year 1304, for example, the sergeant
Laurence of Beaune became commander of Epailly in Burgundy,
where a few years earlier the knight Hugh of Chalon had held
office. In the same way, the chaplain Robert of St Just was
appointed in the last decade of the thirteenth century as commander of Sommereux, an office earlier held by the knight Walter
of Esta. It may also be noted that some of the most important
posts within Templar provinces in France were at times filled by
sergeants. The last preceptor of the Templar house in Paris was
the sergeant Peter of Tortainville, and the last three Templars in

charge of the bailiwick of Ponthieu were all sergeants. Similarly in 1338, the thirty-four Hospitaller commanderies in the British Isles were by no means all under the control of knights: seventeen were held by sergeants and four by chaplains.

Such appointments meant that knights were sometimes subject to superiors who were either sergeants or chaplains. When the sergeant Peter of Sevrey held the commandery of Bure shortly before the Templars' arrest, the knight Hugh of Chalon occupied a subordinate post within that commandery; and, during the Templar trial, Robert of Reinheval stated that he had made his profession at Loison before a knight who was acting on the orders of John of Villeneuve, the sergeant commander of Ponthieu. This situation is also encountered in the Hospital in England in 1338. Of the seventeen sergeants then holding commanderies, six had authority over one or more knightly brothers, and in one instance a knight was subject to a commander who was a chaplain. At Quenington, in Gloucestershire, where two knights and a sergeant resided, it was the latter who was the commander, and similarly at Greenham in Berkshire, the sergeant Roger of Draycote was in charge and not his colleague, the knight Robert Brayboef. Despite the decrees issued in the thirteenth century, rank was not a significant factor in determining appointments within Templar and Hospitaller provinces which were remote from the borders of Christendom. It is clear that offices in these districts were not always given when possible to knightly brethren: in 1338, fifteen knights were resident in the thirty-four Hospitaller commanderies in the British Isles in addition to the thirteen knightly commanders. Nor can it be argued that all fifteen were too old or infirm to perform administrative duties, for only one of them lived in the infirmary which the order maintained at Chippenham. Ability to perform administrative functions, and possibly also a readiness to undertake such responsibilities, appear to have been more important than status in determining which members were appointed to have charge of houses occupied mainly by lay brethren.

A survey of the ranks to which office holders belonged does not, of course, in itself provide a complete picture of the influence wielded by the various groups within military orders. Although clerics and sisters were subject either directly or indirectly to lay brethren, the latter's authority over them was often restricted in several ways. Lay brothers did not always have full control over

clerical appointments. Admittedly, Templar chaplains must have
been assigned to convents by lay superiors, and a Calatravan
decree of the year 1325 refers to clerical brothers 'who, on the
orders of the said master, have been placed as confessors in the
encomiendas'.[37] Yet, in the order of Santiago, the prior of Uclés
appears to have had some say in the allocation of clerics to houses
in Castile, for in 1228 the papal legate John of Abbeville decreed
that, if the master or the commander of Uclés wanted to send one
of the canons of Uclés to a castle, the prior was to be informed and
was to send the brother if he saw fit: the prior appears to have had
a right of veto. And while heads of convents were normally
imposed from above, houses of clerics and of sisters often had
the right to elect their own prior or prioress. The procedure to be
used at the convent of Uclés was defined by John of Abbeville in
1228: the clerics were to meet in chapter and were to choose five
of their number, who were then to sound out the views of
individual members of the community. The five were then to
make a nomination, and if necessary the choice of three out of the
five was to be accepted. A similar procedure was employed to
select prioresses for the Hospitaller house at Sigena. Election *per
compromissum* was, of course, a method commonly adopted in
religious houses, but in 1298 the Hospitaller sisters at Beaulieu
were given the right to choose a prioress 'either by the method of
scrutiny, or by the method of delegation, or in any other just way
in which an election can and ought to be conducted'.[38] As has
been mentioned, the prior of Calatrava was by contrast nominated by the Cistercian abbot of Morimond, but it is not clear
how the Hospital's conventual prior, the order's leading ecclesiastical official, was appointed: it has been suggested that he was
named by the Pope on the advice of the master, but evidence is
lacking.

In some, though not all, orders, restrictions were also placed on
the powers of lay brethren to judge and punish clerics. In the
Temple, an erring chaplain 'ought to cry mercy in his chapter like
any other brother',[39] and he was then judged by a predominantly
lay assembly. In 1220, Honorius III similarly decreed that
chaplains in the Teutonic order should be subject to their
chapter; but, according to thirteenth-century statutes, clerics
were to confess their faults in the chapter before a clerical prior,
though in the presence of the commander, and the prior was to

pass the appropriate sentence. If no prior was resident in the house, the delinquent was to be sent to a neighbouring convent, or alternatively a clerical brother was to be summoned. A clause in the *Esgarts* of the Hospital implies that clerical brethren in that order were normally under the jurisdiction of their ecclesiastical superiors, and it is clear that all clerics in the orders of Santiago and Calatrava were subject to their priors in matters of justice.

In these two orders, priors alone had the power to admit clerical recruits, and in the Hospital, restrictions were placed on the right of male superiors to receive female postulants. Thus, in 1187, Gregory VIII decreed that in the order of Calatrava, chaplains should make their profession before the prior of Calatrava; and the castellan of Amposta – the head of the Hospitallers' Aragonese province – was not allowed to impose sisters on the convents of Sigena and Alguaire; while the Hospitaller prior of Auvergne was obliged to obtain the prioress's consent before placing more sisters at Fieux than were normally allowed.

It should also be remembered that, in spiritual matters, lay brethren were usually subject to their clerical colleagues. Confessions were normally to be made to these, although some exceptions were allowed. A Hospitaller decree, issued in 1262, which ruled that 'without permission from his superior, a brother should not confess his sins to any one except his prior or another brother chaplain of the house',[40] paralleled regulations in the Temple and the Teutonic order. It is, in fact, clear from the records of the Templar trial that confessions were at times made to outsiders, for non-Templar priests – especially friars – testified that they had heard confessions of Templar brethren; and given the frequent lack of chaplains, some confessing to outsiders was inevitable. There were, however, claims that lay officials within military orders arrogated to themselves the functions of priests in this respect. The author of the *Collectio de scandalis ecclesie* was echoing the words of James of Vitry when he wrote that

> though they are laymen they usurp the functions of priests, imposing and relaxing penance for sins at their will, although the keys have not been committed to them and they ought not to exercise the power of binding and loosing.[41]

But this claim was rejected by many Templars during their trial.

It was mainly in the spiritual sphere that ordained brethren possessed powers and rights, although in some orders the beatings decreed in chapters were administered by chaplains. But in Santiago the convents of clerics also had a right to a tenth of the revenues obtained from properties under the control of lay brethren. Although these convents had their own lands, Alexander III decreed in 1175 that this payment should be made so that the clerics 'may acquire books and suitable ornaments for churches and make appropriate provision for their own bodily needs';[42] any surplus was to be devoted to the poor. This arrangement appears, however, to have been peculiar to that order.

To assess the importance of the various ranks, it is further necessary to consider their roles in counselling and decision-making at chapters and other assemblies. The most precise information on this issue concerns magisterial elections, which in some orders were the responsibility of a specially appointed committee. In the Temple, whose procedure was copied by the Teutonic order, the committee was to consist of eight knights, four sergeants and one chaplain. The Hospital appears not to have favoured knights so strongly, for statutes issued in 1206 decreed merely that the first three chosen to sit on the committee of thirteen were to be a priest, a knight and a sergeant; but in practice knights probably wielded the greatest influence. Certainly when a plan for the reform of central government in the Hospital was advanced in 1295, it was proposed that magisterial elections should be in the hands of the seven diffinitors, who were to be knights, and seven other brothers, of whom it was said merely that they could include sergeants and chaplains. Magisterial elections in the order of Santiago were similarly dominated by knights, for masters were chosen by the *Trece*, membership of which was restricted to *fidalgos*.

In chapter meetings of central convents, as in the *Trece*, the knightly element no doubt had the greatest voice, for knights appear to have been in the majority and held the most important offices. It has even been argued that in the Hospital only the brethren-at-arms were regarded as conventual brothers and could attend meetings of the central chapter. It is true that in that order, as in the Temple, a distinction was made between *frères de couvent* and non-military sergeants; and a clause in the Templar

Customs which refers to the taking of counsel from this group might seem to suggest that *frères de couvent* alone sat in the chapter. Yet objections may be raised to this argument. If the phrase *frères de couvent* excluded non-military sergeants, it could also be interpreted to exclude chaplains, for it was often used in a military context. Yet chaplains had a role to play at chapter meetings and their presence was therefore necessary; and as part of the function of a chapter was to serve as a chapter of faults, all brothers would presumably be expected to attend. There is, moreover, no evidence of separate meetings for non-military sergeants: although the Templar Customs mention a special chapter for squires, they make no reference to a chapter for *frères des mestiers*. The section in the Templar Customs on the convening of chapters states, in fact, that all brothers should attend. The term *frères de couvent* may therefore have been used merely to signify the convent as a fighting body, with no governmental implications. Yet, even if all resident brothers were present at chapter meetings of central convents, the influence of non-military sergeants would have been small, and at general chapters as well, brethren of knightly rank predominated. At provincial chapters, however, the situation varied. In the border regions of Christendom the majority of those present were probably knights, but at provincial meetings in kingdoms away from the frontiers of Christendom, sergeants would have had more say. And at chapter meetings in most Templar and Hospitaller convents in the West, sergeants comprised the most numerous group. At all levels, however, sisters and clerical brethren had little voice in assemblies, except in the convents which were set up especially for them.

Dissension between brethren of different ranks was by no means unknown in religious orders during the twelfth and thirteenth centuries. Examples are provided by Sempringham in the 1160s and by Grandmont two decades later. These involved conflicts between lay and clerical brothers, but in military orders there was also scope for discord between lay brethren of different ranks, as well as between brethren and sisters.

Much of the evidence which has survived about relations between lay brethren in military orders makes no specific reference to rank, and focuses on the attitudes displayed by brothers who were of high birth or position. A Templar sergeant who came from the diocese of Clermont thus testified in 1311 that the leading brothers of his order were proud and arrogant. Long before this, it had been considered necessary to include in the rule of Santiago clauses which threatened flogging to those who boasted of their former wealth or high birth and who vilified those of humble origins. In the early thirteenth century, James of Vitry similarly warned that a brother of a military order 'should not take pride in the nobility of his family' and that 'sick and humble brethren and those born of humble parentage are not to be despised'.[43] Some of these comments could, of course, reflect tension between knights and sergeants, and there are a few sources which do explicitly refer to ill-feeling between ranks of lay brethren. During the Templar trial the sergeant John Senandi, who had been commander of La Fouilhouze, said that when he had asked a knight of the order about the practices which supposedly characterised the Templar admission ceremony, he was told that he was too inquisitive, 'for since he was a brother sergeant – and sergeants were despised by knights – he ought to be deaf, mute and blind'.[44] The reference to the admission ceremony is obviously suspect, but the comment about the relations between knights and sergeants is not necessarily to be rejected. The Templar Customs themselves provide a further indication of tensions by stating that:

> When conventual brothers ask *frères des mestiers* for things they need, they should make the request gently and politely; and the *frères des mestiers* should hand over the items to them politely and without fuss or offence, if they have them in stock. If the *frères des mestiers* do not have the items, they should turn down the request gently and politely. If they behave any differently, they should be punished, for such conduct can occasion discord between brothers.[45]

The wording suggests ill-feeling between the military elements and sergeants employed on more menial duties. Distinctions of rank within military orders reflected those of society at large, of course, and would be expected by recruits. Yet, however expected such distinctions might be, they could occasion tension, especially when brothers of different rank followed the same rule and in some cases fulfilled the same functions. Sergeants might be resentful of the fact that, although in some respects they were treated as the equals of knights, in other ways they were not; and in this situation knights might be anxious to stress their superiority: the Templar regulation that sergeant commanders could not admit a knightly recruit or deprive a knight of his habit may be an expression of this concern. Yet there is no evidence of large-scale conflict involving knights and sergeants, which could in any case occur only at an order's headquarters and the few other places where there were numerous brethren of both ranks. Many convents of the leading orders in Western Europe probably housed only sergeants, and in small communities – where office was not monopolised by knights – tension was likely to take the form of personal animosity rather than strife between ranks.

In the Temple, conflict between lay and clerical brethren was also minimal. Some individual clerics certainly did resent being subjected to the authority of laymen: in 1255, for example, the Aragonese provincial master was complaining to Alexander IV about several chaplains who held benefices and who had ignored a summons to answer charges of wasting the properties under their control and of leading dissolute lives. Yet Templar clerics did not live together in groups and could not easily assert themselves as a body; nor did they enjoy rights which lay brethren coveted. By contrast, in the orders of Santiago and Calatrava the authority of lay officials over clerics was subject to limitations, and in Santiago groups of clerics lived together in their own convents. It was mainly in these orders that conflict between cleric and lay occurred, with lay officials seeking to assert claims over their clerical colleagues and to reduce the latter's rights. In the thirteenth century the convent of Uclés complained repeatedly that the master and lay brethren of Santiago were abusing their powers. In a judgement given in 1228, the papal legate John of Abbeville sought to check lay encroachment in various spheres: he confirmed that jurisdiction over clerics rested with the prior, not the master, and ruled that no clerical recruit was to be admitted to the convent at Uclés except by the prior or his deputy; he reaffirmed the right of election to the post of prior, after the master had ousted the existing incumbent and himself set up a new one; he also ordered the restitution of the convent's property which had been appropriated by the lay brethren, and confirmed the clerics' right to a tenth of the revenues of their lay colleagues. Yet these rulings did not put an end to discontent at Uclés. Although the clerical brethren of Calatrava did not live in separate convents, in that order the master was similarly accused of seeking to extend his rights: in 1265, for example, the chaplains of Calatrava were complaining to Clement IV that the master was admitting clerical recruits to the order.

Although there were clashes between Sigena and the castellan of Amposta, there is less evidence of prolonged conflict between lay officials and convents of sisters, despite the fact that the latter were often a financial burden to their male colleagues. The right of election to the post of prioress seems usually to have been respected, and the only known attempt to suppress a female house in the twelfth and thirteenth centuries was made for financial reasons in 1267, when the master of the Hospital sought the Pope's permission to revoke the grant of Hospitaller property made in 1250 for the establishment of a convent for sisters at Alguaire in Catalonia. But sisters were not as closely integrated as clerical brethren into the life of military orders.

Conventual Life

THE life of the members of a military order was governed primarily by a rule which was usually based on, or adapted from, existing regular observances, although the regulations of many military orders were in time amended and expanded through the enactment of new statutes and the compilation of codes of customs. The first Templars were said to have imitated the canons of the Holy Sepulchre, but their early practices were modified at the Council of Troyes, partly under the influence of St Bernard, and the rule then drawn up included some borrowings from that of St Benedict. The rule compiled for the Hospitallers by the second master Raymond of Le Puy was based on that of St Augustine, and the order of Calatrava received its first rule from the general chapter of Cîteaux in 1164, while the orders affiliated to Calatrava – as well as that of Mountjoy – similarly followed a modified form of Cistercian observance.

Yet, if life in the military orders was modelled on that of existing religious institutions, on some points there were divergences. Although, in most military orders, recruits took the normal monastic vows of poverty, chastity and obedience, in Santiago only conjugal chastity was required: married men could become full members even though they retained their wives. One explanation which has been advanced for this innovation is that some of the first members were already married and were unwilling to put away their spouses. Since for more than a century the Church had been seeking to enforce clerical celibacy, it may well have been this issue which caused Alexander III to delay before giving his approval of the order, for the texts and arguments used both in the papal confirmation of 1175 and in Santiago's rule to justify the acceptance of married brethren could well have been applied elsewhere in the Church. The rule of Santiago, for example, includes the statement from Corinthians that 'it is better to marry than to burn', and the papal confirmation similarly quotes from Corinthians in asserting that 'it is good that a man should not touch a woman; because of immorality, however, let each man have his own wife'.[46] It is not surprising that the Pope was careful to point out that celibacy was better. Unmarried members of Santiago were not, however, allowed to take wives without the master's permission, and there was clearly a desire to keep the numbers of married brethren within limits: in 1208, when some brothers were apparently claiming that permission to marry should be granted automatically, Innocent III decreed that permission should not be extorted from the master; and in 1259, the general chapter imposed a further restriction by ruling that a brother who had remained celibate for five years should not be allowed to marry. The proportion of married brethren is, however, not known.

Married members of Santiago lived with their wives and families outside the order's convents, although they were obliged to abandon their spouses and move into a convent during periods of fast: and the wives were themselves at these times to reside in a sisters' house. Other members of military orders were expected to follow a coenobitic form of life within a convent, eating in a refectory and sleeping in a dormitory. Thus the seventeenth clause of the Teutonic order's rule states that 'if possible, all brothers who are healthy are to sleep together in one place',[47] and most rules, like that of St Benedict, include regulations concerning conduct in the dormitory. Brethren were forbidden to sleep naked; they were not to share beds; and a light was always to be kept burning. As Gerald of Causso testified during the Templar trial in 1310, this was done 'lest the hostile enemy give them occasion to sin'.[48] But, although a common life was regarded as the norm in military orders, in many places in Western Europe this can scarcely be said to have existed, for many houses contained no more than two or three brothers, and some brethren lived by themselves on granges.

Within convents, the daily routine was based on the normal monastic *horarium*. All brothers were obliged to attend services, although in practice most took little active part. As many lay brethren were illiterate, they were merely expected to listen as chaplains recited offices, and to say a certain number of paternosters for each of the canonical hours. Templar regulations state that 'when the brothers are in chapel and matins are said, each ought to remain silent and hear the service quietly and in peace';[49] and according to the rule of the Teutonic order, all brothers were to attend services, with the clerics chanting and reading, and the lay brothers saying paternosters, unless they were capable of participating. In the Temple and the Teutonic order, lay brothers were obliged to say thirteen paternosters for matins, nine for vespers and seven for each of the other offices, together with the same number for the hours of the Blessed Virgin Mary. In the order of Santiago, six were said for each office except matins and vespers, for which thirteen and ten respectively were recited. This practice is obviously to be contrasted with the observances of monks, but it was similar to that adopted in other institutions, including hospitals, where laymen led a religious life.

As regulations were based on monastic rules, they were inevitably concerned mainly with life within a convent; but the Templar rule did make provision for absences by stating that 'if any brother happens to be away on the affairs of Christendom in the East – which we do not doubt has often occurred – and through such absence cannot hear divine service' he should say the required number of paternosters.[50] Yet the disruption of the daily observance occasioned by warfare should not be exaggerated. On no front was fighting continuous, and in the leading orders only a small proportion of brethren was ever involved in warfare. The majority of Templars and Hospitallers lived in Western Europe and most – particularly those belonging to the rank of sergeant – spent the whole of their careers residing peacefully in the West: during the trial of the Templars many testified that they had never been out to the East. It is, of course, true that many small houses in Western Europe had no brother chaplains of their own to recite offices, but they usually had priests in their employ: in 1338, the personnel of all Hospitaller commanderies in England included priests, even if most of these were not members of the order.

In convents, the periods between services were occupied with practical pursuits. As the majority of brethren were laymen, meditative reading or literary and intellectual activity was not expected of them, and little time appears to have been devoted to these pursuits. These kinds of activity were not, of course, completely absent, although in some cases there is merely a presumption that a historical or other work concerning a military order was written by a brother. It is clear, however, that the author of Anglo-Norman versions of the Hospitaller rule and of the *Miracula* concerning the order's foundation was a Hospitaller: he was probably a chaplain, and possibly resident at Clerkenwell. And, in the late thirteenth century, the Hospitaller William of San Stefano not only made a collection of sources concerning the history of his order but also wrote on the origins of the Hospital and discussed its constitution, making use of Aristotle, Cicero and the Christian fathers, although his own knowledge of Latin appears to have been limited. At about the same time, Hugh of Langenstein, a brother of the Teutonic order, was completing his poem on St Martina which, even if of no great literary merit, ran to 33,000 lines. Occasional references also occur to works which were translated for particular brothers. In the twelfth century, a version of the *Book of Judges* was made for the Templars Richard of Hastings and Odo of St Omer, and several vernacular works, including a *Lives of the Fathers*, were dedicated to the Templar Henry Darcy; while a vernacular Psalter which survives from the turn of the thirteenth and fourteenth centuries bears a dedication to Simon Rat, who was at one time marshal of the Hospital. Some of the texts produced for brethren even reveal the orders as patrons of manuscript illuminators. Yet during the Templar trial the only books which were reported to have been found in most Templar houses were those needed for the conduct of services: works of other kinds were rare. Reading and literary activity were limited to a small minority.

Manual work as decreed in the Benedictine rule was not expected of all brethren of military orders either. It was not a regular part of the daily routine: in Templar regulations, manual labour is mentioned only as a form of penance. The omission is understandable in view of the orders' military obligations. Yet in practice, many non-military sergeants devoted most of their time to manual work, including farming, household tasks and the pursuit of crafts. Templar sources from Aragon, for example, reveal that brothers working inside a convent sometimes performed the functions of cook, butler or porter, or were craftsmen: some houses had Templar shoemakers, while Miravet in 1241 had a brother Dominic as tailor, and Monzón at times possessed a Templar smith and tanner. Many Templars employed outside convents in Aragon worked the land or had charge of animals. A brother Andico was a gardener at Castellote in 1237, and G. of Albesa in 1212 worked in the vineyards at Gardeny. A brother Ferrer was a cowherd at Miravet in 1228, and Arnold of Corbins was 'preceptor of sheep' at Gardeny in 1182, while Templar oxherds are recorded at Zaragoza and Huesca.

Some brothers of all ranks were involved in administration, and this must have been the main function of many brethren in the small houses which characterised much of Western Europe. In several orders there were also members who cared for the sick and poor or undertook other charitable work. In fact, all orders to some extent provided hospitality, even if in the Temple it amounted to little more than entertaining friends or occasionally supporting an itinerant royal household. When they were living in convents, brethren of the military orders were by no means cut off from the world.

Little information survives, however, about the military training of warrior brethren or of military exercises undertaken during periods of peace. Rules and regulations seek merely to ensure that some activities which were characteristic of secular knighthood were shunned. The rule of the Teutonic order commands brothers to avoid *collectas militum* – presumably a reference to tournaments, which were, of course, condemned by the Church. There were also frequent prohibitions on hunting and hawking. The Templar rule explained the ban by stating that 'it is not appropriate for a religious order to indulge in this way in worldly pleasures'.[51] In some regulations, such as that issued by the Hospital in 1262, the prohibition was complete, but in many orders exceptions were made. James of Vitry reports that when members of Calatrava were living in waste lands, they were permitted to relieve their poverty by eating animals they had hunted, and the rule of Santiago contains a similar provision, while that of the Teutonic order includes the clause:

> we allow brethren to pursue wolves, lynx, bears and lions, killing them not for the sake of hunting but for the common welfare, and without hunting dogs; they can also shoot from time to time at birds in order to practise their archery skills.[52]

As is apparent from the regulations about hunting in the orders of Calatrava and Santiago, in matters of food the military orders were not as strict as monasteries. Whereas monks were expected to abstain completely from eating the flesh of four-footed animals, members of military orders – like regular canons – were usually permitted meat on specified days each week. In the early rule of the Hospitallers, the eating of meat on Wednesdays and Saturdays was forbidden, but the later *Esgarts* also banned it on Mondays; and in most orders the eating of meat was restricted to Sundays, Tuesdays and Thursdays. Although the compilers of the Templar rule regarded a superfluity of meat as a 'burdensome corrupting of the body',[53] meat-eating was probably allowed in order to ensure that brethren were strong enough to fight. Yet, as has been seen, many members of military orders were not, in fact, involved in warfare. It was presumably for this reason that the Cistercian general chapter in 1233 decreed that brethren of Calatrava living outside Spain should observe normal Cistercian regulations concerning the eating of meat. This step was not imitated by other military orders; but, whereas for Calatrava the ruling marked a reversion to normal Cistercian practice, other orders would have been departing from their original regulations if they had introduced such a restriction.

Fasts were, of course, observed in military orders, but they were more restricted than in other religious foundations. In all military orders fasts were imposed in Advent and Lent, although the date for the beginning of the Advent fast varied from one order to another. During these periods brethren took only one meal a day, and there were also restrictions on the kinds of food which they could consume: the Teutonic rule, for example, specifically states that brothers should fast 'on Lenten food'.[54] Brethren of the Temple, the Hospital and the Teutonic order also fasted on all remaining Fridays between All Saints and Easter – in 1300 Hospitaller regulations were amended to include all Fridays from Michaelmas – and in the order of Santiago fasting took place on all remaining Fridays between Michaelmas and Pentecost. During the summer months, brethren of these orders were allowed to eat twice on Fridays, but they were to have only Lenten food. The greatest demands, however, were made on brothers of Calatrava who, in addition to fasting in Advent and Lent, were expected to have only one meal on three days of each of the remaining weeks between 14 September and Easter. Yet in most religious orders only one meal a day was taken throughout the period from mid-September until Easter.

The main periods of fasting fell in the winter months and – except in the Baltic region – did not normally coincide with a campaigning season. It was made clear, however, in the regulations of Calatrava, that the decree about fasting on three days a week from 14 September was binding only on those brothers who were living in convents: the master was to exercise discretion concerning the food allowed to any who were in the field fighting against the Muslims. There was also a common concern to ensure that brethren did not undertake additional fasts, which would have rendered them incapable of fighting properly. The Templar rule recommended that brothers should eat in pairs 'so that extreme austerity of life and furtive abstinence may be avoided at the common table',[55] and it also decreed that no additional fasts were to be undertaken without permission, a ruling which was backed up by papal letters. In the rule of Santiago, fighting was, in fact, seen as more demanding than fasting: 'it is much more difficult for a person to expose himself to great and indescribable dangers than in peace and tranquillity at home to afflict his body with prolonged fasting'; it was also considered better than fasting and therefore 'if anyone weakens his body by abstaining from food and by persistent fasting, and lacks the strength to defend the law of God and his brothers, he should realise that he is doing a wicked thing, for which he must stand to judgement'.[56]

In the monastic world, mealtimes were occasions when silence was to be observed, and similarly in the military orders, brethren were usually expected to refrain from talking when eating. But in matters of silence normal monastic practice was again adapted to meet particular needs. In the Templar rule it was accepted that brothers might have to speak at mealtimes through ignorance of the sign language usually employed in monasteries, and Templar regulations also allowed brothers to talk to their squires after compline, when they were checking their horses and equipment.

In clothing and equipment, simplicity was to be maintained and extravagance avoided. In his *De laude novae militiae*, St Bernard contrasted the Templars' appearance with that of secular knights:

> When battle is imminent, they protect themselves inwardly by their faith and outwardly by iron, not gold, so that, armed and not adorned, they strike fear into the enemy rather than arousing his greed. They seek to have strong and swift horses, not ones decked out in many colours. They are intent on fighting not pomp, victory not glory, and they strive to inspire terror not admiration.[57]

Peter of Dusburg claims that early brothers of the Teutonic order even had clothes made out of old flour sacks. The Syrian heat was, however, taken into account in clothing regulations, for the Templars were allowed a linen shirt from Easter to All Saints, and brethren of the Teutonic order could wear linen undergarments at all times.

To try to ensure that members adhered to the rules governing their lives, the military orders – like other religious institutions – devised graded schemes of penalties for breaches of regulations. There was no absolute uniformity either in the categories of offences and punishments or in the penalties inflicted for particular failings, but the schemes were basically similar. In the Teutonic order, there were four categories of offences and punishments. For a 'most serious' (*gravissima*) crime the penalty could be expulsion from the order; for offences categorised as 'very serious' (*gravior*) a penance of a year was imposed, during which the offender had to live with the slaves, if there were any, wear a habit without a cross, fast for three days a week on bread and water, and be beaten on Sundays; a 'serious' (*gravis*) offence was punished in the same way but for a shorter period, while a minor

offence incurred a penalty of up to three days' penance, sometimes
accompanied by a beating. In the Hospital, expulsion from the
order was similarly the heaviest penalty, and the others comprised
loss of the habit for a period, which meant a temporary expulsion;
the *quarantaine* and *septaine*, of forty and seven days' length
respectively, during which the offender fasted and ate on the
ground; and the minor punishment of being deprived of cooked
food or wine. In both of these orders, and in the Temple as well,
sodomy incurred the penalty of permanent expulsion, but crimes
were not always punished in so uniform a manner. Loss of the
habit was the punishment in the Hospital and Temple for
fornication, while in the Teutonic order, Santiago and Calatrava
a year's penance was imposed; and whereas those who struck
another brother were in the Temple deprived of the habit, in
Santiago they received a penance of six months and in the
Hospital they were subjected to the *quarantaine*.

Obviously, threats of punishment could not, in fact, prevent
breaches of discipline, and there were in addition some permitted
relaxations of observance. The ideal of the common life was not
maintained in its entirety through the twelfth and thirteenth
centuries. In the sources for the leading orders there is a growing
number of references to the rooms or quarters of individual
brothers. The master of the Hospital apparently had his own
quarters before 1170, and the master's chamber is mentioned both
in the Templar Customs and in the statutes of the Teutonic order.
In the thirteenth and early fourteenth centuries references also
occur not only to rooms occupied by other leading officials at an
order's headquarters but also to those belonging to provincial
masters and preceptors within provinces. In 1311, for example,
the chamber of the preceptor of Lammens was mentioned in
evidence given by one Templar, and after the arrest of the
Aragonese Templars, a royal official reported finding considerable sums of money in the room occupied by the commander of
Miravet. At the headquarters of the Hospital it would seem that
even ordinary brothers were acquiring rooms or cells of their own
by the end of the thirteenth century, for statutes issued in 1301
state that chambers in the order's hospice at Limassol were to be
at the disposal of the marshal, and he could assign them to
brothers of the same *langue* as those previously occupying them.
This set of statutes also implies that some brothers had their own

quarters outside the hospice, for it was decreed that other chambers – by which was presumably meant those outside the hospice – were at the disposition of the grand commander, and in the same statutes there is a reference to chaplains going to hear the confessions of, and give communion to, brothers in the town.

The expanding households of leading officials would also suggest a movement away from the common life, but the possession of rooms and attendants did not necessarily mean that a brother no longer shared in it at all. Although the Templar Customs and the statutes of the Teutonic order refer to the master's chamber, they also expect the master normally to eat with the convent: the Templar master was allowed to take food in his chamber only when he had just returned from the field, when he had been bled or was ill, and when he had secular guests. The cook assigned to him was, therefore, perhaps to provide for his needs mainly when he was travelling outside the convent, not when he was resident in it. But eating outside the refectory seems to have been a growing custom: although in the Hospital, the *quarantaine* was the penalty for eating in chambers without permission, in statutes issued in 1206 it was envisaged that permission might be given to brothers who were not ill. There is also little doubt that those who possessed chambers normally slept in them rather than in a dormitory. A Templar decree allowing a sick master to lie in his chamber instead of going to the infirmary and a Hospitaller regulation permitting sick brothers to eat in their chambers imply that such rooms usually contained beds. Nevertheless, there was still a dormitory at the Hospital's headquarters at Limassol at the beginning of the fourteenth century, and the records of the Templar trial include numerous references to dormitories both in leading and in smaller houses. The common life had not been altogether abandoned.

In monasteries, the taking of food outside the refectory was a common means of avoiding prohibitions on meat-eating, and this may have been the case in the military orders as well. In 1300, a Hospitaller decree even conceded the right to eat meat on Mondays outside the refectory. Nor was this the only permitted relaxation concerning food. In 1247, Innocent IV allowed brethren of Santiago to eat meat regularly when they were in the field, and in 1295 Hospitallers on campaign were given permission by the Pope to eat meat on any day except Friday.

These decrees were obviously prompted by military considerations, but there was no such justification for the pittances of extra
food and drink which became customary in military orders, just as
they were in most other religious foundations. In the Hospital, a
pittance of bread and wine was allowed on double festivals, and in
1303 the general chapter decreed that the master could grant a
pittance on the first Monday in Lent. Pittances were sometimes
linked with blood-letting, which came to be regarded as a means
of securing a break from the regular routine of convent life. A
clause in the Hosillaller Customs states that 'it is the custom that
the brethren should be bled on Saturdays, provided they have
permission, and that they should have a pittance at dinner and at
supper on the Saturday, and at dinner on the Sunday';[58] while
the Templar Customs rule that when healthy brothers were bled,
they could have three meals at the table of the infirmary, where
the normal regulations about food were not enforced.

There was no relaxation of rules concerning dress and equipment, but considerable difficulty was encountered in ensuring that
they were observed. In Calatravan statutes issued at the turn of
the twelfth and thirteenth centuries, warnings were already being
included about the use of silk and gold on equipment and in
clothing, and later *difiniciones* of Calatrava contain numerous
strictures on extravagances of dress. The fullest comment on the
period up to the early fourteenth century, however, is provided by
Hospitaller statutes, for these include repeated condemnations of
excesses in clothing and equipment: the possession of embroidered
clothes was prohibited in 1262, 1283, 1288 and 1295, while the
use of gold and silver on equipment was banned in 1265, 1270 and
1288. Clearly these rulings were of little avail, and by the early
fourteenth century it was coming to be accepted that Hospitallers
would possess clothing and equipment of this kind.

If in these matters the difference between brethren of military
orders and secular knights was diminishing, the former also
engaged in the pursuits of secular knighthood. Prohibitions on
hunting were not rigorously observed. Privileges were not infrequently accepted which allowed brothers to hunt on patrons'
lands: in 1233 the count of Dampierre conceded to the Hospital
that 'whoever is master or bailiff of St Amand can hunt in all my
warrens whenever he wishes',[59] and twenty years later Henry III
gave the prior of the English Hospitallers the right to course with

his dogs against hare, fox or cat in the royal forests of four counties. That brothers did, in fact, engage in these pastimes is apparent from a pardon given by Henry III in 1259 to the Templar master in England for taking a stag in the forest of Pickering. Yet hunting was regarded as a relatively minor offence and was punished severely only if loss or damage occurred: on one occcasion, a Templar in Cyprus who had chased a hare was condemned to lose his habit, but this was only because his horse had fallen and died of the injuries sustained.

Even if they breached regulations, most brothers remained members of an order until death; but there were some who sought to abandon the religious life altogether and return to the world. In 1209, Innocent III condemned those Hospitallers who,

> rejecting the religious habit, go back, like dogs to the vomit, to the illicit pleasures of the world, which for their salvation they had earlier abandoned, and who presume in their rashness to contract marriages *de facto* – since they cannot marry lawfully – and shamefully involve themselves in secular affairs as if they were laymen, refusing to return to the said order even when they are earnestly admonished to do so;[60]

and there were numerous other papal letters dealing with the same problem in this and in other military orders.

One explanation for breaches of regulations and for desertions is to be found in the motives which led recruits to enter an order: they were not always joining for the purposes listed in the account of the Templar admission ceremony. A further factor was the frequent absence of a novitiate, since this would have allowed both a postulant and those who received him to assess his suitability for the religious life, and would also have provided an opportunity for instruction. Admittedly, many military orders did at first follow current monastic practice and insist on a period of probation, although there is no evidence to show that a novitiate was ever the norm in the Hospital or the order of Santiago. According to the Templar rule, recruits were to undergo a novitiate whose length was to be determined by the master, and Calatrava – basing itself on Cistercian practices – similarly demanded a novitiate, as did the order of the Blessed Virgin Mary. Yet while Calatrava continued to insist on a period of probation, the version of the Teutonic order's rule which was drawn up in the middle of the thirteenth century allowed recruits to forgo the novitiate, and in 1257 Alexander IV confirmed that order's right to admit postulants without a probationary period. In the Temple, the novitiate completely disappeared. During the Templar trial all brethren admitted that recruits were accepted immediately as professed brethren. It is not known when the change took place, but it was certainly well before the end of the thirteenth century, for some brethren who were interrogated were of the opinion that postulants had never been subjected to a probationary period. One reason for abandoning the insistence on a novitiate was probably the need to make good the losses sustained in severe defeats in battle. Several Templars at their trial explained the lack of a probationary period by saying that profession was made immediately so that brothers could be sent at once to the East, and in 1257 Alexander IV gave as the justification for his concession to the Teutonic order the fact that

> a number of the brethren of your order, as we understand, have been cruelly killed by the infidel in the Holy Land and in the districts of Livonia and Prussia when fighting in defence of the catholic faith; whence it is that the order is known to be in great need of being replenished with new brothers.[61]

Most orders at times incurred heavy losses, and this would appear to have been a factor in the decline or disappearance of the novitiate.

Even when there was no novitiate, orders did, of course, attempt to provide some instruction for recruits. In the Temple, this was done in the first instance at the admission ceremony. After a postulant had received the habit, the brother conducting the ceremony was required to inform him about the penalties for certain offences and to give him details about sleeping arrangements and the daily routine, including the number of paternosters to be said. The section in the Templar Customs concerning admissions provides a summary of the necessary information, and in some instances this may have been read out: it may be noted in this context that the most worn part of a Catalan version of the Templar Customs is the section on admissions. But brothers conducting admission ceremonies were not always able to read,

and it is possible that on some occasions no one present was able
to do so. Nor should it be assumed that a copy of the rule and
Customs was always available. Some Benedictine monasteries are
known to have lacked copies of their rule in the thirteenth
century, and the Teutonic order found it necessary to decree
that a copy of its rule should be kept in every house. Some who
admitted recruits may have relied merely on memory when giving
instruction. Yet, in whatever way it was done, instruction at this
point could not have been a very effective method of informing a
recruit, who was likely to be confused by a long catalogue of
regulations and would probably remember little of what he was
told. Some knowledge would in time be gained just by living in a
community: Templars who did not know when to kneel during
services, for example, were told to position themselves at the back
of the chapel, and from this vantage point they would learn when
to genuflect. But not all regulations could be assimilated merely
by observation. Brethren were therefore encouraged to ask for
guidance; but a more formal arrangement was mentioned by an
English Templar, who testified during the Templar trial that
when he was received he had been placed in the charge of a
literate brother sergeant for a month. In the Temple this was not
a regular practice, but a similar measure is mentioned in a late
medieval account of the admission ceremony of the order of
Santiago, where it was presumably a more normal custom. A
Templar who had made his profession at Villemoison in the
diocese of Auxerre about the year 1303 further stated during his
interrogation that the brother admitting him had handed him a
copy of the order's regulations; but this could hardly have been a
common method of learning, for copies of rules were not numerous, and there were restrictions on the circulation of those which
did exist. And although all orders probably had vernacular
versions of their rules and customs, it may be doubted whether
most brethren would have benefited much from possessing a copy
of them.

Whether there was a novitiate or not, however, the problem
was not only to assimilate rules and regulations in the first
instance, but also to remember those regulations which had been
learned but which did not become fixed in the mind through daily
practice. The military orders adopted the custom – widespread in
other religious foundations – of having periodic public readings of

their rules: the rule of Santiago, for example, contains the provision that 'the rule is to be read once each month',[62] and a decree issued by the Teutonic order stipulated that brothers should hear the rule read at least six times a year. Yet if some houses lacked copies of rules, and if some brothers only infrequently attended chapters, this may not always have been a very effective means of instruction.

Certainly, during the Templar trial some brethren displayed an accurate and detailed understanding of many regulations, but there was also widespread ignorance and inaccurate knowledge among Templars at that time. Four brothers provided precise details of the number of paternosters to be said for each of the canonical hours, but none of the accounts tallied exactly with any of the others, and one brother – who provided information 'as it seemed to him'[63] – gave an account which at no point coincided with what was set down in the order's Customs. There was similar diversity of opinion on the matter of confession. Although some brothers understood the regulation about confessing to non-Templar priests, a number merely expressed ignorance; several thought that there was a total ban on outside confessions; the view was also expressed that there was complete freedom; and lastly a few were of the opinion that confessions could be made only to certain outsiders, such as Carmelites. During the trial, some brothers quite openly admitted their ignorance about many of the order's regulations. Thomas of Quentin, a sergeant from the diocese of Bayeux who had been in the Temple for about ten years, confessed that 'he knew little of the affairs of the order, because he worked on the land'.[64] But clearly ignorance was not peculiar to brothers who devoted their time to agricultural or household tasks: those who during questioning revealed the inadequacy of their knowledge included brothers who were preceptors and had charge of Templar convents.

The absence of a novitiate and the illiteracy of many brothers inevitably created special problems, but breaches of regulations and declining standards occurred not only in military orders. In many monasteries there were similar relaxations of observance: episcopal visitations of religious houses in the thirteenth century reveal numerous abuses, which could not easily be stamped out. Nor were all who contravened rules in military orders seeking a more lax way of life. In the early thirteenth century James of Vitry wrote in a sermon that

> we have encountered some knights of your order who were so intent on fasting and afflicting their bodies that in warfare and battles against the Saracens they easily succumbed because of excessive weakness. We heard of one who was very devout, but not wisely so, since in battle against the Saracens he fell from his horse at the first blow of a lance; another brother, at great danger to himself, helped him to remount, but he immediately fell again to another blow.[65]

And naturally the sources have more to say about abuses than about praiseworthy conduct. Yet Peter of Dusburg, in his Prussian chronicle, does single out some members of the Teutonic order for commendation: a brother from Westphalia, for example, who was serving in the castle of Christburg, is described as

> a man of wonderful devotion and abstinence, wholly given up to the service of God, who among other virtuous works adopted the particular custom of wearing an iron breastplate as a shirt next to his skin, and by the time of his death he had used up four such breastplates, worn out with age and rust.[66]

Peter no doubt had a didactic purpose in inserting such comments, but they are not for that reason to be wholly discounted.

6.   Criticism and Change

The Orders' Critics

THE criticism which had attended the emergence of the military order continued to be voiced in some quarters throughout the twelfth and thirteenth centuries, for not all accepted that warfare could in any circumstances be a meritorious activity. Although the views he expressed on military orders were not altogether consistent, in the later twelfth century Walter Map wrote at one point in his *De nugis curialium* that the Templars in the Holy Land

> take up the sword for the protection of Christendom, which was forbidden to Peter for the defence of Christ. There Peter was taught that peace should be sought by patience: I do not know who taught these to overcome force with force. They take up the sword and perish by the sword. They nevertheless assert: 'All laws and all law codes allow the repelling of force by force'. He, however, rejected that ruling, who, when Peter was striking a blow, refused to call on the legions of angels.[1]

In a sermon written early in the next century, James of Vitry reported that some in his time were arguing from scripture that fighting was unlawful and were therefore asserting that military orders should not take up the material sword for any purpose and should not engage in a physical struggle against the enemies of the Church; and when later in the thirteenth century Aquinas discussed whether a religious institution could be established for military purposes, the main objections he examined were those which maintained that warfare was sinful and a secular matter.

During the course of the twelfth and thirteenth centuries, however, as the orders grew in wealth, power and responsibilities, they came to be criticised more frequently for other reasons. It has been said that pride was regarded in the West as the leading vice up to the end of the tenth century, when it was joined by avarice: brethren of the military orders were commonly accused of both. Apart from specific charges made by secular clerics relating to the abuse of ecclesiastical privileges, many more general comments on these faults have survived in letters, chronicles, poetry and other sources. In a letter written in 1207, Innocent III complained that Templars

who abandon the Lord and depart from the purity of their order are so unbridled in their pride that they do not hesitate to disfigure their mother, the church of Rome, which by its favours has not ceased to cherish the brethren of the knighthood of the Temple

and in the same letter he wrote of their being 'consumed by greed'.[2] When dealing with a complaint against the Hospitallers in 1252, the English king, Henry III, asserted that the Templars and Hospitallers had acquired such wealth that they had become swollen with pride. Several English chroniclers relate the tale that Richard I proposed to bequeath his pride to the proud Templars (or Hospitallers), and a similar comment was attributed in a German source to the emperor, Frederick II. When describing the origins of the Templars, the St Albans chronicler Matthew Paris followed William of Tyre in condemning them for abandoning their early humility, and further comments on their pride occur elsewhere in his work. Earlier in the thirteenth century, the poet Guiot of Provins had castigated the Templars for their greed and pride, and in the anonymous poem *Sur les états du monde*, probably also written in the first half of the thirteenth century, it was claimed that the Templars 'know well how to look after themselves, but they love money far too much'.[3] Later in the century, the poet Daspol wrote that the Templars and Hospitallers were 'full of pride and avarice', and Rostanh Berenguier commented on the Templars that 'their pride is so great that one cannot look them straight in the eye'.[4] In his sermons, James of Vitry not only commented on greed but also claimed that

some, indeed, who were poor and wretched in the secular world, become so haughty and insolent after being admitted to a noble order that, when they are assigned the task of guarding the door or given some other minor post, they have the audacity to provoke and abuse secular knights because they have been told to uphold the habit of their order and the honour of their houses.[5]

Although comment of this kind persisted, there was also growing criticism about the uses to which the military orders put their wealth. Early in the thirteenth century, James of Vitry warned the orders that 'they should take great care how they spend the wealth of the Church and the resources given for the defence of the Church'.[6] Several lines of attack were developed on this point. It was commonly held that brethren lived a life of ease and luxury and devoted their revenues to this end. Rostanh Berenguier asserted that 'on this side of the sea many knights of the Temple ride about on their plentiful grey horses or recline in the shade', and in the poem *Ordre de bel ayse*, which was a satire on religious orders, also written at the end of the thirteenth century, it was claimed that the Hospitallers 'have fine long robes, which trail at their feet, seemly shoes and *chausses*, and large, easy-pacing palfreys'.[7] The leading orders were thought in consequence not to be maintaining as many knights in the Holy Land as they could. In his survey of the events of the year 1244 – when Jerusalem fell and the Christians suffered severe losses at the battle of La Forbie – Matthew Paris, in his *Chronica majora*, argued that a fully equipped knight could be maintained in the Holy Land from the revenues of each of the Temple's 9000 and the Hospital's 19,000 manors:

> therefore Christians, reflecting on these matters, always assume that they are hiding some fraud and are concealing wolfish deceit under sheep's clothing; for if there were no deceit or fraud, a great number of valiant western knights would forcibly overcome the resistance of all the eastern peoples.[8]

Thirty years later, another Englishman, Richard of Mepham, who was dean of Lincoln, asserted at the Council of Lyon that the possessions of the military orders were sufficient to provide for the defence of the Holy Land if proper use were made of them. In Church councils summoned after the fall of Acre it was similarly maintained that the orders were not providing as much assistance as they could for the Holy Land, and in the next decade the French propagandist Pierre Dubois argued that 'the Hospitallers, Templars and members of other orders founded to aid and defend the Holy Land have enormous resources, incomes and possessions on this side of the Mediterranean, which up till now have brought little benefit to the Holy Land'.[9] This kind of argument was elaborated mainly with reference to the Holy Land, but the orders' reluctance to give service in Spain in the later thirteenth century inevitably provoked complaints of the same nature. At the beginning of 1287, for example, the Aragonese king, Alfonso III, pointed out that the Templars had been given lands and privileges on the understanding that they would always be ready to fight against the infidel; he therefore threatened to confiscate some of their property and use it to obtain other troops, implying that the Templars were not providing the service they were capable of giving.

The brethren who did reside in frontier regions of Christendom were censured for using resources in fighting against fellow Christians, instead of devoting them exclusively to the conflict with the infidel. In the later thirteenth century, the Dominican Humbert of Romans wrote that brothers of the military orders should be exhorted

> not to convert wars which they ought to have against infidels into conflicts among themselves, fighting each other because of discord, or turning against brethren of other military orders who are their neighbours or against prelates.[10]

Brethren of the Teutonic order in the Baltic region were frequently criticised for using force against Western Christians. In 1310, Clement V could refer to numerous past complaints, and claim that the brothers 'have become domestic enemies and foes within the family, taking up arms not in the name of Christ against those who oppose the faith, but in their support' and that 'leaving the militia of Christ, they now wage a wretched war with their evil weapons against the faithful of Christ'.[11] Among earlier complaints were those made in 1240 by the bishop of Prussia, who claimed that the order was attacking and seizing episcopal property; in 1257 by a papal legate who passed sentence of excommunication for an attack on the territory of voluntary converts; and in 1299 by the archbishop and the city of Riga, and the bishop of Oesel, who all argued that the order was using force against them. In Syria, most attention was focused on conflicts between the military orders themselves, especially the Templars and Hospitallers, whose relations were seen to be characterised by a deep-seated rivalry and hostility. In 1235, for example, Gregory IX was complaining that the Templars and Hospitallers were waging war on each other merely over claims to some mills in the Holy Land, and Matthew Paris reported that in 1259

> the Hospitallers all rose against the Templars, when some deadly dispute had broken out between them; although they lost a large part of their own men, they are said to have completely destroyed the Templars... never has so great and so wretched a slaughter been reported amongst Christians, especially among men of military orders.[12]

Greed was often seen to be the motive. When reproving the orders in 1235, Gregory wrote that 'many people have been forced to the conclusion that your chief aim is to increase your holdings in the lands of the faithful, when it should be to prise from the hands of the infidel the lands consecrated by the blood of Christ', and the author of the *Collectio de scandalis ecclesie* was merely repeating comments made earlier by James of Vitry when he stated that 'it is commonly said that the Templars and Hospitallers cannot abide each other. The reason is greed for worldly goods. There is jealousy between them if one house acquires what the other wants'.[13]

Rivalry between orders was thought not only to occasion the diversion of resources and energy away from the conflict with the infidel but also to hamper co-operation in battle against the Muslims. Defeats were blamed, at least in part, on discord between military orders. This explanation is found in a number of accounts of the loss of Acre in 1291. The Dunstable annalist wrote that 'it is said that this grievous misfortune occurred because of discord between the Templars and Hospitallers', while the author of the *Annales Eberhardi* reported that 'it was the opinion of many that if the brothers of the houses there – namely the Hospital, the Temple and the Teutonic order – and other people had been in complete agreement among themselves the city would not have been taken';[14] and similar accusations were made by the Sicilian chronicler Bartholomew of Neocastro and in the *De excidio civitatis Acconis*.

Effective action against Muslims in the East was also seen to be hindered by the independence enjoyed by the military orders, as well as by other elements in the Holy Land. The Franciscan Fidentius of Padua, who had experience of Syria, included in his *Liber recuperationis Terre Sancte* a section headed 'The lack of a leader is harmful', in which he argued:

> The inhabitants of the Holy Land do not have one leader whom they obey and follow; for the Venetians, Genoese, Pisans, Templars, Hospitallers, brothers of the Teutonic order and barons residing in those parts do not obey, and are unwilling to obey, the king of Jerusalem.[15]

There were also more specific comments about the harm caused by the orders' independence. In 1231, Frederick II complained to Gregory IX that the Templars were intending to break a truce with the Muslims, and the Pope therefore wrote to the master of the Temple, ordering that 'you do nothing at all which can endanger the Holy Land or those visiting it, for such action could easily bring confusion to the whole Christian people'.[16] In a letter sent to Richard of Cornwall in 1245, Frederick further maintained that the Templars' refusal to accept the treaty made with Egypt and their siding with Damascus had led the sultan of Egypt to call upon the assistance of the Khwarismians, to whom Jerusalem had fallen.

There was also criticism of the orders' apparent reluctance to adopt sufficiently aggressive policies towards the Muslims in the eastern Mediterranean. During the third crusade, when the Templars and Hospitallers advised against attacking Jerusalem, they incurred the hostility of French crusaders wishing to march on the city. Half a century later, Philip of Nanteuil, captured at the battle of Gaza in 1239, lamented in an Egyptian prison: 'If the Hospital and the Temple and the brother knights had given our people a good example of how to fight, our grand force of knights would not now be in prison, nor the Saracens still alive'.[17] Although his own crusade to the East in 1269 had ended at Aigues Mortes, at the Council of Lyon in 1274 James I was similarly critical of the Templars for their unenthusiastic response to Aragonese proposals for action against the infidel.

To some, the orders in the Holy Land appeared to be on much too familiar terms with the infidel. The German chronicler Otto of St Blasien reported that in 1197 crusaders in Syria were offended

by the familiarity which existed between the orders and the
Muslims, and Frederick II, in his letter to Richard of Cornwall
in 1245, criticised the Templars for allowing Muslim leaders into
their houses and permitting them to perform religious ceremonies
there. Such feelings were expressed even by some brethren.
During the Templar trial, the master James of Molay said that
he and some of his fellow knights had grumbled because, during a
truce made by the English prince, Edward, the then Templar
master William of Beaujeu 'showed respect to the sultan and
remained on good terms with him'.[18]

Yet while some critics felt that the orders were not sufficiently
aggresssive in Syria, the English Franciscan Roger Bacon criticised them in his *Opus maius* for fighting at all. He maintained that
by their actions they were impeding the conversion of the infidel
both in the Holy Land and in the Baltic region:

> The Templars and Hospitallers and the brothers of the
> Teutonic order hinder the conversion of the infidel through
> the wars which they are always waging and through their
> desire to establish total dominion. There is no doubt that all the
> nations of infidels beyond Germany would have been converted
> long ago, had it not been for the aggressiveness of the Teutonic
> order, for the pagan people has on many occasions been ready
> to receive the faith peacefully through preaching. But those of
> the Teutonic order are unwilling to allow this, because they
> want to subjugate the pagans and to reduce them to servi-
> tude.[19]

This argument was one of expediency and therefore different from
that advanced by those who thought all fighting to be sinful. But,
like the latter argument, it represented only a minority opinion.
Although there were others, such as the Dominican, William of
Tripoli, who felt that warfare was not necessary, it was not the
prevalent view that force should be altogether abandoned. The
orders in the Baltic region were, however, frequently criticised for
failing to use resources for missionary purposes and for pursuing
policies which hindered, rather than aided, the process of Christianisation. After receiving complaints from the bishop of Riga
about the partitioning of conquered territories, Innocent III was
in 1213 already castigating the Swordbrethren:

less anxious to propagate the name of the Christian faith than to add house to house and field to field right up to the frontiers of the region...you do not fear to impede the teaching of Christ, provided that you can increase your possessions and revenues[20]

and ten years after the Teutonic order established itself in Prussia the local bishop was complaining that it was not allowing Prussians to be baptised; was preventing churches being built; and was causing converts to apostasise because of the harsh treatment they suffered at the hands of the order. Despite an agreement made at Christburg in 1249 concerning the conditions under which the native population was to live, complaints on all these issues continued, and in the fourteenth and fifteenth centuries it was frequently said that the Prussians were still hardly Christian.

These various criticisms must obviously be seen in perspective. The military orders were by no means the only religious institutions to be censured in the twelfth and thirteenth centuries: all religious orders had their detractors. Nor were all commentators critical of the military orders. In the later twelfth century, for example, the English writer Ralph Niger was careful to exclude the Templars and Hospitallers from his censures on those living in the Holy Land; and in 1258 the warden of the Franciscans at Thorn on the Vistula was vigorously defending the Teutonic order against charges of hindering and neglecting the Christianising of the Prussians.

Of those who did censure the orders, not all expressed unmitigated hostility. It has been seen that, despite his criticisms, William of Tyre acknowledged the Templars' and Hospitallers' diligence in defending frontier castles. Humbert of Romans made a number of laudatory comments, and wrote of the brethren of the Teutonic order:

They have many praiseworthy traits. They are devoted to the blessed Virgin, whom they have as their special patron. They are also pious and poor. They are strenuous in arms against the Saracens. They are charitable to men of their own race. They maintain a humble and devout obedience to their superiors. They are strict in the observances of true religion and display great zeal.[21]

Similarly, in spite of hostile comments voiced by some popes, the activities of the orders were praised in many bulls issued by the papacy, which continued to support the military orders through the granting of privileges and in other ways; and in 1218 Honorius III was staunchly defending the orders against their critics: in a letter to Sicilian prelates he said that he had had inquiries made in the East about the accusations which were being voiced, and had found them to be 'frivolous and fictitious'.[22] In his *Abbreviatio chronicorum*, Matthew Paris went so far as to withdraw the accusation of betraying Frederick II which he had earlier made against the Templars in his *Chronica majora*; and although in the opening years of the fourteenth century the Aragonese king, James II, reproached the military orders for failing to give service, on hearing of the arrest of the Templars in France he wrote in November 1307 to Philip IV that 'during our reign they have faithfully given us very great service, in whatever we required of them, in repressing the enemies of the faith'.[23]

It should also be remembered that many leading critics were scarcely unbiased. As has already been mentioned, the views of the secular clergy were inevitably influenced by the losses of income and authority they suffered as a result of the orders' papal privileges and immunities, while the crusading taxes imposed by the papacy in the thirteenth century no doubt help to explain the clergy's readiness to criticise the orders for failing to provide an adequate defence for the Holy Land: the opinions expressed by the dean of Lincoln at Lyon in 1274 were voiced at a time when Gregory X was demanding a sexennial tenth in aid of the Holy Land – from which the military orders were, of course, exempt. In the Baltic region, many critics were rivals of the Swordbrethren or of the Teutonic order and had their own ambitions, which clashed with those of the orders. The complaints made by the bishop of Prussia in 1240, for example, are to be seen against the background of the events of the previous decade, when the imprisoned bishop had been outmanoeuvred by the Teutonic order and had lost claims in Prussia. In his Egyptian prison, Philip of Nanteuil was seeking to blame his predicament on others rather than admitting his own and his colleagues' foolhardiness; and many were seeking more generally to find a scapegoat for the misfortunes of the Holy Land: as responsibility for the defence of the crusader states fell increasingly on the military orders, these became an obvious target. It should also not be forgotten that papal letters which censured the orders were often based on information supplied by those who were by no means impartial.

Some criticism, moreover, did not reflect personal experience but was merely the expression of what had become the conventional view. This could be said of a number of comments about pride and avarice, and also about rivalry between military orders. Although some critics who wrote of pride and avarice were referring to particular incidents, in other cases generalised comment was being made. And many were putting forward a conventional explanation when they attributed misfortunes in the Holy Land to rivalry between the orders: this appears to have happened with regard to the fall of Acre, for although in many sources the orders were blamed, some better-informed reports do not advance this explanation. The frequency of references to pride, avarice and rivalry may therefore be indicative of the state of popular opinion rather than of the truth.

Critics were, in fact, often ill-informed or had only a limited understanding of the orders' situation. Many commentators probably held an exaggerated view of the wealth of the leading military orders. Because these had estates in all parts of western Christendom it was assumed that they possessed enormous resources. Yet the important issue was not the extent of their properties but the amount of money which these properties could provide for the struggle against the infidel; and it has been seen that in the thirteenth century many orders were experiencing financial difficulties. No doubt many would have argued that these problems arose because revenues were being wasted and devoted to the wrong purposes; and that there were excesses in clothing and equipment is certainly apparent from statutes issued by the Hospital in the later thirteenth century. But these decrees do not necessarily indicate that the order's revenues were being misused, for postulants were expected to provide their own clothing and equipment when they joined an order. A recruit to the Hospital's male house at Sigena in Aragon promised in 1227 to come equipped with a horse, clothing and a bed 'as is decreed in the order of the Hospital';[24] and a postulant's responsibility to provide clothing was reiterated in a Hospitaller statute issued in 1273, while decrees promulgated by the chapter of Santiago in the early 1270s, and also by the Templars, required recruits to the rank of knight to be knighted – and thus provided with knightly equipment – before they made their profession. Evidence drawn from the trial of the Templars suggests that it was, in fact, common for recruits to be knighted shortly before they entered the order. Often, therefore, a brother's family or friends paid for extravagances of dress and equipment. Inventories of Templar houses compiled in the early fourteenth century after the arrest of the brethren certainly do not suggest an affluent lifestyle: it was only in the order's chapels that valuable goods were commonly found, and here a display of wealth could be considered a sign of devotion.

That the orders were constantly devoting their energies and resources to conflicts with each other was also an exaggeration. Admittedly, both in the struggle against the infidel and in political disputes within the Holy Land, such as the war of St Sabas, the Templars and Hospitallers at times pursued conflicting policies, and in all regions there were inevitably property disputes which were not always quickly ended. But it is questionable whether in Syria the Hospitallers always adopted a royalist stance and the Templars a baronial one, as has sometimes been suggested, and it should not be assumed that on all issues the two orders automatically took opposing sides. There were many occasions when brethren of these orders co-operated in the field or at the negotiating table, and the references to the Hospitallers in the Templar Customs reveal a not unfriendly attitude. On various occasions, procedures were agreed for settling disputes which did occur between military orders, and in the later thirteenth century leading officials of the Temple and Hospital appear to have been particularly anxious to bring conflicts to a speedy conclusion: in 1274 quarrelling Templars and Hospitallers in Aragon were commanded by their superiors to settle their differences without delay, and the master of the Temple was at pains to point out that 'between us and the venerable order of the Hospital peace and concord should by God's will be fostered, so that no one has occasion to complain, which would be to the scandal of both orders'.[25] It is true that this statement was made at a time when demands were being voiced for an amalgamation of the two orders, but it does show that they were responding to criticism.

Complaints that the orders in the Holy Land did not pursue the struggle against the infidel with sufficient vigour and that they were too friendly towards their supposed opponents are to be explained in part by differences of attitude and by misconceptions. Crusaders coming from the West usually knew little of Islam or of Muslims, and many regarded the infidel merely as someone to be killed. They could not understand the more tolerant attitudes which characterised regions on the borders with Islam. The difference is illustrated by Usamah's account of his experience while praying on one occasion in Jerusalem: the Templars repeatedly intervened to restrain a newcomer from the West who was trying to force Usamah to pray in a Christian manner; and Frederick II's letter to Richard of Cornwall in 1245, written shortly after the Templars had given hospitality in their Acre house to al-Mansur Ibrahim, the ruler of Homs, was clearly intended to provoke ill-feeling towards the Templars by playing on such differences of outlook. Newcomers also often lacked a clear understanding of the political situation in Syria and did not perceive where the long-term interests of the crusader states lay: they tended to favour aggressive policies, without thought for the consequences. Many did not remain in the East long enough to moderate their stance, although during his stay in Syria after his disastrous Egyptian crusade, the French king, Louis IX, came to appreciate the value of alliances with the Muslims; and, in the early fourteenth century, James of Molay explained to his interrogators that the brethren who had criticised William of Beaujeu were young men, 'eager for war, as is usual among young knights, who want to participate in deeds of arms'; they were, however, finally persuaded that

> the master could not have done anything else, because at that time the order was responsible for, and had under its protection, numerous cities and many fortresses on the borders of the lands of the said sultan, and the master could not have defended them in any other way.[26]

Roger Bacon similarly revealed the limitations of his knowledge and understanding when writing about preaching in the Baltic region. And in defence of the Teutonic order against other criticisms concerning the conversion of the Prussians, it may be pointed out that it was not a missionary as well as a military order of the kind envisaged by Raymond Lull in his *Epistola summo pontifici Nicolao IV*; that total Christianisation was in any circumstances a very slow process; and that the order's more material needs could not be ignored if it was to maintain the struggle against the infidel.

Yet the military orders, like other religious foundations which attracted criticism in the twelfth and thirteenth centuries, were by no means blameless. Not only were the Templars and Hospitallers in the Holy Land at times pursuing conflicting policies, which did not help the Christian cause; there was also a readiness among some brethren to engage in feuds with other orders. Although in 1274 leading officials in the Temple and Hospital were anxious to settle the dispute between their subordinates in Aragon, the latter showed little inclination to reach a compromise, and the quarrel dragged on for several years. The property dispute between Santiago and the archbishop of Toledo in 1242 shows that military orders were prepared to use force against Christians not only in the defence of established rights; and the Teutonic order's determination to achieve independence in Hungary and Prussia suggests that its interests lay not just in promoting the struggle against the infidel. The examples could be multiplied. Since many recruits entered military orders with little sense of vocation, it would have been surprising if brethren had always adhered to their orders' stated objectives. Many complaints against them were, in fact, justified.

Whatever the exact validity of criticisms, towards the end of the thirteenth century the view was certainly widely held that the military orders were in need of reform. Most of those who composed crusading treatises or proffered advice on crusading in the later thirteenth and early fourteenth centuries gave consideration to this issue, and on a number of occasions the ecclesiastical authorities devoted attention to it as well. In some instances it was argued that the orders' independence must be curbed: thus in a letter sent to the Pope after discussions at a London council in 1292, Archbishop Pecham of Canterbury maintained that the military orders should be compelled to obey the leader of the crusading expedition which was expected to take place shortly and that they should later be subordinated to the king of Jerusalem. More attention was focused, however, on the question of rivalry and the contribution in manpower and resources which the orders made to the defence of the Holy Land.

In his *Tractatus de modo convertendi infideles*, written shortly after the fall of Acre, Raymond Lull sought a solution to the problem of rivalry by suggesting that, once the Holy Land had been recovered, the military orders should fight on different fronts: one of the two leading orders should be stationed in North Africa and the other in *Turquia*, while the Teutonic order should be located in Lycaonia. He maintained that in this way 'they will remain in concord and amity'.[27] In another work written at about the same time, however, Lull sought a more immediate remedy through the amalgamation of the military orders. A similar proposal was advanced in several of Lull's later writings, including the *Liber de fine*, which contains his most detailed crusading plans. A union of some or all of the military orders was also advocated in many other crusading treatises and plans produced at this time. About the year 1291, Charles of Naples supported an amalgamation of this kind, as apparently did the French king in 1305, and a union of the military orders was again suggested by Pierre Dubois in his *De recuperatione Terre Sancte*.

In proposing an amalgamation, the authors of these plans were merely echoing a commonly held view, and the question of union was, in fact, considered on a number of occasions by the papacy and ecclesiastical councils. It was discussed at the Council of Lyon in 1274, while in the summer of 1291 – a few months after the fall of Acre – Nicholas IV ordered the summoning of provincial councils to consider the matter. A series of assemblies was held, and all the conciliar recommmendations which have survived – from England, France, Germany and Italy – were in favour of union.

The councils held in 1291–2 also discussed the utilisation of resources. In several it was argued that the properties of the Templars and Hospitallers should be assessed to discover how many knights could be maintained from their lands, and it was held that the orders should be obliged to keep that number in the East. A proposal of this kind was made at the London council which met in 1292, and the archbishop of Canterbury therefore advised the Pope that

when their rents and revenues have been assessed at their true value, the orders should be compelled to furnish constantly for the recovery and defence of the Holy Land as many valiant

warriors as can reasonably be maintained with their resources'.[28]

A similar suggestion was made at the council of Arles, and some
years later the same argument was advanced by Philip IV's
counsellor, William of Nogaret. The implication was, of course,
that few brethren should reside in the West, and this was
explicitly stated in a letter sent to Nicholas IV by the French
clergy. While prelates attending the council of Reims in 1292
appear to have envisaged the eventual confiscation of possessions
if an adequate force was not maintained in the East, some
theorists wanted to proceed more directly to the appropriation
of the orders' property. In his *De recuperatione Terre Sancte*, Dubois
argued that the Templars and Hospitallers should subsist from
their possessions in the Holy Land and Cyprus: their lands in the
West should be confiscated and used to provide subsidies for
crusaders and to endow schools, whose purpose was to be the
furtherance of the Christian cause in the East.

Although such proposals sprang from dissatisfaction with the
orders' conduct, especially in Syria, some theorists nevertheless
thought that, once an amalgamation had taken place, the single
military order which emerged should assume the main burden of
government and defence in the Holy Land: there was still
confidence in the institution. It was argued that the new order
should not only make a major contribution in manpower but also
take over the leadership of the Christian cause in the eastern
Mediterranean. Charles of Naples advocated that the master of
the order should also become king of Jerusalem, and this idea was
taken up later by Raymond Lull and by the author of the *Memoria
Terre Sancte*. Lull also assumed that a *passagium* for the recovery of
the Holy Land would be under the control of the master: thus in
the *Liber de fine* he proposed that a war of reconquest should be led
by a *rex bellator*, who was to be the head of the order. In some
works it was further envisaged that the order's role during a
crusading expedition would extend beyond the leadership of land
and sea forces to include control over the disbursement of
crusading monies, which in the past had often been diverted
from their true purposes.

These roles were assigned to the proposed military order partly
because it was thought capable of providing continuity in leader-

ship and manpower. In the *Memoria Terre Sancte* it was argued that a crusade led by the master of the military order would be assured of continuous direction, for

> if a passage was decided upon, and there was one king, or several, the passage could be brought to nothing by the death of one or two men; but if the said order was founded...and its master should happen to die, another could be appointed in his place immediately[29]

and in his *Liber de fine*, Lull similarly argued that the election of a new *rex bellator* immediately after the death of his predecessor would ensure continuity of leadership. It was also assumed that a military order could guarantee a constant supply of manpower because its members would be stationed permanently in the East and brethren who died could quickly be replaced. In Charles of Naples's plan, the 2000 knights to be maintained at the order's central convent were each to have two squires and these 'should be such that, if their master should happen to die, one of the two could be made a brother';[30] and Lull, in the *Liber de fine*, likewise argued that on the death of one knight another could be admitted to the order.

For various reasons nothing was done to implement the proposed changes. Nicholas IV died in April 1292, before he could act on the suggestions of the recent provincial councils. Even if he had lived, however, he would have encountered opposition to any attempted reform. The proposal to amalgamate the military orders was clearly not welcomed in all quarters. It was reported that nothing came of the discussions about union at the Council of Lyon because opposition was anticipated from Spanish rulers; and that there was hostility to union within the existing orders is clear from a memorandum addressed to Clement V by the Templar master, James of Molay. Some of the points which he raised were in themselves of little significance and merely demonstrated the strength of feeling against amalgamation, but he also advanced some valid criticisms: if, as claimed, there was rivalry between Templars and Hospitallers, existing animosities would be transferred to the combined establishment, which would be rent by faction; in addition, some officials would become redundant, and the consequent dismissals would be resisted by those deprived of office. New problems would, in fact, have been created by the implementation of a number of the proposed reforms. The suggestion that most members of the leading orders should be stationed in the East was, for example, rather simplistic. Supplies would have had to be sent out from the West for many who would have been of little use in Syria: some were too old or infirm, and many were *frères des mestiers* who would have contributed little to the orders' fighting strength. To have transferred most brethren to the East would also have necessitated the entrusting of properties in the West to secular officials – possibly by the farming out of estates, as was later suggested by Gregory XI – and this would not have provided a very reliable form of administration. It may further be doubted whether the employment of lay administrators would have saved much expense, and the abolition of most Western convents would have had a harmful effect on recruitment and patronage. Considerations of this nature may have helped to check the implementation of reforms, while some changes could in any case not have been undertaken immediately: proposals concerning the kingship of Jerusalem were dependent not only on the amalgamation of the orders but also on the recovery of the Holy Land.

Changing Roles

CHANGE resulted not from the reform of the military orders but from altered circumstances in the frontier regions of western Christendom, which led to a modification of the orders' roles. This occurred most gradually in Spain, where the orders became less involved in fighting against the infidel and increasingly concerned with the internal politics of the Christian kingdoms and the relationships between Christian states. It has been seen that by the middle of the thirteenth century the reconquest had either been completed, as in Aragon and Portugal, or come to a halt. Although the orders continued to give service against Muslims, in some parts of the peninsula their function had become limited to intermittent action of a mainly defensive nature, and even that they were increasingly reluctant to perform. On the other hand, besides becoming involved in internal conflicts within Christian kingdoms, they were in the later thirteenth century expected to give service against neighbouring Christian states. The fullest information on this trend comes from Aragon, for which a series of royal registers survives, although it was not peculiar to that kingdom. In 1283, in the aftermath of the Sicilian Vespers, the Templars and Hospitallers were ordered by the Aragonese king, Pedro III, to give service when an attack from the French was expected, and two years later the brothers of Santiago and Calatrava, as well as those of the Temple and Hospital, were assigned the task of defending the Catalan coast against the French fleet. James II similarly demanded service against Castile in 1300 and 1301. Brethren of the orders were, admittedly, not called out on all possible occasions but, probably in part because of loyalty to their king and partly through fear of the consequences of refusal, they did on a number of occasions give service. As the Templars reminded James II in 1308 after he had ordered their arrest,

> when the king of France invaded the land to conquer it, brother Berenguer of San Justo, who was master, and all the brethren of the Temple of the bailiwick of Aragon did not desert the lord king Pedro, like the men of Barcelona and elsewhere, some of whom fled and thought that all was lost; the brethren fortified and garrisoned their castles with their forces with the intention of dying with the lord king or preserving the kingdom for him, and they defended him and his land.[31]

At the other end of the Mediterranean, the final collapse of the crusader states in 1291 might appear to provide a more obvious turning point. Yet this event did not, as has often been suggested, immediately destroy the orders' *raison d'être*, for it would not have been so apparent to contemporaries as it is to modern commentators that the Holy Land had been lost for good. The numerous crusading proposals and plans put forward at the end of the thirteenth and in the early years of the fourteenth centuries show that the West had not lost all interest in the recovery of the kingdom of Jerusalem, even if few practical measures were taken. In 1291, the Templars and Hospitallers, together with the small order of St Thomas of Acre, transferred their headquarters to Cyprus, which was only a hundred miles from the Syrian coast; and, although time was needed for regrouping and consolidation, in the following years the two leading orders did not altogether abandon hostilities against the Muslims. It has been seen that the Templars and Hospitallers were developing their naval arm at this time and participated in expeditions which attacked Muslim coasts in the year 1300; the Templars garrisoned the island of Ruad, off Tortosa, and held it until 1303. In the opening years of the fourteenth century the Hospitaller master also undertook two expeditions to Armenia, where the orders still retained possessions. At this time, moreover, the Temple and Hospital made several contributions to current discussions about the recovery of the Holy Land. Both the Templar master, James of Molay, and the Hospitaller master, Fulk of Villaret, put forward proposals to the Pope, while another Hospitaller treatise, advocating preliminary expeditions to weaken the enemy, has also survived from the early fourteenth century. In 1291, the Teutonic order admittedly transferred its headquarters much further west to Venice; but it has been pointed out that this was equidistant from the Baltic and the Holy Land, which until then had been the order's two areas of operations, and the move does not therefore indicate a loss of interest in the eastern Mediterranean: the order had been founded in the Holy Land and its headquarters had remained there, despite a growing commitment in the Baltic region. Yet if the collapse of the crusader states in 1291 did not occasion an immediate revision of objectives, it paved the way for changes which took place in the earlier part of the fourteenth century.

For the Teutonic order, the year 1309 marked a turning point, for it was then that its headquarters were transferred from Venice to Marienburg in Prussia, although the question of the order's future had apparently already been an issue for some years before that date: earlier differences of opinion on this matter are implied by criticisms made in 1299 by brethren in Prussia, who felt that inadequate support was being given to those in the Baltic region. By 1309, it must have become apparent that there was little point in keeping Venice as the order's headquarters, as it was obviously not well-situated for localised military action against the Muslims. The continued involvement of the Teutonic order in warfare against the infidel in the eastern Mediterranean was, in fact, dependent on a crusading initiative from the West which might restore a Western presence in Syria. Despite all the plans and proposals formulated at this time, however, no major crusading expedition took place. The Teutonic order nevertheless had to seek to justify itself, for by 1309 the trial of the Templars was already in progress, and it was against this background that Frederick, archbishop of Riga, was at the papal court at Avignon, seeking to pursue his claims against the Teutonic order and reviving old accusations against it. The order needed to show that, in spite of criticism, it was still performing a useful function for western Christendom. It is perhaps also significant that the transfer took place at a time when the Teutonic order was incorporating Pomerelia into its territories at the expense of Brandenburg and Poland, for this was likely to have consequences which would demand the attention of those in authority within the order.

From 1309 onwards, the Teutonic order's military interests inevitably became concentrated in the Baltic region. It did still retain some properties in the kingdoms of Cyprus and Armenia, but these were – at least for a time – linked administratively with Sicily, and no evidence survives of continued military activity on the part of the brethren in these two countries. In the fourteenth century, the order did maintain a military presence in Latin Greece, but this was of minor significance compared with that in the Baltic. In the north, fighting continued against the pagan Lithuanians, although in the fourteenth century warfare was characterised by raiding rather than by the conquest of territories. But there was at this time also growing conflict between the Teutonic order and its Christian neighbour Poland, while fighting against the Lithuanians did not cease when their ruler became a Christian.

While the Teutonic order was transferring its attention to the Baltic, between 1306 and 1310 the Hospitallers created a new role for themselves by conquering the island of Rhodes, off the southwest corner of Asia Minor, and establishing their headquarters there. In explaining this decision it is necessary to avoid using hindsight. It can hardly be linked with the impending fall of the Temple, for although the French king had apparently discussed rumours concerning the Templars with the Pope late in 1305, it would not have been obvious in the spring of the following year that the Temple was soon to be abolished. Even if reports of these discussions had reached Cyprus in 1306, it would not have been apparent that they were of any greater consequence than earlier deliberations about the shortcomings of the military orders. Nor can a move westwards, away from Syria, be seen purely as a response to critics who were stressing the failings of the orders in general, for the Holy Land remained the chief concern of Western commentators. The explanation seems to lie mainly in the problems which the Hospitallers were encountering in Cyprus and in the difficulty of providing effective aid for the Holy Land. In Cyprus, the order's resources were limited, and there was tension over taxation between the Hospital and the king, Henry II. Yet, if assistance was not forthcoming from the West, there was no possibility of recovering the Holy Land: the Hospitallers by themselves could achieve little against the Mamluks. The only place on the mainland to which the Hospitallers could have transferred their headquarters was Armenia, but a move of this kind would have created its own problems. In establishing themselves on Rhodes, the Hospitallers were moving into a region where other Westerners, especially the Italians, already had interests, and the order itself possessed properties in Greece. The Hospitallers were not isolating themselves from their fellow Christians. Rhodes was, of course, a Greek possession, although parts may have been under Turkish control; but Western action against schismatic Greeks had become commonplace. In the preceding decades there had been various attempts or plans to restore the Latin Empire of Constantinople, and the seizure of Rhodes itself had formed part of some Western schemes shortly before the Hospitaller conquest.

Once the Hospitallers were established on the island of Rhodes, their attention became focused mainly on Asia Minor and other areas to the north. Already, in 1312, they were gaining footholds on the mainland of Asia Minor, and in the course of the fourteenth century they were involved in a number of expeditions against the Turks there, including that which captured Smyrna in 1344. As Ottoman power expanded into Europe, they also gave assistance against the Turkish advance further north: the crusader force which was defeated at Nicopolis in 1396 included a contingent of Hospitallers. It is true that Hospitallers were also present on the expedition to Alexandria led by Peter of Cyprus in 1365, and there is evidence of occasional involvement in Armenia during the fourteenth century. But Armenia at that time was of peripheral significance to the Hospitallers, and their main sphere of action was to the north of Rhodes. Even in this region, however, their military activities were limited.

While the Hospital and the Teutonic order retained their military character, the lesser orders which had fought in the East in time abandoned their military functions. In the first decade of the fourteenth century there was a schism in the order of St Thomas of Acre, with rival masters in Cyprus and England, but this appears to have been occasioned by a proposed amalgamation with the Temple rather than by differing views about the order's role. Yet in 1318, Henry of Bedford, who held authority in Cyprus, journeyed to England, seeking to oust his rival and to establish his own headquarters in London. This implied the abandonment of the order's military character. Henry was, however, opposed by brothers in Cyprus, and a new master was set up there. For a time there was again schism. In the 1340s, the brethren in Cyprus were apparently still trying to preserve the order's military status, but in the second half of the century the attempt was abandoned, and the headquarters were transferred permanently to London. The order became an establishment whose members followed the Augustinian rule; it appears to have undertaken some charitable work, and in the sixteenth century there was a grammar school at St Thomas of Acre in London.

The history of the order of St Lazarus is more obscure. It has been argued that after 1253, when the order suffered heavy losses near Ramleh, its headquarters were located at Boigny in France; and certainly at times in the second half of the thirteenth century the master was in the West. But the order was still active in the Holy Land after that date, and according to one chronicler – admittedly not an eyewitness – the master took part in the defence of Acre in 1291. It was probably after the collapse of the crusader states that the headquarters were permanently transferred to France, where the order was based in the fourteenth century.

The Trial of the Templars

WHILE other orders which had been based in the Holy Land were finding new roles, the Temple was suppressed. On 13 October 1307, when the order's headquarters were still in Cyprus, the Templars in France were suddenly arrested, on the orders of

Philip IV. They were accused of heresy, idolatry and immorality: among specific charges were the denial of Christ, spitting on the cross and indecent kissing – all of which were said to occur when a recruit was admitted to the order – and also the encouragement of homosexual practices. Although it was claimed that action was being taken at the request of the papally-appointed inquisitor in France, protests were quickly voiced by Pope Clement V, who in the preceding summer had already made known his own intention of investigating the rumours which were then circulating about the Templars. Yet confessions of guilt were soon being obtained from James of Molay and numerous other Templars in France, and on 22 November 1307 Clement himself instructed rulers elsewhere to detain the members of the order and to seize their possessions. James II ordered the arrest of the Aragonese Templars at the beginning of December, after hearing of the confessions in France and before he had received Clement's instructions; but he was the ruler who encountered the greatest difficulty in apprehending the brethren of the order. The Aragonese Templars possessed well-fortified strongholds, and most of them grouped themselves in some half-dozen castles, where they defied the king. Lengthy sieges had to be conducted, and it was not until the later months of 1308 that most of the strongholds surrendered, while Monzón held out until May 1309. Yet Aragon was the only country where prolonged opposition was encountered. Attempts to resist arrest in Cyprus and Castile were short-lived, and in most countries away from the borders of Christendom, brethren were in no position to defend themselves against the Crown, although probably in every country there were some brethren who managed to avoid being captured. Even in France, where the Templars appear to have received no advance warning of Philip's plans, some brothers evaded arrest.

In the early months of 1308, further investigation of the charges was delayed by renewed differences between the Pope and the French Crown. Clement suspended the proceedings which were being conducted in France, possibly after hearing that James of Molay and some other Templars had retracted their confessions. He was also seeking to secure control of the persons and possessions of the Templars. The French government resisted papal demands on this point, and wanted proceedings to be restarted. As an alternative, however, it was also demanding the immediate abolition of the order, on the grounds that guilt had already been established: all that was needed was a papal decree suppressing the Temple. In the early months of 1308, the Crown sought to gain support against Clement from the masters of theology at the University of Paris and from the Estates General, which were convoked in May 1308. Anonymous pamphlets attacking the Pope were also being circulated in France. Lastly, in June 1308, arrangements were made for seventy-two Templars to be brought before Clement at Poitiers, and almost all of these again confessed their guilt. On 5 July, the Pope agreed to lift his earlier suspension. Proceedings against individual French Templars – except some leading officials who were to be investigated by the Pope – were now to be continued by the French prelates and the inquisitor, who were to act in conjunction with other clerics to be nominated by Clement. The Pope in addition appointed a commission which was to hear evidence in France about the order as a whole. Guidelines were also laid down at this time for the proceedings which were to take place in other countries, and a series of articles of accusation to be used in the inquiries was issued by the papal chancery on 12 August 1308. The fate of individual Templars was to be decided by provincial councils, while the future of the order was to be determined at a general council which was to meet at Vienne in October 1310.

The interrogations of Templars and of non-Templar witnesses which took place between 1307 and 1311 produced varying results. In France, almost all of the brethren questioned in the later part of 1307 confessed to at least some of the more serious accusations. Yet the outcome of later episcopal inquiries in that kingdom was not always so uniform: of sixty-nine Templars questioned by the bishop of Clermont in 1309, twenty-nine maintained their innocence of the main charges. And in February and March 1310, a growing number of brothers from all parts of the kingdom travelled to Paris, ready to defend the Temple before the commissioners appointed by the Pope to hear evidence about the order as a whole: by the end of March the number had reached nearly six hundred. Their spokesmen denounced the accusations as false, and vigorously asserted that earlier confessions were untrue. But on 12 May 1310, fifty-four Templars were burnt following judgement at a provincial council presided over by the archbishop of Sens, Philip of Marigny, who was the brother of Philip IV's adviser, Enguerrand of Marigny. After that date, attempts to defend the order in France rapidly collapsed, and the vast majority of the Templars who later appeared before the papal commissioners admitted their guilt. In Italy, confessions were obtained in the kingdom of Naples, in the papal states and in Florence, but in most parts of Southern Europe the Templars denied the main charges against them. No confessions on the more important accusations were made in Cyprus, Aragon, Mallorca, Castile or Portugal. Further north, in England, only three Templars admitted any of the more serious charges. There were similarly variations in the evidence given by non-Templars: the testimony of outsiders in Cyprus was in the main very favourable to the Templars, but in England many non-Templar witnesses testified against the order.

It was against this confusing background that the Council of Vienne finally met in October 1311, a year after the date originally set. Shortly after the council had opened, a small group of Templars arrived with the intention of defending the order, and most of the prelates attending the council were in favour of allowing them an opportunity to state their case. But at the end of December, Philip IV summoned the Estates General to assemble on 10 February 1312 at Lyon, not far from Vienne, and it was also at the end of December that Henry Ffykeis, an English proctor at the papal court, reported the news that the French king 'is coming in anger and with a large following'.[32] Philip did not go immediately to Vienne, but in the middle of February a royal embassy arrived at the council; on 2 March, Philip wrote from Mâcon, urging Clement to suppress the order; and on 20 March, Philip appeared in person, accompanied by a considerable following of troops. Two days later, in the bull *Vox in excelso*, Clement V decreed the suppression of the Temple. The Templars at Vienne had received no hearing.

Once the Temple had been abolished, a decision had to be made about the future of its possessions. This was an issue which was already being discussed at Vienne well before 22 March, and three main possibilities were being considered: Templar property might be assigned to the Hospitallers; it might be used to endow a new military order, which would replace the Temple; or it might be administered by the Church and the revenues utilised for general crusading purposes. There was limited support for the third proposal, but the majority of the prelates at Vienne favoured the creation of a new order. On 2 May, however, Clement ruled that in most countries Templar possessions should be assigned to the Hospitallers. The reasons which the Pope gave for his decision were in the main not very convincing. James II's envoys at the Council reported that one of the Pope's objections to a new order was that there would be no one to instruct its members concerning a rule: but as new orders often borrowed regulations from existing foundations, this was hardly an insuperable obstacle. A more plausible objection to a new foundation would have been the difficulty of immediately recruiting the personnel needed to take over the role of the Templars; and the renewed danger of rivalry could also have been stressed. But Clement also advanced more positive reasons for favouring the Hospitallers. In his bull of 2 May, he praised both their military exploits and their devotion: yet in view of the widespread criticism of the Hospital which had earlier been expressed, and was still being voiced at the Council of Vienne, his words hardly carried conviction. There was, however, more substance in his claim that 'once their power has been augmented by increased resources, they will be able more easily and lightly to bear the burdens which the execution of so great a task imposes'.[33] The financial situation of the Hospital, which was already deteriorating in the thirteenth century, was made worse by the costs of the conquest of Rhodes. The order was certainly in need of additional resources, and with its network of houses throughout the West it could take over Templar possessions without having to maintain all existing Templar convents in Western Europe. Possibly the real reason for Clement's decision, however, was the stance of the French Crown, for Philip was reported in April 1312 to be advocating that Templar property should be assigned to the Hospital.

In May 1312, Templar possessions in the Iberian peninsula and in the kingdom of Mallorca were excluded from the Pope's general ruling because of opposition from some Spanish kings. The surviving sources mostly relate to the Aragonese king, James II, who clearly feared the power – and therefore the independence – which the Hospital would enjoy if it added the extensive Aragonese properties of the Temple to its own considerable possessions in the kingdom. He also wanted to ensure that the revenues from these lands were used inside the peninsula, and claimed that donations had been made to the Aragonese Templars so that they could defend the Church in Spain. Yet, although in the settlements which were finally reached concerning Templar possessions in Aragon and Portugal John XXII stressed the threat posed by the Muslims in Spain, in the early fourteenth century neither Aragon nor Portugal bordered on Muslim territories: it was for other reasons that the Aragonese king was interested in Templar revenues. In various letters, James suggested the establishment of a magistracy of the order of Calatrava in Aragon, and this proposal led to the creation of the order of Montesa in 1317. John XXII assigned to the new foundation the properties of both the Temple and the Hospital in Valencia, although the Hospitallers were to receive Templar rights in Aragon and Catalonia: in this way the Hospital in fact gained rather more than it lost. John XXII also agreed to the founding on the other side of the peninsula of the order of Christ, which was to be endowed with Templar possessions in Portugal. The lands of the Temple in Castile and Mallorca, on the other hand, were awarded by the Pope to the Hospital.

In these countries, as in others, the Hospital encountered difficulties in securing possession of Templar rights. In Mallorca, it had to pay an annual rent as well as a lump sum to king Sancho in order to obtain Templar property. In 1313, the French Hospitallers similarly undertook to pay Philip IV the sum of 200,000 *livres*, and a further payment of 50,000 *livres* was agreed in 1318, although such concessions did not ensure a smooth transfer. In England, Edward II ordered the surrender of Templar properties to the Hospital in 1313, but many English estates of the Templars in fact passed into the hands of private lords, and it was not until 1324 that it was decreed by Parliament that Templar lands were no longer to be claimed as escheats. Even then the Hospital had difficulty in actually securing the property, and it often had to make concessions and to agree to compromises. It did gradually make gains – between 1328 and 1338 its annual income from the lands of the English Templars rose from £458 to £1442 – but in 1338 it was calculated that property worth nearly £800 a year had still not been recovered. In many parts of the West many Templar possessions never, in fact, came under Hospitaller control.

Of the Templars themselves, James of Molay and Geoffrey of Charney, who had been master in Normandy, were burnt in 1314 after retracting their confessions, but most brethren appear to have been reconciled to the Church at provincial councils and pensioned off. In England, they were sent after the trial to live in convents belonging to other religious orders – an arrangement which in some cases satisfied neither the Templars nor their hosts. But there was greater disquiet in Aragon, where in the years following 1312 the brethren continued to live in their own houses, free from outside supervision. Inevitably, complaints were soon made about their conduct, and in 1318 John XXII felt obliged to decree that within three months all Templars should enter houses belonging to other religious orders, either as full members – if their hosts would accept them as such – or as lodgers. He also sought to regulate the Templars' pensions, which in some areas were regarded as excessive in amount. Yet, as the years passed, the numbers of Templars gradually dwindled. References to them become less frequent, and the last brethren died unobtrusively in the middle years of the fourteenth century.

Ever since October 1307, the trial of the Templars has been a subject of discussion and controversy. The two main issues of contention have been the validity of the charges against the Templars and the motives behind the attack on the order in 1307. Although there has been endless debate about the guilt or innocence of the Templars, it is difficult to believe that they had committed the more serious offences of which they were accused. The absence of incriminating material evidence, such as idols and copies of secret statutes, is admittedly in itself not a conclusive proof of innocence. Outside France brothers would have had time to conceal or destroy such evidence after hearing of the action taken against the French Templars, and even within France brethren could have disposed of incriminating material when rumours began to circulate; but to explain away the lack of idols and secret statutes in France it would have to be assumed that, although they were not anticipating the arrests and seizures which took place in October 1307, the French Templars had already undertaken a very thorough destruction of all incriminating material in every part of the kingdom.

Clearer evidence of innocence is provided by the testimonies of brothers who admitted the main charges, for these were often self-contradictory and unconvincing. The account of the reception ceremony given by some Templars comprised a series of incompatible statements, which juxtaposed orthodoxy and error; and while admitting to spitting on the cross during the reception ceremony, some brothers then proceeded to state that on Good Friday the cross was adored by brethren. There are also considerable variations not only between the admissions of guilt made by different brothers – if accepted at their face value these would imply a bewildering variety of practice – but also between confessions made at different times by the same brother.

Nor in the testimonies were any convincing explanations advanced for the supposed adoption of practices which were in direct contradiction to the avowed purposes of the order. Most of the brothers who made any comment at all merely stated that these practices were customary in the order and were decreed by its statutes. When more particular explanations were put forward, they hardly carried conviction. According to Geoffrey of Gonneville, the Templar master of Aquitaine and Poitou, the denial of Christ was thought by some brothers to be in imitation of Peter's denying Christ, while others held that the practice had been introduced by a Templar master who had to agree to it in order to secure his release from a Muslim prison. In 1311, the Templar Hugh of Narsac told the papal commissioners that the errors had originated in the East,

> where there was frequent contact with Saracens, and brother William of Beaujeu, sometime master of the order, and brother Matthew Sauvage, knight, established a close friendship with the sultan and the Saracens; the said brother Matthew kept company with them and the aforesaid brother William had some Saracens in his pay when he wanted; and they said they did this for their greater security; but others spoke differently about this.[34]

Another witness appearing before the papal commissioners in 1311 said that he had been told that the denial of Christ was intended both as a test and as a joke, but he did not elaborate further. In the same year, however, the English Templar John of Stoke – one of the three in England to admit guilt – spoke of the denial as a test of obedience. On the other hand, another witness before the papal commisioners in 1311 advanced the suggestion that it was a test to see if brothers would deny their faith if they were captured by the infidel. This suggestion can hardly be taken seriously; and had a test of any sort been involved, the recruit would have needed to know what kind of test it was: he might otherwise have given the wrong response. And other testimonies imply that the denial was meant to be genuine.

Furthermore, although in France many confessed, none sought to defend, or to adhere to, the practices attributed to the order. In 1310, many French Templars retracted earlier confessions – the guilty would have had little to gain by doing this – and some were killed for maintaining their innocence, but none went to the flames in defence of the supposed practices. Many of those admitting the charges sought, in fact, to distance themselves from what was said to have happened by stating that they had been coerced into denying Christ and into countenancing other blameworthy acts; that the denial had been made with their mouths but not with their hearts; and that they had spat near, but not on, the cross. The confessions convey the impression that large numbers of Templars were doing what not one of them believed in.

Had the practices attributed to the Templars been customary throughout the order for any length of time, they would scarcely have escaped detection until the early years of the fourteenth century. It was not unusual for brethren to leave the order, either to transfer to another – normally stricter – religious foundation or to return to the world, and these brothers would have undoubtedly have made known what had been happening. As the abandoning of a religious order was a serious offence, those who had left the Temple merely to revert to secular life would hardly have ignored a means of justifying their flight. Nor is it credible that all who entered the order believing it to be orthodox would have stayed in it if they had been forced to submit to the practices which were said to occur at admission ceremonies. As a Templar spokesmen told the papal commissioners on 23 April 1310,

many noble and powerful men from various lands and regions, some of them of considerable age and many of them well-known in the secular world, honest men born of high-ranking families, have made their profession in the Temple, burning with zeal for the orthodox faith, and have remained in it until they died. If men of such standing had known, seen or heard of anything dishonourable in the order of the Temple, especially the deplorable insulting and blaspheming of the name of Jesus Christ, they would have vehemently protested, and brought everything to the notice of the whole world.[35]

It was not only Templars or former Templars who could have revealed irregularities, for confessions were often made by brethren to non-Templar priests. Yet, although during the trial some Templars claimed to have confessed their crimes to outside priests well before 1307, no outsider admitted to hearing unorthodox confessions. All the non-Templar priests who testified during the trial and who had heard Templar confessions stated that these had been orthodox. As admission ceremonies and chapters were held in private, it was, of course, difficult for most outsiders to discover what happened on these occasions; but this in itself throws doubt on the hostile evidence given by some non-Templar witnesses, which in any case usually consisted of second-, third- or fourth-hand reports. The hostile testimony provided by non-Templars seems, in fact, to reflect general attitudes to the order rather than to indicate where the truth lay: this would explain why in England, where the Templars would have been known mainly as wealthy and privileged landowners, there was a considerable amount of unfavourable comment, whereas in Cyprus, where there were many who had seen the Templars in action against the infidel, the evidence provided by outsiders was almost wholly supportive of the order.

It should lastly be remembered that the charges levelled against the Templars were not very original. Precedents can be found for almost all of them in earlier accusations against alleged heretics or against Muslims; some of the same offences had even been imputed to Pope Boniface VIII only a few years before the Templars' arrest. That old charges were being repeated also throws doubt on the suggestion that, even if the order was innocent, there may have been occasional acts of what amounted to horseplay at admission ceremonies which could explain some of the accusations.

That confessions were obtained from innocent men should occasion little surprise. Persistent and skilful interrogation, deprivation and torture have often produced this result. It is, of course, true that in some regions the Templars maintained their innocence despite persistent questioning, and in 1311 Aragonese brothers refused to confess even when they were subjected to torture. Much, in fact, seems to have depended on the determination of those controlling proceedings. In Aragon, where there was considerable sympathy for the Templars, the conditions of imprisonment during the trial were much less severe than in France, and torture was used only at a late stage when the Pope insisted on it. In France, on the other hand, every available means was used from the outset to obtain confessions, with royal officials playing a leading role in the early interrogations. In France, the Templars were also taken by surprise, totally unprepared for what they were to experience, whereas elsewhere there was time for some mental adjustment to the new situation.

It is not so easy to discern the motives behind the events of October 1307. There is first the problem of the relative influence of the king himself and of his advisers: on this issue historians are by no means agreed. Yet even if it is argued that government was under the control of ministers, it does not necessarily follow that the king exercised no influence over general lines of policy. Whoever was taking the initiative, however, motivation should be considered in the light of what was actually said and done during the trial: discussions of motive have too often been conducted in a vacuum.

Many contemporaries were of the opinion that the motive was greed: Philip wanted to secure the revenues of the Templars. It was a view which became so widely expressed that the French government felt the necessity of seeking to rebut it. It is also a verdict which has been reached by many modern commentators, who have pointed to the financial difficulties experienced by the Crown during the reign of Philip IV; and in preceding decades it had not, of course, been unknown for crusading taxes to be diverted by secular rulers to more mundane purposes. Two forms of financial gain were possible: a short-term benefit, through the seizure and retention of Templar revenues for a limited period, and a long-term advantage, through securing more permanent access to Templar resources. In the short term, the French government clearly did profit: it held Templar lands during the trial, was slow to release them after the order had been suppressed, and gained compensation for their final surrender. But such action does not necessarily indicate the primary motive for the attack on the Templars. All rulers in the West, when presented with the opportunity, sought to gain in this way. As the French Crown was demanding in the spring of 1308 that the Temple should be suppressed immediately without any further investigation, it was, in fact, pursuing a policy which would have limited the opportunities for profit of this kind. It could be argued, however, that at that time Philip and his advisers were hoping to secure more permanent, though not necessarily direct, control over Templar properties. The issue was raised in two of the questions put to the masters of theology in Paris early in 1308:

> Sixthly, it is inquired concerning the property which the Templars possessed in common as if their own, is it to be confiscated in a case of this kind to the benefit of the prince in whose area of authority it is situated, or is it instead to be assigned to the Church or to the business of the Holy Land, in consideration of which it was given to, or in other ways gained by, the Templars? Seventhly, if by right or through the devotion of princes it is assigned to the business of the Holy Land, to whom should the control, management and administration of such property belong: to the Church or to princes, especially in the kingdom of France, where all the possessions of the Templars are known to have been under the protection and guardianship of the king and his predecessors for a very long time?[36]

In the first of these questions, the point that is stressed is that the Templars had held the property for the benefit of the Holy Land: no case is made for assigning it to the prince. In the second question, on the other hand, the royal role is emphasised. Yet if the French government was anxious to assert a more permanent control over Templar possessions, it is surprising that it did not pursue this objective more vigorously. Although, in 1311, Philip's adviser, William of Nogaret, was maintaining that Templar revenues should be held by the king so that they could be employed for crusading purposes, in the following year Philip did not support the proposal – even though it had some clerical backing at the Council of Vienne – that Templar goods should be administered by the Church in the interests of the Holy Land: this was the solution then under discussion which would have provided the greatest surplus of income and which would have made Templar revenues most easily accessible to the Crown. A financial motive cannot be ruled out, but it is not so obvious as some have claimed.

A further suggestion is that the order was an independent, military and aristocratic organisation which could not be tolerated by a government which was seeking to extend its sway. But in France the Temple was hardly a military organisation: most convents in the kingdom contained only a handful of brothers, the majority of whom were sergeants, and little military equipment was discovered when the arrests took place. Since most French Templars were sergeants, the Temple can scarcely be considered an aristocratic body either. Nor should its independence of the Crown be exaggerated: the king could seek to influence appointments to Templar posts within France, and the resident brethren were almost all of French origin and therefore likely to feel some allegiance to the French king. The order's subjection to the Pope affected the episcopate more than the king, and although the Temple enjoyed privileges and immunities, these could be reduced without destroying the order. And there were, of course, a number of other ecclesiastical institutions in France whose position was similar to that of the Templars: it is, for example, difficult to differentiate in this respect between the Templars and the Hospitallers. It should also be remembered that in 1312 Philip was reported to be supporting the proposal to assign Templar property to the Hospital rather than to a new order: this made the Hospital in France a more powerful institution than the Temple had ever been. On this issue Philip did not adopt the stance taken by James II of Aragon.

The trial has further been seen in a more general context as an affirmation of the temporal over the spiritual, of the monarchy over the papacy. The French were certainly able to browbeat Clement V and the Temple was suppressed, although the extent of the French victory depends upon the other objectives attributed to the Crown. Yet a case involving heresy and idolatry was not the best issue on which to assert temporal claims: at the outset, the French government was having to legitimise its arrest of the Templars by stating that it was acting at the request of the inquisitor and the Church; the masters of theology in 1308 made clear the limited extent of a secular ruler's rights in such matters; and Philip and his ministers had to accept that the suppression of an order was a matter for the Pope.

Some contemporaries discussed the trial in the context of proposals involving the Capetians and the Holy Land. Towards the end of 1307, the Genoese Christian Spinola told James II that Philip and the Pope had acted partly because they wanted the military orders amalgamated into a single foundation, the head of which was to be one of the king's sons: this had been opposed by the Temple. In an anonymous letter, sent to a correspondent in Mallorca early in 1308, it was asserted that after the death of his wife in 1305 Philip wanted the military orders to be amalgamated: he would then abdicate and become the head of the order; this also was said to have been opposed by the Templars. In 1309, the bishop of Lérida informed James II that a cardinal had asserted that Philip wanted all the goods of the Temple to go to one of his sons, who would become king of Jerusalem. This report is also found in several chronicle sources. It is, of course, true that Capetian interests had been expanding in the later thirteenth and early fourteenth centuries. In the year of the Templars' arrest, for example, Philip's brother, Charles of Valois, was seeking to pursue claims to the former Latin Empire of Constantinople. Yet it is not easy to explain the trial of the Templars against this background. If it is argued that the king was seeking vengeance on the Temple for its opposition to union, it may be doubted whether the Hospital was, in fact, any more ready to accept amalgamation, even though there is no surviving Hospitaller statement comparable to the extant memorandum on the subject written by James of Molay. If Philip wanted to promote proposals for an amalgamation of the orders, the most obvious course would have been to press for the implementation of this measure, which – as has been seen – had very widespread support in the West, even if there was opposition within the orders themselves. The granting of Templar lands to the Hospital did achieve a kind of union – of property if not of personnel – but there is no sign that the French Crown sought to intrude itself into the leadership of the Hospital in the way suggested. Nor is there any first-hand evidence during the trial of Philip's seeking to have Templar property used to endow a king of Jerusalem. In fact, none of the reported proposals is mentioned in a document emanating from the royal chancery: they all occur in private correspondence or in chronicle sources. The possibility cannot be discounted that they were merely rumours which had their origins not in the mind of the king but in the writings of crusader theorists, such as Raymond Lull and Pierre Dubois, whose treatises contain proposals which are not altogether dissimilar.

There remains the question of whether Philip or his advisers actually believed the charges against the Templars. It seems quite probable that at least the king did so. It has been argued that, particularly after the death of his wife, he became increasingly preoccupied with matters of religion and salvation, and that he saw himself as responsible for the spiritual welfare of his subjects and the purity of the Church. Heresy, which had flourished in the thirteenth century, had to be eradicated and the machinations of the Devil contained. He could, therefore, have been more ready than some of his fellow rulers, or even the Pope, to accept the validity of the rumours which were being put about by such men as Esquiu of Floyran; and he could have distrusted the Pope's willingness to take what he regarded as the necessary measures: hence the attitude displayed towards Clement which might otherwise appear unscrupulous. The treatment of the Templars themselves, which to modern eyes might seem a cynical attempt to find the innocent guilty, could be interpreted as revealing a determination to root out evil, particularly when torture was regarded as a legitimate means of ascertaining the truth.

It is clearly difficult to speak with any certainty of the motivation behind the attack on the Templars. The surviving evidence will admit of more than one possible explanation; and there may well have been more than one factor at work, especially if policy-making and government action were not under the exclusive control of one man. Facile and over-confident assertions are to be eschewed.

Conclusion

WITHIN two hundred years of the emergence of the institution of the military order, the earliest foundation of this kind had been suppressed, and the defence or recovery of the Holy Land, which had been the original function of military orders, was no longer being actively pursued. Orders were devoting a declining amount of time and resources to fighting the infidel, and in some regions they were increasingly confronting their fellow Christians in the field. It is not surprising that in the fourteenth century criticism continued to be voiced. In 1310, a year after the Teutonic order's headquarters were established at Marienburg, Clement V was denouncing its brethren and appointing a papal commission to investigate charges against them. In 1320, John XXII instructed his legate in Spain to obtain information about the revenues of Santiago, Calatrava and Alcántara and to ensure that these orders maintained as large a force as they could on the Muslim frontier. In 1343, Clement VI threatened that, if the Hospitallers declined to give greater service against the infidel in the East, he would use some of their property to endow a new order, and a similar threat was made by Innocent VI in 1355, while in 1373 Gregory XI ordered inquests of Hospitaller properties as a preliminary to reform. The military orders were clearly at fault: the inactivity of the Hospital in the eastern Mediterranean, for example, cannot be explained wholly by financial difficulties, and the policies pursued by the Teutonic order in Prussia were becoming indistinguishable from those of a secular state.

Yet few religious orders of any kind managed to adhere fully to their original objectives and their early standards; nor were the failings of the military orders up to the fourteenth century all of their own making. Slowness of communications and the inadequacies of medieval administrative methods hindered effective government, while the illiteracy of many recruits hampered the proper instruction of brethren. In the military sphere, the very success of the Spanish reconquest reduced the need for military service against the infidel, and in this situation Spanish rulers were anxious to utilise the orders' manpower and revenues against Christian enemies. At the other end of the Mediterranean it was failure which deprived them of their original purpose, but it was not a failure of the orders alone. In the twelfth and thirteenth centuries, the crusader states were viable political units only at times when the neighbouring Muslim world was fragmented: without more extensive conquests and further Western colonisation, the resources derived from the kingdom of Jerusalem and from the other Western principalities in Syria were insufficient to contain any formidable threat from Islam; and in the thirteenth century the situation was made worse by the frequent lack of a king in the kingdom of Jerusalem. These states depended on aid from the West for survival. But in the thirteenth century fewer large crusading expeditions were dispatched to the East, and financial assistance to the rulers of the crusader states was provided only intermittently. Despite calls for crusades and the proliferation of crusading plans and proposals, the defence – and later the recovery – of the Holy Land was left increasingly to the military orders, which could, of course, call on reserves of manpower and money in Western Europe. Yet the orders' ability to defend the Holy Land was at the same time being diminished by the actions of Westerners. Just as crusading activity declined, so the initial enthusiasm for military orders waned. Their privileges and exemptions were reduced, and increasing financial demands were made on them by popes and Western secular rulers. The limited patronage which the orders did receive in the later thirteenth century often involved them in expenditure, such as the costs of maintaining chantry priests. At times even their dispatching of men and supplies to the East was impeded by Western kings. Although the Temple, the Hospital and the Teutonic order provided garrisons for numerous castles in the crusader states, as on other Christian frontiers, and could usually put a disciplined and experienced force into the field, they could not by themselves undertake the defence of the Holy Land, and their ability to render assistance was being reduced. Admittedly, they seem to have encountered few recruiting difficulties, partly because the Church was still regarded as a suitable career for younger sons, but they were hampered by the inadequacy of their financial resources.

Some criticism of the orders was, of course, valid, but in making it appear that these institutions were constantly failing to achieve what they were capable of doing, critics such as Richard of Mepham were seeking in part to relieve themselves of responsibility for the Holy Land and therefore to exonerate themselves from blame for the lack of success against Islam in the eastern Mediterranean. The failure was, in fact, that of Western Christendom as a whole, without whose continuous support it was impossible to maintain a distant Christian outpost amidst surrounding Muslim territories. Although most Westerners continued to pay lip-service to crusading ideals, and wanted the reform rather than the abolition of military orders, the Holy Land was a cause which had lasted too long.

Abbreviations

ACA	Archivo de la Corona de Aragón, Barcelona
AHN	Archivo Histórico Nacional, Madrid
AN	J. B. Pitra, *Analecta novissima: Spicilegii Solesmensis altera continuatio* (Paris, 1885–8)
BC	*Bullarium ordinis militiae de Calatrava*, ed. I. J. Ortega y Cotes, J. F. Alvarez de Baquedano and P. de Ortega Zúñiga y Aranda (Madrid, 1761)
CH	J. Delaville Le Roulx, *Cartulaire général de l'ordre des Hospitaliers de Saint-Jean de Jérusalem* (Paris, 1894–1906)
CTP	Peter of Dusburg, *Chronicon terrae Prussiae*, ed. M. Toeppen, *SRP*, vol. I
HCL	*Heinrici Chronicon Livoniae*, ed. L. Arbusow and A. Bauer, *MGH, Scriptores rerum germanicarum in usum scholarum* (Hanover, 1955)
MGH	*Monumenta Germaniae Historica*
OOS	J. L. Martín, *Orígenes de la orden militar de Santiago (1170–1195)* (Barcelona, 1974)
PL	J. P. Migne, *Patrologiae cursus completus. Series latina* (Paris, 1844–55)
PT	J. Michelet, *Procès des Templiers* (Paris, 1841–51)
PUTJ	R. Hiestand, *Papsturkunden für Templer und Johanniter* (Göttingen, 1972–84)
RHC Occ	*Recueil des historiens des croisades: historiens occidentaux* (Paris, 1844–95)
RHC Or	*Recueil des historiens des croisades: historiens orientaux* (Paris, 1872–98)
RSJ	E. Gallego Blanco, *The Rule of the Spanish Military Order of St James, 1170–1493* (Leiden, 1971)
RT	*La règle du Temple*, ed. H. de Curzon (Paris, 1886)
SBO	*Sancti Bernardi opera*, ed. J. Leclercq and H. M. Rochais (Rome, 1957–77)
SDO	M. Perlbach, *Die Statuten des Deutschen Ordens nach den ältesten Handschriften* (Halle, 1890)
SRP	*Scriptores rerum Prussicarum*, ed. T. Hirsch *et al.* (Leipzig, 1861–)

References

1. INTRODUCTION

1. *Liber ad milites Templi de laude novae militiae*, cap. 1, in *SBO*, III.214; *RT*, p. 58 caps. 51 (Latin), 57 (French).

2. FOUNDATIONS AND LOCATIONS

1. *Relatio de peregrinatione Saewulfi ad Hierosolymam et Terram Sanctam*, ed. W. R. B. Brownlow (Palestine Pilgrims Text Society, 1892) p. 36.
2. *The Rule of St Benedict*, cap. 4, ed. T. Fry (Collegeville, 1981) p. 182.
3. *Commentaria in regulam sancti Benedicti*, in *PL*, CII.696.
4. J. Leclercq and L. P. Bonnes, *Un maître de la vie spirituelle au XIe siècle, Jean de Fécamp* (Paris, 1946) pp. 201–2.
5. *Liber de vita christiana*, VII.28, ed. E. Perels (Berlin, 1930) pp. 248–9.
6. R. Somerville, *The Councils of Urban II. 1. Decreta Claromontensia* (Amsterdam, 1972) p. 74.
7. *RT*, pp. 12–13.
8. H. Hagenmeyer, *Epistulae et chartae ad historiam primi belli sacri spectantes* (Innsbruck, 1901) p. 137; Baldric of Dol, *Historia Jerosolimitana*, I.4, in *RHC Occ*, IV.15.
9. *PUTJ*, I.206 doc. 3.
10. *Gesta Dei per Francos*, I.1, in *RHC Occ*, IV.124.
11. St Bernard, *De laude novae militiae*, cap. 1, in *SBO*, III.214.
12. *Liber miraculorum sancte Fidis*, I.26, ed. A. Bouillet (Paris, 1897) p. 68.
13. *Rodulphi Glabri historiarum libri quinque*, II.18, ed. N. Bulst (Oxford, 1989) p. 82.
14. *SBO*, III.214.
15. J. Leclercq, 'Un document sur les débuts des Templiers', *Revue d'histoire ecclésiastique*, LII (1957) p. 87; C. Sclafert, 'Lettre inédite de Hugues de Saint-Victor aux chevaliers du Temple', *Revue d'ascétique et de mystique*, XXXIV (1958) p. 292.
16. Leclercq, 'Un document', p. 87; Sclafert, 'Lettre inédite', p. 292.
17. Leclercq, 'Un document', p. 88; Sclafert, 'Lettre inédite', p. 294.
18. *SBO*, III.217.
19. *CH*, I.98 doc. 116.
20. E. Strehlke, *Tabulae ordinis theutonici* (Berlin, 1869) p. 25 doc. 28.
21. *SDO*, p. 160.
22. *CH*, I.107 doc. 130.
23. *Les registres de Grégoire IX*, ed. L. Auvray (Paris, 1890–1955) II.254 doc. 2944.

24. *Historia Hierosolimitana*, cap. 66, in J. Bongars, *Gesta Dei per Francos* (Hanover, 1611) II.1085.

25. *Willelmi Chronica Andrensis*, ed. I. Heller, *MGH, Scriptores*, XXIV (Hanover, 1879) p. 769.

26. Marquis d'Albon, *Cartulaire général de l'ordre du Temple, 1119?–1150* (Paris, 1913) p. 25 doc. 33.

27. Ibid., p. 204 doc. 314; *Colección de documentos inéditos del Archivo general de la Corona de Aragón*, ed. P. de Bofarull y Mascaró, IV (Barcelona, 1849) p. 93 doc. 43.

28. *CH*, I.141 doc. 181.

29. J. González, *Regesta de Fernando II* (Madrid, 1943) p. 444.

30. *PUTJ*, I.280–1 doc. 89.

31. *Roderici Ximenii de Rada Historia de rebus Hispaniae sive Historia Gothica*, VII.14, ed. J. Fernández Valverde (Corpus Christianorum, Continuatio Mediaevalis, vol. LXXII, Turnhout, 1987) p. 235.

32. *RSJ*, p. 78.

33. J. M. Font Rius, *Cartas de población y de franquicia de Cataluña*, I (Madrid-Barcelona, 1969) p. 294 doc. 214.

34. *Cortes de los antiguos reinos de León y de Castilla*, I (Madrid, 1861) p. 94.

35. *OOS*, p. 227 doc. 53.

36. *Preussisches Urkundenbuch*, ed. R. Philippi, I.I (Königsberg, 1882) p. 51 doc. 69.

37. *HCL*, p. 18.

38. *Urkundenbuch zur Geschichte der Deutschen in Siebenbürgen*, ed. F. Zimmermann and C. Werner, I (Hermannstadt, 1892) p. 13 doc. 22.

39. Ibid., p. 40 doc. 49.

40. Ibid., p. 29 doc. 40.

41. *CH*, II.658 doc. 2445.

42. *AN*, II.405.

43. Strehlke, *Tabulae ordinis theutonici*, p. 134 doc. 133.

44. *MGH, Epistolae saeculi XIII*, ed. C. Rodenburg (Berlin, 1883–94) II.401 doc. 568; J. L. Huillard-Bréholles, *Historia diplomatica Friderici II* (Paris, 1852–61) VI. 624.

45. G. Meersseman, 'Etudes sur les anciennes confréries dominicaines. IV. Les milices de Jésus-Christ', *Archivum fratrum predicatorum*, XXIII (1953) p. 286.

46. *Registres de Grégoire IX*, I. 476 doc. 753.

47. D. M. Federici, *Istoria de' cavalieri gaudenti* (Vinegia, 1787) II, Codex diplomaticus, p. 20.

3. MILITARY ACTIVITIES

1. *OOS*, p. 252 doc. 73.

2. *HCL*, p. 126.

3. Ibid., pp. 160–1, 167.
4. *CTP*, III.27, 70, in *SRP*, I.65, 91.
5. *The Livonian Rhymed Chronicle*, trans. J. C. Smith and W. L. Urban (Bloomington, 1977) p. 52.
6. *CTP*, III.77, in *SRP*, I.94.
7. J. González, *Alfonso IX* (Madrid, 1944) II.453 doc. 346.
8. J. González, *El reino de Castilla en la época de Alfonso VIII* (Madrid, 1960) II.306 doc. 183.
9. F. D. Gazulla, 'La orden del Santo Redentor', *Boletín de la sociedad castellonense de cultura*, IX (1928) p. 375.
10. *HCL*, p. 68.
11. *RT*, p. 112 cap. 141.
12. *SDO*, p. 110 cap. 42.
13. *RT*, p. 129 cap. 172.
14. *Historia aecclesiastica*, XII.29, ed. M. Chibnall, VI (Oxford, 1978) p. 310.
15. Albon, *Cartulaire du Temple*, p. 308 doc. 499.
16. *Liv-, Esth-, und Curländisches Urkundenbuch nebst Regesten*, ed. F. G. von Bunge *et al.* (Reval, 1853–1914) I. 109 doc. 91.
17. R. B. C. Huygens, *De constructione castri Saphet. Construction et fonctions d'un château fort franc en Terre Sainte* (Amsterdam, 1981) p. 36.
18. *Itinerarium peregrinorum et gesta regis Ricardi*, ed. W. Stubbs, I (Rolls Series, 1864) p. 289.
19. *Chronique d'Ernoul et de Bernard le trésorier*, ed. L. de Mas Latrie (Paris, 1871) pp. 27–8.
20. J. Riley-Smith, 'The Templars and the Castle of Tortosa in Syria: An Unknown Document concerning the Acquisition of the Fortress', *English Historical Review*, LXXXIV (1969) p. 284–5.
21. *CH*, I.492 doc. 783.
22. Abu-Shama, *Le livre de deux jardins*, in *RHC Or*, IV. 379.
23. *Les gestes des chiprois*, cap. 303, ed. G. Raynaud (Paris, 1887) p. 162.
24. *CH*, I.227 doc. 313.
25. Abu-Shama, *Le livre de deux jardins*, in *RHC Or*, IV. 206.
26. *Die Schriften des Kölner Domscholasters, späteren Bischofs von Paderborn und Kardinal-Bischofs von S. Sabina Oliverus*, ed. H. Hoogeweg (Tübingen, 1894) pp. 170–1.
27. Huygens, *De constructione*, p. 39; Burchard of Mount Sion, *Descriptio Terre Sancte*, ed. J. C. M. Laurent, in *Peregrinationes medii aevi quatuor* (Leipzig, 1864) p. 34.
28. M. Benvenisti, *The Crusaders in the Holy Land* (Jerusalem, 1970) p. 298.
29. *BC*, p. 451.
30. *Colección de documentos inéditos*, IV.209 doc. 77.
31. *HCL*, p. 84.
32. Font Rius, *Cartas de población*, I.401 doc. 276.
33. ACA, Archivo del gran priorato de Cataluña, pergaminos de Gardeny, no. 1786.
34. *CH*, II.125 doc. 1357.

35. Ibid., IV.292 doc. 3308.
36. *Ayyubids, Mamlukes and Crusaders: Selections from the Tarikh al-Duwal wa'l Mulūk of Ibn al-Furāt*, trans. U. and M. C. Lyons, II (Cambridge, 1971) p. 146.
37. *CTP*, III.118, in *SRP*, I.110.
38. *BC*, p. 41.
39. *Chronicon Magni presbyteri*, ed. W. Wattenbach, *MGH, Scriptores*, XVII (Hanover, 1861) p. 507.
40. Cap. 74, ed. C. Rosell (Biblioteca de autores españoles, vol. LXVI, Madrid, 1953) p. 58.
41. *CTP*, III.71, in *SRP*, I.91.
42. Ibn al-Athīr, *Kamel-Altervarykh*, in *RHC Or*, I.571–2.
43. Ibid., I.679.
44. Ibid., I.688.
45. Ibid., I.736.
46. *RSJ*, p. 98 cap. 11; D. W. Lomax, *La orden de Santiago (1170–1275)* (Madrid, 1965) p. 224 cap. 15.
47. C. Kohler, 'Deux projets de croisade en Terre-Sainte, composés à la fin du XIIIe siècle et au début du XIVe', *Revue de l'orient latin*, X (1903–4) p. 442.
48. Ibid.
49. Odo of Deuil, *De profectione Ludovici VII in orientem*, lib. 7, ed. V. G. Berry (New York, 1948) p. 124.
50. *OOS*, p. 273 doc. 92.
51. *CH*, II.343, 482 docs. 1824, 2105.
52. Ibid., II.415 doc. 1975.
53. M. Rivera Garretas, *La encomienda, el priorato y la villa de Uclés en la edad media (1174–1310)* (Madrid–Barcelona, 1985) pp. 388–9 doc. 183.
54. ACA, Cancillería real, registro 70 fol. 93.
55. *Recueil des historiens des Gaules et de la France*, ed. M. Bouquet *et al.*, XVI (Paris, 1878) p. 157 doc. 469.
56. J. Torres Fontes, 'La orden de Santa María de España', *Miscelanea medieval murciana*, III (1977) pp. 110–11 doc. 10; J. Menéndez Pidal, 'Noticias acerca de la orden militar de Santa María de España', *Revista de archivos, bibliotecas y museos*, XVII (1907) p. 177 doc. 4.
57. *Epistola summo pontifici Nicolao IV*, ed. J. Rambaud-Buhot, in *Beati magistri R. Lulli opera latina*, III (Palma, 1954) p. 96.
58. *BC*, p. 38.

4. RESOURCES AND MANPOWER

1. *Historia rerum in partibus transmarinis gestarum*, XII.7, in *RHC Occ*, I.521.
2. A. L. Javierre Mur, *La orden de Calatrava en Portugal* (Madrid, 1952) p. 49 doc. 3; J. González, *Reinado y diplomas de Fernando III*, III (Córdoba, 1986) p. 319 doc. 754.

3. *CH*, III.316 doc. 3562.
4. J. H. Hennes, *Codex diplomaticus ordinis sanctae Mariae Theutonicorum*, I (Mainz, 1845) p. 37 doc. 35.
5. *CH*, II.231 doc. 1590.
6. *Cartulaire de la commanderie de Richerenches de l'ordre du Temple (1136–1214)*, ed. Marquis de Ripert-Monclar (Avignon-Paris, 1907) p. 233, appendix doc. 6.
7. *CH*, II.492 doc. 2124; *Documentos de Sigena*, ed. A. Ubieto Arteta, I (Valencia, 1972) p. 218 doc. 147.
8. *CH*, IV.26 doc. 4555.
9. AHN, Ordenes militares, Montesa, documentos reales, no. 134.
10. Rivera Garretas, *Uclés*, p. 283 doc. 69.
11. *The Cartulary of the Knights of St John of Jerusalem in England*, ed. M. Gervers (Oxford, 1982) p. 215 doc. 372.
12. E. de Hinojosa, *El régimen señorial y la cuestión agraria en Cataluña* (Madrid, 1905) p. 89 note 3.
13. *Statutes of the Realm*, I (London, 1810) p. 87.
14. *Cartulaires des Templiers de Douzens*, ed. P. Gérard and E. Magnou (Paris, 1965) p. 209 doc. 26.
15. AHN, Montesa, documentos particulares, no. 582.
16. *SDO*, p. 30.
17. *PUTJ*, I.207 doc. 3.
18. AHN, Códices, cód. 470, pp. 72–3 doc. 86.
19. AHN, cód. 467, pp. 258–9 doc. 265.
20. ACA, Cancillería real, pergaminos de Jaime II, no. 2360.
21. *CH*, IV.291 doc. 3308.
22. J. Villanueva, *Viage literario a las iglesias de España*, V (Madrid, 1806) p. 277.
23. L. de Mas Latrie, *Histoire de l'île de Chypre sous le règne des princes de la maison de Lusignan*, II (Paris, 1852) p. 82.
24. L. B. Larking, *The Knights Hospitallers in England* (Camden Society, 1857) pp. 13 and 183.
25. *BC*, p. 44.
26. *PL*, CLV.1085.
27. London, Mercers Company, Register of Writings, I.8.
28. González, *Reino de Castilla*, III.140 doc. 641.
29. Ibid., III.165 doc. 658.
30. *CH*, III.484 doc. 3917.
31. H. Finke, *Acta aragonensia*, III (Berlin, 1922) p. 146 doc. 65.
32. *CH*, IV.19–20 doc. 4549 cap. 23.
33. Ibid., III.158 doc. 3261.
34. Ibid., II.557 doc. 2213 cap. 121.
35. K. Schottmüller, *Der Untergang des Templer-Ordens*, II (Berlin, 1887) p. 45.
36. *RT*, pp. 25–6 cap. 62.
37. *SDO*, p. 51 cap. 30.

38. *Curia Regis Rolls, 1223–1224* (London, 1955) p. 176.
39. *CH*, I.673 doc. 1082.
40. *Les registres d'Innocent IV*, ed. E. Berger, III (Paris, 1897) p. 21 doc. 5548.
41. Madrid, Biblioteca Nacional, MS 8582 fol. 44v.
42. *CH*, II.556 doc. 2213 cap. 121.
43. *Urkundenbuch des Deutschordens-Ballei Hessen*, ed. A. Wyss, I (Leipzig, 1884) p. 185 doc. 241.
44. *CTP*, I.5; III.133, in *SRP*, I.31, 116.
45. *CH*, II.556 doc. 2213 cap. 121.
46. *AN*, II.410.
47. *PT*, I.416.
48. *RT*, p. 340 cap. 663.
49. *Summa theologiae*, II.II.188.6, Blackfriars edn, XLVII (London, 1973) p. 206.
50. H. Finke, *Papsttum und Untergang des Templerordens* (Münster, 1907) II.4 doc. 4.
51. *Les deux rédactions en vers du Moniage Guillaume*, ed. W. Cloetta, I (Paris, 1906) pp. 72–3.
52. *CH*, III.541 doc. 4050.
53. Ed. H. R. Luard, II (Rolls Series, 1890) p. 287.

5. STRUCTURES AND REGULATIONS

1. J. M. Canivez, *Statuta capitulorum generalium ordinis Cisterciensis*, I (Louvain, 1933) p. 520.
2. *SDO*, p. 60 cap. IIb.
3. Ibid., p. 59 cap. II.
4. ACA, Cancillería real, Cartas reales diplomáticas, Templarios no. 173.
5. *SDO*, p. 59 cap. IIb.
6. *CH*, III.448 doc. 3839.
7. *SDO*, p. 32 cap. 6.
8. Ibid., p. 96 cap. 7.
9. *RT*, p. 85 cap. 97.
10. *SDO*, p. 76 cap. 31.
11. *CH*, II.548 doc. 2213.
12. *SDO*, p. 102 cap. 17.
13. ACA, Cartas reales diplomáticas, Templarios no. 290.
14. *SDO*, p. 97 cap. 8.
15. *RT*, pp. 23, 26, 49 caps. 58 (Lat), 14 (Fr), 45 (Fr), 67 (Lat).
16. *CH*, III.229 doc. 3396 cap. 22.
17. Ibid., I. 277 doc. 403.
18. Paris, Bibliothèque Nationale, MS Fr. 6049 fol. 244.
19. *CH*, III.655, 673 docs. 4267, 4293.
20. Ibid., II.677–8 doc. 2488.

21. *SDO*, p. 49 cap. 27.
22. H. Finke, 'Nachträge und Ergänzungen zu den *Acta aragonensia* (I–III)', *Spanische Forschungen der Görresgesellschaft: Gesammelte Aufsätze zur Kulturgeschichte Spaniens*, IV (1933) pp. 451–2 doc. 14.
23. A. J. Forey, *The Templars in the Corona de Aragón* (London, 1973) p. 414 doc. 44.
24. *RSJ*, pp. 122–4 cap. 46.
25. *PL*, CCXVII.283.
26. Javierre Mur, *La orden de Calatrava en Portugal*, p. 46 doc. 1.
27. *RT*, p. 69 cap. 56.
28. *BC*, p. 4.
29. *RT*, p. 234 cap. 431.
30. *PUTJ*, I.207 doc. 3.
31. *SDO*, p. 52 cap. 31.
32. *RT*, p. 28 cap. 17.
33. *SDO*, p. 38 cap. 11.
34. *PUTJ*, I.208 doc. 3.
35. *RT*, p. 113 cap. 143.
36. Madrid, Biblioteca Nacional, MS 8582 fol. 46v.
37. J. F. O'Callaghan, 'The Earliest "Difiniciones" of the Order of Calatrava, 1304–1383', *Traditio*, XVII (1961) p. 269 cap. 1.
38. *CH*, III.738 doc. 4413.
39. *RT*, p. 165 cap. 270.
40. *CH*, III.52 doc. 3039 cap. 38.
41. A. Stroick, '*Collectio de scandalis ecclesiae*: nova editio', *Archivum franciscanum historicum*, XXIV (1931) p. 57.
42. *OOS*, p. 252 doc. 73.
43. *AN*, II.406–7.
44. *PT*, II.137.
45. *RT*, p. 187 cap. 321.
46. *RSJ*, p. 84; *OOS*, p. 250 doc. 73.
47. *SDO*, p. 44.
48. *PT*, I.385.
49. *RT*, p. 171 cap. 282.
50. Ibid., p. 22 cap. 10.
51. Ibid., p. 57 cap. 55.
52. *SDO*, p. 47 cap. 23.
53. *RT*, p. 35 cap. 26.
54. *SDO*, p. 43 cap. 15.
55. *RT*, p. 35 cap. 25.
56. *RSJ*, pp. 94–6 caps. 9–10.
57. Cap. 4, in *SBO*, III.220–1.
58. *CH*, II.551 doc. 2213 cap. 105.
59. Ibid., II.450 doc. 2044.
60. Ibid., II.101 doc. 1322.
61. Strehlke, *Tabulae ordinis theutonici*, p. 387 doc. 560.

62. *RSJ*, p. 92 cap. 7.
63. *PT*, I.194.
64. Ibid., I.555.
65. *AN*, II.412.
66. *CTP*, III.146, in *SRP*, I.122.

6. CRITICISM AND CHANGE

1. *De nugis curialium*, I.20, ed. M. R. James, C. N. L. Brooke and R. A. B. Mynors (Oxford, 1983) p. 60.
2. *PL*, CCXV.1217–18.
3. *Anglo-Norman Political Songs*, ed. I. S. T. Aspin (Anglo-Norman Texts, vol. XI, Oxford, 1953) p. 123.
4. P. Meyer, 'Les derniers troubadours de la Provence', *Bibliothèque de l'Ecole des Chartes*, XXX (1869) pp. 289, 497–8.
5. *AN*, II.410.
6. Ibid.
7. *Anglo-Norman Political Songs*, p. 134.
8. Ed. H. R. Luard (Rolls Series, 1872–83) IV.291.
9. Pierre Dubois, *De recuperatione Terre Sancte*, cap. 9, ed. A. Diotti (Florence, 1977) p. 126.
10. Humbert of Romans, *De eruditione praedicatorum*, II.34, in *Maxima biblioteca veterum patrum*, ed. M. de La Bigne, XXV (Lyon, 1677) p. 471.
11. A. Theiner, *Vetera monumenta Poloniae et Lithuaniae*, I (Rome, 1860) p. 119 doc. 204; *Liv-, Esth-, und Curländisches Urkundenbuch*, II.48 doc. 630.
12. *Chronica majora*, ed. Luard, V.745–6.
13. Stroick, '*Collectio de scandalis ecclesiae*', p. 57.
14. *Annales de Dunstaplia*, in *Annales monastici*, ed. H. R. Luard, III (Rolls Series, 1866) p. 366; *Annales Eberhardi*, ed. P. Jaffé, *MGH Scriptores*, XVII (Hanover, 1861) p. 594.
15. Cap. 11, in G. Golubovich, *Biblioteca bio-bibliografica della Terra Santa e dell'oriente francescano*, II (Quaracchi, 1913) p. 15.
16. Huillard-Bréholles, *Historia diplomatica Friderici II*, III.266–7; *MGH, Epistolae saeculi XIII*, I.346 doc. 427.
17. 'Continuation de Guillaume de Tyr de 1229 à 1261, dite du manuscrit de Rothelin', in *RHC Occ*, II.549; J. Bédier, *Les chansons de croisade* (Paris, 1909) p. 223.
18. *PT*, I.45.
19. *Opus maius*, III.13, ed. J. H. Bridges (London, 1900) III.121–2.
20. *Liv-, Esth-, und Curländisches Urkundenbuch*, I.41–3 doc. 36.
21. *De eruditione praedicatorum*, II.37, in *Maxima biblioteca*, XXV.473.
22. *CH*, II.254 doc. 1633; *MGH, Epistolae saeculi XIII*, I.58 doc. 79.
23. Finke, *Papsttum und Untergang des Templerordens*, II.56 doc. 37.
24. Ubieto Arteta, *Documentos de Sigena*, I.175 doc. 118.

25. ACA, Archivo del gran priorato de Cataluña, Casas antiguas, perga-minos no. 46.
26. *PT*, I.44–5.
27. Ed. J. Rambaud-Buhot, in *Beati magistri R. Lulli opera latina*, III.101.
28. *Councils and Synods, with other Documents relating to the English Church*, ed. F. M. Powicke and C. R. Cheney, II (Oxford, 1964) p. 1113.
29. Kohler, 'Deux projets', pp. 442–3.
30. G. Bratianu, 'Le conseil du roi Charles: essai sur l'internationale chrétienne et les nationalités à la fin du moyen âge', *Revue historique du sud-est européen*, XIX (1942) p. 358.
31. Finke, *Papsttum und Untergang des Templerordens*, II.72 doc. 48.
32. C. V. Langlois, 'Notices et documents relatifs à l'histoire du XIIIe et du XIVe siècle', *Revue historique*, LXXXVII (1905) p. 75.
33. *Regestum Clementis papae V*, annus septimus (Rome,1887) p. 67 doc. 7885.
34. *PT*, II.209.
35. Ibid., I.202–3.
36. G. Lizerand, *Le dossier de l'affaire des Templiers* (Paris, 1964) pp. 60–2; Finke, *Papsttum und Untergang des Templerordens*, II.109 doc. 70.

Further Reading

Books and articles in English are listed where possible, but most of the works which have been published on the military orders are in other languages.

1. GENERAL

Few attempts have been made to produce general surveys of the military orders since the publication of H. Prutz, *Die geistlichen Ritterorden* (Berlin, 1908): D. Seward, *The Monks of War* (London, 1972) is not altogether reliable. Recently, however, several collections of essays on various orders have appeared, such as J. Fleckenstein and M. Hellmann, eds., *Die geistlichen Ritterorden Europas* (Vorträge und Forschungen, XXVI, Sigmaringen, 1980), which includes several important papers, and *Anuario de estudios medievales*, XI (1981), which contains essays on military orders in Spain.

There are numerous surveys of individual orders, and also regional studies which cover a variety of topics. There is no detailed history of the Templars in English, but E. Burman, *The Templars: Knights of God* (London, 1986) is generally sound, and M. Barber, 'The Social Context of the Templars', *Transactions of the Royal Historical Society*, 5th series, XXXIV (1984) briefly raises a wide range of issues. See also M. Melville, *La vie des Templiers* (Paris, 1951) and M. L. Bulst-Thiele, *Sacrae domus militiae Templi Hierosolymitani magistri: Untersuchungen zur Geschichte des Templerordens, 1118/19–1314* (Göttingen, 1974). Regional studies of the Templars include T. W. Parker, *The Knights Templars in England* (Tucson, 1963); J. A. Durbec, 'Les Templiers en Provence. Formation des commanderies et répartition géographique de leurs biens', *Provence historique*, IX (1959); A. J. Forey, *The Templars in the Corona de Aragón* (London, 1973); and P. Schickl, 'Die Entstehung und Entwicklung des Templerordens in Katalonien und Aragon', *Spanische Forschungen der Görresgesellschaft: Gesammelte Aufsätze zur Kulturgeschichte Spaniens*, XXVIII (1975). Among regional studies which discuss both Templars and Hospitallers, see A. M. Legras, *Les commanderies des Templiers et des Hospitaliers de Saint-Jean de Jérusalem en Saintonge et en Aunis* (Paris, 1983) and M. L. Ledesma Rubio, *Templarios y Hospitalarios en el reino de Aragón* (Zaragoza, n.d.).

The standard work on the Hospital is J. Riley-Smith, *The Knights of St John in Jerusalem and Cyprus, c.1050–1310* (London, 1967); this largely supersedes J. Delaville Le Roulx, *Les Hospitaliers en Terre Sainte et à Chypre* (Paris, 1904) and E. J. King, *The Knights Hospitallers in the Holy Land* (London, 1931). Regional studies of the Hospitallers are provided by W. Rees, *History of the Order of St John in Wales and on the Welsh Border* (Cardiff, 1947) and S. A. García Larragueta, *El gran priorado de Navarra de la orden de San Juan de Jerusalén* (Pamplona, 1957). B. B. Szczesniak, *The Knights Hospitallers in Poland*

and Lithuania (The Hague–Paris, 1969), has little on the twelfth and thirteenth centuries.

I. Sterns, 'The Teutonic Knights in the Crusader States', in K. Setton, ed., *History of the Crusades*, V (Wisconsin, 1985), gives a short survey of some aspects of the history of the Teutonic order. C. Krollmann, *The Teutonic Order in Prussia* (Elbing, 1938) is very dated. General works on the Teutonic order in German include M. Tumler, *Der Deutsche Orden im Wenden, Wachsen und Wirken bis 1400* (Vienna, 1955) and the shorter M. Tumler and U. Arnold, *Der Deutsche Orden. Von seinem Ursprung bis zur Gegenwart* (Bad Münstereifel, 1981), while H. Boockmann, *Der Deutsche Orden. Zwölf Kapitel aus seiner Geschichte* (Munich, 1981) also provides a useful survey. On the Teutonic order in Mediterranean lands, see K. Forstreuter, *Der Deutsche Orden am Mittelmeer* (Bonn, 1967). The leading work on the Swordbrethren is F. Benninghoven, *Der Orden der Schwertbrüder: Fratres milicie Christi de Livonia* (Cologne, 1965). The military orders in the Baltic region are discussed in W. Urban, *The Baltic Crusade* (DeKalb, 1975) and *The Prussian Crusade* (Lanham, 1980); more perceptive is E. Christiansen, *The Northern Crusades: The Baltic and the Catholic Frontier, 1100–1525* (London, 1980).

On the order of St Lazarus, S. Shahar, 'Des lepreux pas comme les autres: l'ordre de Saint-Lazare dans le royaume latin de Jérusalem', *Revue historique*, CCLXVII (1982) is more useful than P. Bertrand de la Grassière, *L'ordre militaire et hospitalier de Saint-Lazare de Jérusalem* (Paris, 1960). On the order of St Thomas of Acre, J. Watney, *Some Account of the Hospital of St Thomas of Acon, in the Cheap, London, and of the Plate of the Mercers' Company* (London, 1892) and A.J. Forey, 'The Military Order of St Thomas of Acre', *English Historical Review*, XCII (1977) may be consulted.

The best work on the Spanish order of Santiago is D. W. Lomax, *La orden de Santiago, 1170–1275* (Madrid, 1965); see also his lecture *Another Sword for St James* (Birmingham, 1974). For regional studies of this order, see R. Sáinz de la Maza Lasoli, *La orden de Santiago en la Corona de Aragón: La encomienda de Montalbán (1210–1327)* (Zaragoza, 1980) and E. Benito Ruano, 'La orden de Santiago en Francia', *Hispania*, XXXVII (1977). J. F. O'Callaghan, 'The Affiliation of the Order of Calatrava with the Order of Cîteaux', *Analecta sacri ordinis Cisterciensis*, XV (1959) and XVI (1960) (reprinted in his *The Spanish Military Order of Calatrava and its Affiliates* (London, 1975)) covers more ground than its title suggests and is the most important study of Calatrava in English. F. Gutton, *L'ordre de Calatrava* (Paris, 1955), *L'ordre de Santiago* (Paris, 1972) and *L'ordre d'Alcantara* (Paris, 1975) are all sketchy on the twelfth and thirteenth centuries. The most recent survey of the order of Mountjoy is A.J. Forey, 'The Order of Mountjoy', *Speculum*, XLVI (1971), and on the foundation at Alcalá, see D.W. Lomax, 'Las dependencias hispánicas de Santa María de la Selva Mayor', *Príncipe de Viana*, XLVII (1986). The order of Santa María de España is discussed in J. Menéndez Pidal, 'Noticias acerca de la orden militar de Santa María de España', *Revista de archivos, bibliotecas y museos*, XVII (1907) and J. Torres Fontes, 'La orden de Santa María de España', *Miscelanea medieval murciana*, III (1977).

There are no satisfactory studies of the orders established to fight against Western Christians, but on the order of the Faith and Peace, see M. Branet, 'L'ordre de Saint Jacques de la Foix et de la Paix', *Bulletin de la Société archéologique du Gers*, I (1900), and on the order of the Blessed Virgin Mary, D. M. Federici, *Istoria de' cavalieri gaudenti* (Vinegia, 1787) and A. de Stefano, 'Le origini dei frati gaudenti', *Archivum romanicum*, X (1926).

2. FOUNDATIONS AND LOCATIONS

The views expressed in the first part of Chapter 2 are elaborated more fully in A.J. Forey, 'The Emergence of the Military Order in the Twelfth Century', *Journal of Ecclesiastical History*, XXXVI (1985). For a different interpretation, see E. Lourie, 'The Confraternity of Belchite, the Ribāt, and the Temple', *Viator*, XIII (1982). On the development of crusading ideas, C. Erdmann, *The Origin of the Idea of Crusade*, trans. M.W. Baldwin and W. Goffart (Princeton, 1977) is still valuable; and on concepts of knighthood, M. Keen, *Chivalry* (London, 1984) and J. Flori, *L'essor de la chevalerie, XIe–XIIe siècles* (Geneva, 1986) should be consulted. The early history of the Temple is covered by M. Barber, 'The Origins of the Order of the Temple', *Studia monastica*, XII (1970). The letter of Hugh to the Templars is discussed and published by J. Leclercq, 'Un document sur les débuts des Templiers', *Revue d'histoire ecclésiastique*, LII (1957) and C. Sclafert, 'Lettre inédite de Hugues de Saint-Victor aux chevaliers du Temple', *Revue d'ascétique et de mystique*, XXXIV (1958). R. Hiestand, 'Kardinalbischof Matthäus von Albano, das Konzil von Troyes und die Entstehung des Templerordens', *Zeitschrift für Kirchengeschichte*, XCIX (1988) argues convincingly that the Council of Troyes was held in 1129.

On the early history of the Hospital, see R. Hiestand, 'Die Anfänge der Johanniter', in *Die geistlichen Ritterorden Europas*; and T.S. Miller, 'The Knights of St. John and the Hospitals of the Latin West', *Speculum*, LIII (1978) places its hospitaller role in context. Its transformation into a military order is considered by A.J. Forey, 'The Militarisation of the Hospital of St John', *Studia monastica*, XXVI (1984).

On the early history of the Teutonic order, see M.L. Favreau, *Studien zur Frühgeschichte des Deutschen Ordens* (Stuttgart, n.d.), and U. Arnold, 'Entstehung und Frühzeit des Deutschen Ordens', in *Die geistlichen Ritterorden Europas*. U. Arnold discusses the date of the *Narracio de primordiis ordinis theutonici* in 'De primordiis ordinis theutonici narratio', *Preussenland*, IV (1966). *Die geistlichen Ritterorden Europas* also contains H. Zimmermann, 'Der Deutsche Ritterorden in Siebenbürgen', which discusses its establishment in Hungary, and G. Labuda, 'Die Urkunden über die Anfänge des Deutschen Ordens im Kulmerland und in Preussen in den Jahren 1226–1235', dealing with its arrival in Prussia. A further essay looks at the creation of the order of Dobrin: Z. H. Nowak, 'Milites Christi de Prussia. Der Orden

zu Dobrin und seine Stellung in der preussischen Mission'. On the estab-
lishment of military orders in Central and Eastern Europe, see also W.
Kuhn, 'Ritterorden als Grenzhüter des Abendlandes gegen das östliche Heidentum',
Ostdeutsche Wissenschaft, VI (1959) and Z. H. Nowak, 'Der Anteil der
Ritterorden an der preussischen Mission (mit Ausnahme des Deutschen
Ordens)', *Die Rolle der Ritterorden in der Christianisierung und Kolonisierung des
Ostseegebietes*, ed. Z. H. Nowak (Torun, 1983).

The origins of Santiago are discussed by J. L. Martín, *Orígines de la orden
militar de Santiago (1170–1195)* (Barcelona, 1974); those of Alcántara are
treated in J. F. O'Callaghan, 'The Foundation of the Order of Alcántara,
1176–1218', *Catholic Historical Review*, XLVII (1962) and R. P. de Azevedo, 'A
ordem militar de S. Julião do Pereiro, depois chamada de Alcântara', *Anuario
de estudios medievales*, XI (1981). The latter writer has also discussed the early
history of Avis in 'Primórdios da ordem militar de Evora', *Boletim cultural da
junta distrital de Evora*, VIII (1967). For proposals to extend the Spanish orders'
activity to North Africa and the East, see A. Ballesteros, 'La toma de Salé en
tiempos de Alfonso X el Sabio', *Al-Andalus*, VIII (1943), and E. Benito
Ruano's articles 'Balduino II de Constantinopla y la orden de Santiago: un
proyecto de defensa del imperio latino de oriente', *Hispania*, XII (1952) and
'Santiago, Calatrava y Antioquía', *Anuario de estudios medievales*, I (1964).

The use of military orders against Western Christians is discussed in G.
Meersseman, 'Etudes sur les anciennes confréries dominicaines. IV. Les
milices de Jésus-Christ', *Archivum fratrum predicatorum*, XXIII (1953); E.
Delaruelle, 'Templiers et Hospitaliers en Languedoc pendant la croisade
des Albigeois', *Paix de Dieu et guerre sainte en Languedoc au XIIIe siècle* (Cahiers
de Fanjeaux, IV, Toulouse, 1969); N. J. Housley, 'Politics and Heresy in
Italy: Anti-Heretical Crusades, Orders and Confraternities, 1200–1500',
Journal of Ecclesiastical History, XXXIII (1982); and A. J. Forey, 'The Military
Orders and Holy War against Christians in the Thirteenth Century', *English
Historical Review*, CIV (1989).

3. MILITARY ACTIVITIES

The orders' military activities are best studied by reading the chronicles
which describe warfare on the various fronts. Many of these are available in
English. On crusades to the eastern Mediterranean, see Odo of Deuil, *De
profectione Ludovici VII in orientem*, ed. and trans. V. G. Berry (New York,
1948); Ambroise, *The Crusade of Richard Lion-Heart*, trans. M. J. Hubert (New
York, 1941); Oliver of Paderborn, *The Capture of Damietta*, trans. J.J.
Gavigan (Philadelphia, 1948) (this translation also appears in E. Peters,
ed., *Christian Society and the Crusades, 1198–1229* (Philadelphia, 1971)); and the
biography of Louis IX by Joinville, of which translations have been
published by Everyman (1908) and Penguin (1963). On the crusader states
in the twelfth century, see William of Tyre, *History of Deeds done beyond the Sea*,

trans. E. A. Babcock and A. C. Krey (New York, 1943). Muslim sources in English for this region include *The Damascus Chronicle of the Crusades*, trans. H. A. R. Gibb (London, 1932) and *Ayyubids, Mamlukes and Crusaders: Selections from the Tarikh al-Duwal wa'l-Mulūk of Ibn al-Furāt*, trans. U. and M. C. Lyons (Cambridge, 1971). Extracts from Muslim sources are published in F. Gabrieli, ed., *Arab Historians of the Crusades* (London, 1969). On the Baltic region, see *The Chronicle of Henry of Livonia*, trans. J. A. Brundage (Madison, 1961); *The Livonian Rhymed Chronicle*, trans. J. C. Smith and W. Urban (Bloomington, 1977); and *The Chronicle of Novgorod, 1016–1471*, trans. R. Michell and N. Forbes, (Camden Society, 3rd series, XXV, London, 1914). For Spain there is *The Chronicle of James I, King of Aragon*, trans. J. Forster (London, 1883).

Information about the orders' military activities is to be found in general works dealing with each front, such as S. Runciman, *History of the Crusades* (Cambridge, 1951–4) and D. W. Lomax, *The Reconquest of Spain* (London, 1978). On military personnel and methods of warfare, see R. C. Smail, *Crusading Warfare, 1097–1193* (Cambridge, 1956); P. Contamine, *War in the Middle Ages*, trans. M. Jones (Oxford, 1984); and M. Bennett, 'La Règle du Temple as a Military Manual or How to Deliver a Cavalry Charge'; in C. Harper-Bill, C. J. Holdsworth and J. L. Nelson, eds., *Studies in Medieval History presented to R. Allen Brown* (Woodbridge, 1989).

On castles in the Holy Land, P. Deschamps, *Les châteaux des croisés en Terre Sainte* (Paris, 1934–39), T. S. R. Boase, *Castles and Churches of the Crusading Kingdom* (London, 1967), and M. Benvenisti, *The Crusaders in the Holy Land* (Jerusalem, 1970) are all useful. More particularly, see J. Riley-Smith, 'The Templars and the Castle of Tortosa in Syria: An Unknown Document concerning the Acquisition of the Fortress', *English Historical Review*, LXXXIV (1969); A. W. Lawrence, 'The Castle of Baghras', in T. S. R. Boase, ed., *The Cilician Kingdom of Armenia* (Edinburgh, 1978); R. B. C. Huygens, 'Un nouveau texte du traité "De constructione castri Saphet" ', *Studi medievali*, VI (1965) and *De constructione castri Saphet* (Amsterdam, 1981), together with the comments on this work by D. Pringle, 'Reconstructing the Castle of Safad', *Palestine Exploration Quarterly*, CXVII (1985); and D. J. Cathcart King, 'The Taking of Le Krak des Chevaliers in 1271', *Antiquity*, XXIII (1949).

On the military orders in the kingdom of Jerusalem in the thirteenth century, see M. L. Bulst, 'Zur Geschichte der Ritterorden und des Königreichs Jerusalem im 13. Jahrhundert bis zur Schlacht bei La Forbie am 17. Oktober 1244', *Deutsches Archiv für Erforschung des Mittelalters*, XXII (1966), and J. Prawer, 'Military Orders and Crusader Politics in the Second Half of the Thirteenth Century', in *Die geistlichen Ritterorden Europas* (see above). The events of the early 1240s have been most recently discussed by P. J. Jackson, 'The Crusades of 1239–41 and their Aftermath', *Bulletin of the School of Oriental and African Studies*, L (1987). The Teutonic order's position in the eastern Mediterranean is considered by W. Hubatsch, 'Der Deutsche Orden und die Reichslehnschaft über Cypern', *Nachrichten der Akademie der Wissen-*

schaften in Göttingen, Phil.-hist Klasse (1955), and 'Montfort und die Bildung des Deutschordensstaates im Heiligen Lande', ibid. (1966). See also M. L. Favreau-Lilie, 'Die Kreuzfahrerherrschaft Scandalion (Iskanderūne)', *Zeitschrift des Deutschen Palästina-Vereins*, XCIII (1977), and 'The Teutonic Knights in Acre after the Fall of Montfort (1271): Some Reflections', in B. Z. Kedar, H. E. Mayer and R. C. Smail, eds, *Outremer: Studies in the History of the Crusading Kingdom of Jerusalem presented to Joshua Prawer* (Jerusalem, 1982); and H. E. Mayer, 'Die Seigneurie de Joscelin und der Deutsche Orden', *Die geistlichen Ritterorden Europas*. On the orders' role in Armenia, and particularly that of the Templars in the Amanus march, J. Riley-Smith, 'The Templars and the Teutonic Knights in Cilician Armenia', *The Cilician Kingdom of Armenia* (see above) should be consulted.

One view of the nature of the conflict in the Baltic region is provided by E. Weise, 'Der Heidenkampf des Deutschen Ordens', *Zeitschrift für Ostforschung*, XII–XIII (1963–4); on this topic see also K. Górski, 'The Teutonic Order in Prussia', *Medievalia et Humanistica*, XVII (1966). Among the essays published in *Die Rolle der Ritterorden in der Christianisierung und Kolonisierung des Ostseegebietes* (see above), is K. Górski, 'Probleme der Christianisierung in Preussen, Livland und Litauen'. On frontier defence, see W. L. Urban, 'The Organization of the Defense of the Livonian Frontier in the Thirteenth Century', *Speculum*, XLVIII (1973).

A general survey of military activities in Spain is provided by A. J. Forey, 'The Military Orders and the Spanish Reconquest in the Twelfth and Thirteenth Centuries', *Traditio*, XL (1984). S. A. García Larragueta, 'La orden de San Juan en la crisis del imperio hispánico del siglo XII', *Hispania*, XII (1952) seeks to minimise the Hospitallers' role, but see M. L. Ledesma, 'Notas sobre la actividad militar de los hospitalarios', *Príncipe de Viana*, XXV (1964). Other studies in Spanish include H. Mota Arévalo, 'La orden de Santiago en tierras de Extremadura', *Revista de estudios extremeños*, XVIII (1962), and J. Rodríguez Molina, 'Las ordenes militares de Calatrava y Santiago en el Alto Guadalquivir (siglos XIII–XV)', *Cuadernos de estudios medievales*, II (1974). J. F. O'Callaghan, '*Hermandades* between the Military Orders of Calatrava and Santiago during the Castilian Reconquest, 1158–1252', *Speculum*, XLIV (1969) discusses agreements between orders, some of which provided for co-operation in the field; see also his recent essay 'The Order of Calatrava: Years of Crisis and Survival, 1158–1212', in V. P. Goss, ed., *The Meeting of Two Worlds* (Kalamazoo, 1986). Strongholds in Spain have not been sufficiently studied, but see *Els castells catalans* (Barcelona, 1967–79) and J. L. Gordillo Courcières, *Castillos templarios arruinados en el sur de la Corona de Aragón* (Valencia, 1974).

For colonisation in frontier areas, see J. Prawer, *Crusader Institutions* (Oxford, 1980); *Cambridge Economic History of Europe*, I (Cambridge, 1966); F. L. Carsten, *The Origins of Prussia* (Oxford, 1954); J. M. Font Rius, *Cartas de población y de franquicia de Cataluña* (Madrid–Barcelona, 1969–83); and M. L. Ledesma Rubio, 'La colonización del maestrazgo turolense por los Templarios', *Aragón en la edad media*, V (1983).

4. RESOURCES AND MANPOWER

Most of the surviving documentation concerning the military orders relates to rights and privileges, and numerous collections of documents have been published, some of them with useful introductions. See, for example, M. Gervers, ed., *The Cartulary of the Knights of St John of Jerusalem in England* (Oxford, 1982); Marquis de Ripert-Monclar, ed., *Cartulaire de la commanderie de Richerenches de l'ordre du Temple (1136–1214)* (Avignon–Paris, 1907); V. Carrière, *Histoire et cartulaire des Templiers de Provins* (Paris, 1919); P. Ourliac and A. M. Magnou, eds, *Le cartulaire de La Selve: la terre, les hommes et le pouvoir en Rouergue au XIIe siècle* (Paris, 1985); and I. B. Cowan, P. H. R. Mackay and A. Macquarrie, eds, *The Knights of St John of Jerusalem in Scotland* (Edinburgh, 1983), although this is mainly concerned with the later Middle Ages. There is also a very good introduction in B. A. Lees, *Records of the Templars in England in the Twelfth Century: The Inquest of 1185, with Illustrative Charters and Documents* (London, 1935).

The general and regional studies listed in the general bibliography usually discuss resources, and there are many more local studies. For England, the volumes of the *Victoria History of the Counties of England* may be consulted: these include articles on Templar and Hospitaller commanderies, but are of uneven quality. Most other local studies relating to England are not very recent: for the Templars in Yorkshire, for example, there are R. V. Taylor, 'Ribston and the Knights Templars', *Yorkshire Archaeological and Topographical Journal*, VII–IX (1882–6); H. E. Chetwynd-Stapylton, 'The Templars at Templehurst', ibid., X (1889); and E. J. Martin, 'The Templars in Yorkshire', *Yorkshire Archaeological Journal*, XXIX–XXX (1929–31).

Local studies in English relating to other countries include A. T. Luttrell, 'Two Templar–Hospitaller Preceptories North of Tuscania', *Papers of the British School at Rome*, XXXIX (1971) and P. Freedman, 'Military Orders in Osona during the Twelfth and Thirteenth Centuries', *Acta historica et archaeologica mediaevalia*, III (1982). Among useful Spanish monographs are M. L. Ledesma Rubio, *La encomienda de Zaragoza de la orden de San Juan de Jerusalén en los siglos XII y XIII* (Zaragoza, 1967); M. Rivera Garretas, *La encomienda, el priorato y la villa de Uclés en la edad media (1174–1301)* (Madrid–Barcelona, 1985); and J. L. Novo Cazón, *El priorato santiaguista de Vilar de Donas en la edad media (1194–1500)* (La Coruña, 1986). C. Estow, 'The Economic Development of the Order of Calatrava, 1158–1366', *Speculum*, LVII (1982) provides a general survey of Calatrava's estates; and conflicts between Calatrava and the archbishops of Toledo are discussed by J. F. O'Callaghan, 'The Order of Calatrava and the Archbishops of Toledo, 1147–1245', *Studies in Medieval Cistercian History presented to Jeremiah O'Sullivan* (Spencer, 1971) (reprinted in *The Spanish Military Order of Calatrava and its Affiliates*). Local studies on the Teutonic order include O. Feger, *Die Deutsch-Ordens-Kommende Mainau: Anfänge und Frühzeit* (Constance, 1958), and R. Schmidt, *Die Deutschordenskommenden Trier und Beckingen, 1242–1794* (Marburg,

1979). U. Arnold, ed., *Zur Wirtschaftsentwicklung des Deutschen Ordens im Mittelalter* (Marburg, 1989) is mainly concerned with the later Middle Ages. Various aspects of colonisation in all parts of the West are discussed in *Les ordres militaires, la vie rurale et le peuplement en Europe occidentale (XIIe–XVIIIe siècles)* (Auch, 1986). There are several studies of the Templars' banking and moneylending activities: L. Delisle, *Mémoire sur les opérations financières des Templiers* (Paris, 1889); A. Sandys, 'The Financial and Administrative Importance of the London Temple in the Thirteenth Century', in A. G. Little and F. M. Powicke, eds, *Essays in Mediaeval History presented to Thomas Frederick Tout* (Manchester, 1925); J. Piquet, *Des banquiers au moyen âge: les Templiers* (Paris, 1939); and D. M. Metcalf, 'The Templars as Bankers and Monetary Transfers between West and East in the Twelfth Century', in P. W. Edbury and D. M. Metcalf, eds, *Coinage in the Latin East* (Oxford, 1980). On the finances of Santiago in the thirteenth century, see E. Benito Ruano, *La banca toscana y la orden de Santiago en el siglo XIII* (Valladolid, 1961) and 'Deudas y pagos del maestre de Santiago, Don Pelayo Pérez Correa', *Hispania*, XXII (1962).

The discussion of recruitment in Chapter 4 is elaborated more fully in A. J. Forey, 'Recruitment to the Military Orders (Twelfth to Mid-Fourteenth Centuries)', *Viator*, XVII (1986). The family backgrounds of recruits have been investigated most extensively with reference to the Teutonic order: M. Hellmann, 'Bemerkungen zur sozialgeschichtlichen Erforschung des Deutschen Ordens', *Historisches Jahrbuch*, LXXX (1961); E. Maschke, 'Deutschordensbrüder aus dem städtischen Patriziat', *Preussenland und Deutscher Orden: Festschrift für K. Forstreuter* (Würzburg, 1958); K. Górski, 'L'ordre teutonique: un nouveau point de vue', *Revue historique*, CCXXX (1963); D. Wojtecki, *Studien zur Personengeschichte des Deutschen Ordens im 13. Jahrhundert* (Wiesbaden, 1971); and K. Scholz, *Beiträge zur Personengeschichte des Deutschen Ordens in der ersten Hälfte des 14. Jahrhunderts: Untersuchungen zur Herkunft livländischer und preussischer Deutschordensbrüder* (Münster, 1971). Simoniacal entry to religious orders has been studied by J. H. Lynch, *Simoniacal Entry into Religious Life from 1000 to 1260: A Social, Economic and Legal Study* (Columbus, 1976).

5. STRUCTURES AND REGULATIONS

The regulations of the Hospitallers and the rule of Santiago are available in English: E. J. King, *The Rule, Statutes and Customs of the Hospitallers, 1099–1310* (London, 1934), and E. Gallego Blanco, *The Rule of the Spanish Military Order of St. James, 1170–1493* (Leiden, 1971), although this translation is based merely on one fifteenth-century manuscript. The regulations of the Temple and the Teutonic order have not been translated into English: H. de Curzon, ed., *La règle du Temple* (Paris, 1886); J. Delaville Le Roulx, 'Un nouveau manuscrit de la règle du Temple', *Annuaire-bulletin de la Société de l'Histoire de France*, XXVI (1889); M. Perlbach, *Die Statuten des Deutschen Ordens nach den ältesten Handschriften* (Halle, 1890). For Calatrava, see D. W. Lomax, 'Algunos estatutos primitivos de la orden de Calatrava', *Hispania*, XXI (1961). The earliest observances of Santiago are discussed by J. Leclercq, 'La vie et la prière des chevaliers de Santiago d'après leur règle primitive', *Liturgica*, II (1958), and those of the Hospitallers have recently been examined by K. V. Sinclair, 'New Light on Early Hospitaller Practices', *Revue bénédictine*, XCVI (1986).

The governmental structure of military orders is discussed in many of the general, regional and local studies listed above. On the Teutonic order, see also R. Ten Haaf, *Deutschordensstaat und Deutschordensballeien* (Göttingen, 1954) and K. Militzer, *Die Entstehung der Deutschordensballeien im Deutschen Reich* (Marburg, 1981). The creation of commanderies in Germany is examined by D. Wojtecki, 'Der Deutsche Orden unter Friedrich II', *Probleme um Friedrich II* (Vorträge und Forschungen, XVI, Sigmaringen, 1974). On the Hospital, B. Waldstein-Wartenberg, *Rechtsgeschichte des Malteserordens* (Vienna, 1969) may be consulted, as well as A. J. Forey, 'Constitutional Conflict and Change in the Hospital of St John during the Twelfth and Thirteenth Centuries', *Journal of Ecclesiastical History*, XXXIII (1982). There are no recent studies of Templar government, but A. Trudon des Ormes, 'Listes des maisons et de quelques dignitaires de l'ordre du Temple en Syrie, en Chypre et en France', *Revue de l'orient latin*, V–VII (1897–1900) is still of some use, and lists of Templar houses and officials in France are provided by E. G. Léonard, *Introduction au cartulaire manuscrit du Temple du Marquis d'Albon* (Paris, 1930), though it should be pointed out that the text of this work is in Latin. On seals, see E. J. King, *The Seals of the Order of St. John of Jerusalem* (London, 1932) and G. Schlumberger, *Sigillographie de l'orient latin* (Paris, 1943). Studies of women's convents include T. Hugo, *History of Mynchin Buckland Priory and Preceptory* (London, 1861), which is inevitably dated, and A. Ubieto Arteta, *El real monasterio de Sigena (1188–1300)* (Valencia, 1966). For more general discussions, see J. Delaville Le Roulx, 'Les hospitalières de Saint-Jean de Jérusalem', *Mélanges sur l'ordre de S. Jean de Jérusalem* (Paris, 1910) and A. J. Forey, 'Women and the Military Orders in the Twelfth and Thirteenth Centuries', *Studia monastica*, XXIX (1987). Information about outsiders who established ties with military orders is provided by E. Magnou, 'Oblature, classe chevaleresque et servage dans les maisons méridionales du Temple au XIIe siècle', *Annales du Midi*, LXXIII (1961), and A. Ubieto Arteta, 'Cofrades aragoneses y navarros de la milicia del Temple (siglo XII). Aspectos socio-económicos', *Aragón en la edad media*, III (1980).

On the relations between Calatrava and other military orders in Spain, see A. L. Javierre Mur, *La orden de Calatrava en Portugal* (Madrid, 1952) and D. W. Lomax, 'Las milicias cistercienses en el reino de León', *Hispania*, XXIII (1963). The relations between Santiago and Iberian rulers are discussed by D. W. Lomax, 'The Order of Santiago and the Kings of León', *Hispania*, XVIII (1958) and 'El rey Diniz y la orden de Santiago', *Hidalguía*, XXX (1982). On Templars in royal and papal service, see M. L. Bulst-Thiele,

'Templer in königlichen und päpstlichen Diensten', *Festschrift Percy Ernst Schramm* (Wiesbaden, 1964). The question of the granting of absolution by lay brethren is covered by H. C. Lea, 'The Absolution Formula of the Templars', in A. C. Howland, ed., *Minor Historical Writings and Other Essays by Henry Charles Lea* (London, 1942). On admission procedures, see M. Rivera Garretas, 'Los ritos de iniciación en la orden militar de Santiago', *Anuario de estudios medievales*, XII (1982), and A. J. Forey, 'Novitiate and Instruction in the Military Orders during the Twelfth and Thirteenth Centuries', *Speculum*, LXI (1986). The Hospitaller William of San Stefano is discussed by L. Delisle, 'Maître Jean d'Antioche et Guillaume de S. Estève', *Histoire littéraire de France*, XXXIII (Paris, 1906); see also J. Folda, *Crusader Manuscript Illumination at Saint-Jean d'Acre, 1275–1291* (Princeton, 1976). For literary activity associated with the Teutonic order, see C. H. G. Helm and W. Ziesemer, *Die Literatur des Deutschen Ritterordens* (Giessen, 1951), and M. E. Goenner, *Mary-Verse of the Teutonic Knights* (Washington, 1943). The compilation of cartularies is discussed by M. Gervers, *The Hospitaller Cartulary in the British Library (Cotton MS Nero E VI)* (Toronto, 1981). Studies of buildings and building decoration include E. Lambert, *L'architecture des Templiers* (Paris, 1955); H. de Curzon, *La maison du Temple de Paris. Histoire et description* (Paris, 1888); S. E. Rigold, 'Two Camerae of the Military Orders: Strood Temple, Kent, and Harefield, Middlesex', *Archaeological Journal*, CXXII (1965); Z. Goldmann, 'The Hospice of the Knights of St John in Akko', *Archaeology*, XIX (1966); and J. Folda, 'Crusader Frescoes at Crac des Chevaliers and Marqab Castle', *Dumbarton Oaks Papers*, XXXVI (1982).

6. CRITICISM AND CHANGE

Translated criticisms of the orders can be found in *Matthew Paris's English History from the Year 1235 to 1273*, trans. J. A. Giles (London, 1852–4), and I. S. T. Aspin, ed., *Anglo-Norman Political Songs* (Anglo-Norman Texts, XI, Oxford, 1953). One particular example of the abuse of rights is discussed by J. Edwards, 'The Templars in Scotland in the Thirteenth Century', *Scottish Historical Review*, V (1908), and a protracted quarrel between Templars and Hospitallers is examined by A. J. Forey, 'A Thirteenth-Century Dispute between Templars and Hospitallers in Aragon', *Durham University Journal*, LXXX (1987–8). A general survey of reform projects is provided by A. S. Atiya, *The Crusade in the Later Middle Ages* (London, 1938), and proposals concerning the military orders are examined by A. J. Forey, 'The Military Orders in the Crusading Proposals of the Late-Thirteenth and Early-Fourteenth Centuries', *Traditio*, XXXVI (1980). On Raymond Lull, see E. A. Peers, *Ramon Lull* (London, 1929), and J. N. Hillgarth, *Ramon Lull and Lullism in Fourteenth-Century France* (Oxford, 1971). One crusading treatise available in English is P. Dubois, *The Recovery of the Holy Land*, trans. W. I.

Brandt (New York, 1956). For proposals produced by the orders themselves, see B. Z. Kedar and S. Schein, 'Un projet de "passage particulier" proposé par l'ordre de l'Hôpital, 1306–1307', *Bibliothèque de l'Ecole des Chartes*, CXXXVII (1979). G. Lizerand, *Le dossier de l'affaire des Templiers* (Paris, 1964) contains a French version of James of Molay's memorandum opposing amalgamation of the military orders, together with French versions of some documents relating to the Templar trial. On James of Molay himself, see M. Barber, 'James of Molay, the Last Grand Master of the Temple', *Studia monastica*, XIV (1972).

On the trial, M. Barber, *The Trial of the Templars* (Cambridge, 1978) provides an up-to-date survey, particularly of events in France. Of the older works, H. Finke, *Papsttum und Untergang des Templerordens* (Münster, 1907) is the most important, and the section on the Templars in H. C. Lea, *History of the Inquisition in the Middle Ages* (New York, 1889) is still well worth reading. N. Cohn, *Europe's Inner Demons* (London, 1975) seeks to place the trial in a broad context. Biographies of Philip IV, such as J. R. Strayer, *The Reign of Philip the Fair* (Princeton, 1980), contain discussions of the trial. R. H. Bautier, 'Diplomatique et histoire politique: ce que la critique diplomatique nous apprend sur la personnalité de Philippe le Bel', *Revue historique*, CCLIX (1978) is an important study of the French king's character. See also M. Barber, 'The World Picture of Philip the Fair', and S. Menache, 'Contemporary Attitudes concerning the Templars' Affair: Propaganda's Fiasco?', both of which appear in *Journal of Medieval History*, VIII (1982).

On events outside France, see C. Perkins, 'The Trial of the Knights Templars in England', *English Historical Review*, XXIV (1909); A. L. Javierre Mur, 'Aportación al estudio del proceso contra el Temple en Castilla', *Revista de archivos, bibliotecas y museos*, LXIX (1961); C. Estepa, 'La disolución de la orden del Temple en Castilla y León', *Estudios sobre la sociedad hispánica en la edad media* (Cuadernos de historia, VI, Madrid, 1975); and A. J. Forey, 'The Beginning of Proceedings against the Aragonese Templars', in D. W. Lomax and D. Mackenzie, eds, *God and Man in Medieval Spain* (Warminster, 1989). The published records of the trial are mostly in Latin, but A. Gilmour-Bryson, *The Trial of the Templars in the Papal State and the Abruzzi* (Vatican City, 1982) and R. Sève and A. M. Chagny-Sève, *Le procès des Templiers d'Auvergne, 1309–1311* (Paris, 1986) contain lengthy and helpful introductions.

For later views on the trial and the development of myths, see P. Partner, *The Murdered Magicians: The Templars and their Myth* (Oxford, 1982) and A. K. Wildermann, *Die Beurteilung des Templerprozesses bis zum 17. Jahrhundert* (Freiburg, 1971). The fate of the English Templars after the trial is discussed briefly by R. Hill, 'Fourpenny Retirement: the Yorkshire Templars in the Fourteenth Century', *The Church and Wealth* (Studies in Church History, XXIV, 1987); and on the disposal of Templar lands in England, see C. Perkins, 'The Wealth of the Knights Templars in England and the Disposition of it after their Dissolution', *American Historical Review*, XV (1909–10), and A. M. Leys, 'The Forfeiture of the Lands of the Templars in England', in F. M. Powicke, ed., *Oxford Essays in Medieval History presented to H. E. Salter*

(Oxford, 1934). J. Delaville Le Roulx, *Les hospitaliers à Rhodes (1310–1421)* (Paris, 1913) includes a chapter on Templar lands and also traces the history of the Hospital in the fourteenth century.

More recently, numerous articles on the fourteenth-century Hospitallers have been written by A. T. Luttrell, many of which have been reprinted in his *The Hospitallers in Cyprus, Rhodes, Greece and the West, 1291–1400* (London, 1978) and *Latin Greece, the Hospitallers and the Crusades, 1291–1440* (London, 1982). Among his latest publications is 'Hospitaller Life in Aragon, 1319–1370', *God and Man* (see above). W. L. Urban, *The Livonian Crusade* (Washington, 1981) surveys events in the Baltic region in the fourteenth century. On the relations between the orders and the papacy at this time, see N. J. Housley, *The Avignon Papacy and the Crusades, 1305–1378* (Oxford, 1986).

Index

The following abbreviations are used: A   Archbishop; B   Bishop;
C   Count; H   Hospitaller; K   King; MO   Military Orders; P   Pope;
T   Templar; TO   Teutonic order, member of Teutonic order